A HISTORY OF BRITISH SOCIALISM
VOLUME I

A HISTORY OF
BRITISH SOCIALISM

BY M. BEER

Author of " Die Geschichte des Modernen
Sozialismus in England," etc.

WITH AN INTRODUCTION BY
R. H. TAWNEY, B.A.
Fellow of Balliol College, Oxford

VOLUME I

G. BELL AND SONS, LTD
LONDON
1929

First published 1919
Reprinted 1920, 1921, 1923
New and cheaper edition 1929

Printed in Great Britain by the Camelot Press Limited
London and Southampton

PREFACE

FROM the thirteenth century to the present day the stream of socialism and social reform has largely been fed by British thought and experiment. Mediaeval schoolmen and statesmen, modern political philosophers, economists, poets and philanthropists of the British Isles have explored its course and enriched its volume, but left it to writers of other nations to name and describe it. The same may be said of all other philosophical and scientific achievements of Britain, and particularly of England. Mr. Kipling's heroic " Explorer " is her true symbol :—-

" Well I know who'll take the credit—all the clever chaps that
    followed—
Came a dozen men together—never knew my desert fears ;
Tracked me by the camps I'd quitted—used the water-holes I'd
    hollowed.
They'll go back and do the talking.   They'll be called the Pioneers ! "

This has been so all along, but it ought not to be so any longer. British students ought to work up and utilise the views which the seminal minds of England have given to the world. The nation needs now all the knowledge, ordered and systematised, of its past labours for socialism and social reform, in order to be able to cope with the social difficulties and weltering movements which are visibly coming to a head.

The English intellect, from its sheer recklessness, is essentially revolutionary, probably more so than the French intellect. But since 1688 it has been the endeavour of English statesmen and educators to impart to the nation a conservative, cautiously moving temper, a distrust of generalisation, an aversion from carrying theory to its logical conclusions. By these means they appear to have succeeded in ballasting and steadying the intellectual swiftness and restlessness of the nation and in producing well-balanced minds. In normal times this ingenious contrivance has worked well—or as Sir Leslie Stephen said, " Illogicality has saved us," and given the English a reputation for being controlled by good sense and sober judgment. In periods of general upheavals, however, when the dynamic forces of society are vehemently asserting themselves, the English are apt to throw their mental ballast overboard and take the lead in revolutionary thought and action. In such a period we are living now.

Since the beginning of the new century a new England has been springing up—" rousing herself like a strong man after sleep and shaking her invincible locks." Her men and women are all astir, their mentality has become sensitive and quickly responsive to doctrinal and moral stimuli— the people are marching on. The intellects of the nation are as bold and active as in the great crises of its stirring past. The old issues are either forgotten or forced to their final fruition, while the masses are joining issue with the classes upon the question of a redistribution of wealth and power. A new Chartist movement has arisen and is daily growing.

The period which now discloses itself to the eyes of the social inquirer exhibits some striking parallels to that of the second quarter of the nineteenth century. The consolidation of the productive and distributive forces that were brought into being by the Industrial Revolution, the contest of the then new middle classes for political power, the agitation for a new commercial policy; the surging-up of the working classes since the repeal of the Combination

Laws (1824-5), the formation of national trades organisations, the alliance between the middle and working classes
against the Tory aristocracy and in favour of the First
Reform Bill (1830-32), the disillusionment of Labour and
the consequent rise of revolutionary trades unionism or
Syndicalism (1833-4), the growth of Chartism or a Socialist
Labour Party (1836-48) ; finally, the rise of the Oxford
Movement, Young England, and Christian Socialism—all
this stupendous mental ferment in the years from 1825 to
1850 appears to be repeating itself now on a larger and
higher scale. Yet, how much do we know of the effects of
the struggle for the First Reform Bill on the then nascent
socialist and labour movement ? And how much of the
effects of the Constitutional struggle since 1909 on organised
Labour ? Or is it a mere coincidence that revolutionary
trades unionism followed in the wake of the agitation for the
Reform Bill, 1832, and that Syndicalism and general strikes
have been treading upon the heels of the Constitutional
crisis that began with Mr. Lloyd George's Finance Bill ?
And will the strengthening of the political action of Labour
which followed upon the collapse of revolutionary trades
unionism, in 1835, be repeated with regard to Syndicalism
and the British Labour Party of to-day ? And is Tariff
Reform destined to mark the close of the social ferment of
the present day as the triumph of Free Trade marked the
close of the Chartist era?

These and many other vital questions suggest themselves
from a comparison of the two periods. I do not pretend
to have supplied adequate solutions of those problems, my
aim having been to stimulate the social and political student,
rather than to offer panaceas. I have but brought together,
as completely as I could, from the vast treasure-houses
of British theology, moral philosophy, political economy,
socialist pamphlets, Labour papers, and general periodical

A2

publications, the materials relevant to our subject. I have classified them according to the theories and general concepts underlying them, and given each phase and leading personality their historical setting, thus bringing them into relation with the social events and mental developments of their time.

From 1790 to 1840 the Francis Place Collections and MSS., which are either in the British Museum Manuscript Department or at the Repository at Hendon, have been of great assistance to me. I take this opportunity to express my thanks to the librarian and assistants of the British Museum for the unfailing courtesy with which they treated my requests and for the facilities they afforded me for my research work.

The correspondence of Robert Owen is now in the keeping of the Co-operative Wholesale Society at Manchester. May I suggest to its administrators to hand it over to the Trustees of the British Museum in order to make it accessible to students ?

While writing this book I often felt the want of an English work on the English schoolmen. It is rather curious that no British student of divinity has ever set himself the task of writing an exhaustive monograph on either Alexander of Hales, or Duns Scotus, or William of Ockham. Or are these leading Minorites and schoolmen regarded as foreigners because the first died at Paris, the second at Cologne, and the third at Munich ?

I have likewise regretted that no English treatise exists on the currency controversies, particularly with respect to paper money, of the crucial period from 1774 to 1819.

The " History of British Socialism " is but a feeble attempt to repay the enormous mental debt which I owe to English life and scholarship. I could not have written it but for my twenty years' residence in this country, which has taught me how high an elevation of political and moral culture a nation must reach before it can embark on a socialistic reconstruction of society. I hope that British social students will assist me, by their criticisms, to make the second edition of the book less defective.

The book is based on my German *Geschichte des Sozialismus in England* (1912), which had a uniformly favourable reception from the press in Great Britain, Germany, Austria-Hungary, and Russia. The English version is practically a new book, it having been completely re-written, and enlarged by a considerable amount of original matter.

In conclusion, I express my cordial thanks to Mr. R. C. K. Ensor for having read and corrected some of the proofs, and to Dr. A. Shadwell for the encouragement and advice he gave me during the writing of the book.

NOTE TO THE REVISED EDITION

The above Preface was written in June, 1914, when the manuscript of the *History of British Socialism* was nearing completion. Owing to the Great War, however, the publication was put off till Peace was declared and public attention again turned to home affairs. The present edition is, with few exceptions, a faithful reprint of the original work which appeared in 1919 and 1920. In Volume II, the chapters XIX and XX, dealing with the years 1914 to 1919, have undergone some alterations, for they seemed to require either corrections or filling up of lacunæ. Moreover, the present edition is enlarged by a supplementary chapter (XXII), covering the years from 1920 to 1928. It is written in the same dispassionate spirit which secured for the original edition the unanimous approval of the British Press and public.

I am glad to have an opportunity of expressing my obligation to Mr. J. S. Middleton, assistant secretary of the Labour
Party, to Mr. Walter M. Citrine, general secretary of the Trades
Union Congress, for information and lending me the Reports of
the Labour Party Conferences and the Trades Union Congresses
respectively, and to Mr. Alfred Mattison, of Leeds, for his great
kindness in sending me his unique notes on the life of John
Francis Bray.

M. BEER.

September, 1928.

CONTENTS

CONTENTS

PART II

(1760—1834)

INTRODUCTION

THE book which is now published under the title " A History of British Socialism, Volume I.," was intended by the author to be the first of two volumes, the second of which would carry the story of British Socialism into the opening decade of the present century. The War intervened before the second volume was ready for the Press, and Mr. Beer, like most other students, was compelled for the time being to lay his literary work on one side. The first volume, therefore, is now published separately; the next, it is hoped, will appear on the return of peace. Together they will form the most complete account of the development of Socialist thought in Great Britain which has yet appeared. The subject of the present volume is the growth of Socialism down to the rise of Chartism, and its readers must remember that there is a sequel in which the story is completed. But the period with which it deals is sufficiently distinct to be studied separately, and the book is a unity, not a mutilated fragment.

Mr. Beer's book is a study of political thought upon the group of problems created by the rise of capitalist agriculture and capitalist industry, as it developed in the country which was the first to experience the transition, and which experienced it most completely. It is called, " A History of British Social- ism," because the particular aspect of that thought with which it is primarily concerned is the effort, partly critical, partly constructive, at once aspiration, theory, prophecy, and pro- gramme, which had as its object to substitute for the direction of industry by the motive of personal profit and the method of unrestricted competition some principle of organization more compatible with social solidarity and economic freedom. Like other summary designations of complex political forces, Socialism is a word the connotation of which varies, not only from generation to generation, but from decade to decade ; and Mr. Beer has wisely refrained from trimming the edges of an experimental and combative history to fit the framework of any neat definition. Instead of formulating a canon of Socialist orthodoxy and grouping the exponents of the faith according to the different degrees of their proximity to it, he has allowed the significance of his title to emerge from the different and sometimes contradictory currents of thought which inte mingle, in their natural complexity and exuberance and crudity, in the pages of his book. His work is not the chronicle of a sect or of a party, but the analysis of a moral and intellectual movement.

As the present volume shows, that movement can claim some classics. But it has developed less through the literary succession of a chain of writers than by the renewed and spontaneous reflection of each generation upon the dominant facts and theories which confronted it. The mental atmosphere of England on the eve of the Industrial Revolution, the reactions of the French Revolution and the long War, the agitation which preceded, and the disillusionment which followed, the first Reform Bill, the influence of Adam Smith, Ricardo, and the Utilitarians form a background without a description of which English Socialism, in its seminal period, is unintelligible. Mr. Beer has set them in the high light which they deserve. He presents the main elements in the political thought of the time, not as specimens in a museum, but in the tumultuous energy and profusion with which they swept across the mind of a tormented generation. The key to the heart of an economic age lies in economics, as to that of a religious age it is religion. What he offers is a study of one side of the great debate upon the merits of modern industrial civilization, which the nineteenth century, at the climax of its triumphant self-confidence, could ignor but could not silence, and which is still unended. His feet are always planted on solid earth, and he is not of those who would convert history into a procession of abstractions. But the main theme of his book is political thought, not political events, and he is more interested in the workshops where doctrines are forged and sharpened than in their use in the field. f there are critics who regard the history of opinion as an unprofitable dilettantism, they may be invited to reconsider their judgment when they have read the second part of the present volume. For the ideas whose development and genesis it traces are not antiquarian curiosities, but a high explosive,—and an explosive which has not yet been fired.

These ideas have a long history, and the first ninety-one pages of the present volume are given to a description of the communistic elements in English thought from the Middle Ages to the beginning of the eighteenth century. Like the Christianity of Plato, the Socialism of the *animae naturaliter socialisticae* of the pre-industrial era bears its name by metaphor or analogy, and the treatment which it receives from Mr. Beer must not be interpreted as implying that he regards a spiritual affinity as a direct affiliation. The importance for him of the earlier thinkers consists in the legacy of political principles which they transmitted. Capitalist industry arose, as he points out, in a country which was intellectually prepared to receive it. It developed, not by a fortuitous series of technical discoveries, but through the concentration of thought upon definite problems to the exclusion of others, and there is a sense in which Locke and Blackstone were as truly its pioneers as Arkwright and Crompton. The first part of the book, therefore, is in the nature of an introduction to its main theme,—the development of political thought under the stress of Industrial Revolution.

The social history of the years from 1760 to 1840 has received more attention in England than that of any other period. Toynbee, Held, Cunningham, and Mantoux have made its main features familiar, and the brilliant books of Mr. and Mrs. Hammond have painted an unforgettable picture of the meaning of the new economic régime to the workers in village and town. The political philosophy which triumphed has been the subject of an elaborate study by Leslie Stephen. Prof. Wallas has described it, while it still had to fight for its existence. Prof. Dicey has shown how in the day of its power it transformed English thought and institutions between 1832 and 1870. What has never been adequately written is the history of the political philosophy which failed. For the victory of the panegyrists of the new industrial order was so complete as to obliterate the very remem-

brance of its critics, and to create the impression that Utilitarianism spoke with the voice of reason itself. That is what seemed
to be the case to the contemporaries who applauded. That is
how it still often appears to-day. There was a leaden obscurant-
ism which would not think. There was a blind movement of
misery among masses hardly capable of thought. But in the
first forty years of the century which saw the establishment of
capitalist industry intelligence was united in its approval, and
an alternative philosophy did not find expression in England
till it was imported in the forties from abroad.

That impression is natural, but the present volume shows
that it is an illusion. In the clash of political ideas in the
early nineteenth century there were not two protagonists,
but three, and the least known had not the least vitality. For
capitalism was no sooner dominant than it produced its critics,
and side by side with the economic theory of Ricardo and the
political theory of Bentham there appeared a body of doctrine
which attacked the fundamental basis of the new order. It is
not the case, therefore, as has sometimes been suggested, that
the classical land of capitalist industry had to wait for an
exposition of Socialism till a German exile disinterred dusty
bluebooks in the British Museum. As Marx himself was well
aware, there was an indigenous English Socialism which, except
for the inspiration to all creative thought given by France, owed
nothing to foreign influences. Spence, Ogilvie, and Paine, of
whom an admirable account is contained in the late Mr. P. A.
Brown's *The French Revolution in English History*, were
agrarian reformers, though Paine was much more as well. Godwin was an anarchist ; Charles Hall was a conservative critic
of capitalism rather than a socialist. But the writings of Gray,
Thompson, Hodgskin, and Bray, all published, except that of
Bray, which appeared in 1839, in the decade 1820–1830, laid
down the main lines of Socialist thought more than twenty years
before the appearance of the Communist Manifesto. Their works
are almost unobtainable. Except in Prof. Foxwell's introduction
to Anton Menger's book, *The Right to the whole Produce of
Labour*, no adequate exposition of their writings has appeared

in English. And, as readers of the present work will discover, they were not isolated eccentrics, but representatives of a current of thought which offered the working classes what in the twenties and thirties they needed most,—a philosophy interpreting the causes of their degradation, and a body of articulate doctrine which could fuse into energy their misery, their passion, and their hope.

It is this current of thought, its antecedents, affinities, and ramifications, its theoretical developments and practical effects in the world of industry and politics, which occupies the greater part of the present volume. Its immediate influence was profound. The word " Socialism " appears first to be used in the *Co-operative Magazine* of November, 1827, in which those who think that Capital should be owned, not individually, but in common, are described as " Communionists or Socialists." Its meaning was not collectivism, but co-operation ; and co-operation not in the specialised sense which it has since assumed of a particular method of conducting trade, but with the larger significance of a social order based on fraternity, not competition. In that sense it was still used by the Rochdale Pioneers of 1844, when they proposed to " arrange the powers of production, distribution, education, and government, or, in other words, to establish a self-supporting home colony of united interests."

Co-operation was a body of social principles before it was an economic device, and, if its practical application owed most to Robert Owen, the intellectual elaboration of the faith was the work of the early English Socialists. Their relation to Chartism and Trade Unionism was equally important. To the former they helped to give the anti-capitalist bias, which, as the excellent work of the late Mr. Hovell shows, was the practical motive to rally the turbulent workers of the North to the decorous political programme enunciated by Lovett and the London Workingmen's Association. Influenced partly by their teaching, which was disseminated in a popular form through the papers read by the working classes, trade unionism assumed a revolutionary and aggressive character as remote from the aims of the sober defensive associations of the sixties and seventies as from those of the local journeymen's clubs of the eighteenth century. That property not earned by labour is theft, that there is necessarily a class-war between the producers and the non-producers, that economic power precedes political power and that salvation must come, not from Parliament, but from syndicalist movements on the part of the organised workers—these were the watch words of the advanced trade unionism of the thirties. " With us, universal suffrage will begin in our lodges, extend to the general union, and finally swallow up the political power " ; " Social liberty must precede political liberty. While we are in a state of social slavery, our rights would be exercised to the benefit of our tyrants, and we should be made subservient to the parties who work us for their purposes." [1] Under the stimulus of such ideas, trade unionism became an effort directed to overthrowing the existing economic system, rather than to improving the condition of the wage-earner within it. Trade union history, which like trade union law, has suffered from the tyranny of over-rigid definitions, requires to be re-written in the light of them. When that is done, movements which now appear novel or ephemeral will possibly be found to be the re-emergence of tendencies which are fundamental and permanent. " The English intellect," writes Mr. Beer, in his preface, " from its sheer recklessness is essentially revolutionary. . . . In periods of general upheaval, when the dynamic forces of society are vehemently asserting themselves, the English are apt to throw their mental ballast overboard and take the lead in revolutionary thought and action. In such a period are we living now." His words are more appropriate to the present moment than to that at which they were written. " Social Reconstruction " is not the invention of the twentieth century ; and those who are concerned with it to-day may find in the intellectual ferment of the period explored by Mr. Beer a medicine to chasten their hopes and to fortify their resolution.

A foreign scholar has certain advantages in writing the history of modern England. He is not scorched by the embers of living controversies. He is free from the prejudices of sect or party, and can view his subject through plain glass. The

[1] See p. 340.

snares of ready-made interpretations are not about his feet, nor conventional judgments upon his lips. His eye for the sharp outline of facts has not been dimmed by a haze of familiar words. He can find a new significance in the obvious and still be surprised at what is surprising. But only scholarship of a high order can give him the learning needed to compose a work like the present volume, and only long familiarity can save him from misinterpreting the atmosphere of a foreign nation. Mr. Beer possesses both. He is an indefatigable student, who knows the social history of England from the middle of the eighteenth century, as it is known only to Professor Graham Wallas, Mr. and Mrs. Sidney Webb, and Mr. and Mrs. Hammond. And his twenty years of residence in England have given him the working acquaintance with the unstated assumptions of English political life which is hardly less necessary than historical knowledge for the task which he has undertaken.

The present book is only part of the work which he had planned. In addition to the second volume, which was almost completed, he had begun, in conjunction with a friend, the task of reprinting the more noteworthy writings of the early English Socialists, and some of them were already in proof when he was interrupted. " I see now," he wrote, in the last week of July, 1914, " that I must use every moment for work. The War will upset all plans, if Germany gets involved in the Austrian madness. I feel more than ever that no agitation and no class-war are of any use. Man is still brutal, and despite all religion, culture, and science, not far removed from the wild animal." At a time when to speak of the unity of Europe seems a cruel jest, a work like that of Mr. Beer, the history by an Austrian scholar of the English contribution to an international movement, is not only a valuable addition to historical knowledge, but a reminder that there are intellectual bonds which preceded the War and which will survive it. English readers will thank him both for the one and for the other, and will hope that, by the publication of his second volume, he will in the near future increase the obligation under which he has already laid them.

R. H. TAWNEY.

PART I

MEDIAEVAL COMMUNISM

I

PRIMITIVE CHRISTIAN INFLUENCES

I.—THE LEGACY OF THE ROMAN EMPIRE

A BROAD current of communistic sentiment runs through the mental life of the Roman Empire in the age of Christ. The widening of the spiritual horizon consequent upon the growing acquaintance with Greek philosophy and oriental speculation ; the political and material forces which were operating upon the social structure since the Punic Wars ; the constant and jarring frictions and contests between the classes ; [1] finally, the increasing corruptions and complications of society, spread dissatisfaction with the existing institutions, and with traditional creeds and concepts. An unquenchable yearning for a return to the simpler past and ruder equality took hold of the minds of poets, patriots, and thinkers.

In that mood the prehistoric past, with its tribal organisation and absence of individual property, appeared to those minds as the reign of Saturn, or the state of nature, where man lived in unconscious innocence and blissful ignorance, knowing nothing of *meum* and *tuum*, good and evil, dominion and servitude. It was a state free from searchings of heart, from wearisome problems concerning social relations and ethical concepts. Vergil, mild and pensive, celebrates the reign of Saturn when—

> " No fences parted fields, nor marks nor bounds
> Divided acres of litigious grounds,
> But all was common."[2]

Strains of rude equality fall on our ear when Horace sings of Scythian institutions :

> " The Scythians of the plains
> More happy are, housed in wandering wains,

---

[1] Cicero, *De Rep.* I. 31.   [2] Vergil, *Georg.* I. 125–28.

3

> More blest the Getan stout,
> Who not from acres mark'd and meted out
> Reaps his fruit and grain.
> A year, no more, he rests in his domain,
> Then, pausing from his toil,
> He quits it, and in turn another tills the soil."[1]

Tacitus inquires, with romantic admiration, into the life of the Germanic tribes ; and Juvenal, conservative and patriotic, pours out his burning zeal in satires upon a civilisation that has forsaken toil and virtue and fallen a prey to luxury and voluptuousness—those insidious foes that paralyse the hands of the world conquerors.[2]

But the most pronounced admirer of primitive communism is Seneca : " The social virtues had remained pure and inviolate before covetousness distracted society and introduced poverty, for men ceased to possess all things when they began to call anything their own. The first men and their immediate descendants followed nature, pure and uncorrupt. When, however, vices crept in, kings were obliged to show their authority and enact penal laws. How happy was the primitive age when the bounties of nature lay in common and were used promiscuously ; nor had avarice and luxury disunited mortals and made them prey upon one another. They enjoyed all nature in common, which thus gave them secure possession of the public wealth. Why should I not think them the richest of all people, among whom there was not to be found one poor man ? " [3]

Josephus, a faithful index of educated opinion of his time, sees in Cain a man striving after possessions and lucre, acquisition of land, while Abel personifies the artless and innocent shepherd, moving about with his herds from pasture to pasture, without occupying any of them. Cain is also supposed by the ancients to have been the first to set bounds to fields.[4]

---

[1] Horace, *Odes* III. 24 (Theodore Martin's translation).
[2] Juvenal, *Satires*, 6 and 13.
[3] Seneca, *Letters*, 90.
[4] Josephus, *Antiq. Jud.*, l. 1, c. 2 (3).   *Cf.* Wycliffe, *Civ. dom.*, III., c. 20 (vol. 4, p. 422) ; John Selden, *Mare Clausum*, l. 1, c. 4.

Private property and civil dominion thus appeared as the origin of evil.

The philosophy underlying these conceptions is of course that of the Stoa, the real origin of the doctrines of the state of nature and of natural rights.

The difficulties and problems that assailed Rome since the Punic Wars had troubled Hellas since the Persian Wars. The old society, in spite of all reforming efforts to maintain it, had given way to individualism ; the old mythology or antique theology was losing authority and its place was being taken by a philosophy that was mainly ethical. The final outcome was the Stoa, whose doctrines are partly a protest against civil society and individual property, and partly a positive guide to an ethical reform of society. It is based on an idealisation of the primitive conditions of tribal society. The appeal to nature implies a censure upon civilisation as well as a summons to mankind either to return to the past or to re-organise their institutions after the ideals drawn from the past. The urbanisation of the land, the bursting of the national bars, the growth of trade and commerce, appeared to the Stoics as an abandonment of natural pursuits, of the simple virtues of country life, and the introduction of artificial conditions, of multitudinous and complicated business, of luxury and corruption. In Stoic philosophy, God appears as the active, rational, and moral principle who saturates and vitalizes the physical nature. The world and the fulness thereof governs itself by the divine law inherent in it, which is equity and goodness. It is infinitely superior to civil law or man-made law, and it applies to all human beings, for men as participators of the divine spirit are free and equal. In the original society, as it issued from the hands of nature, the divine-natural law governed mankind, but in later times corruption set in and man enacted laws. Civil government is thus the effect of the debasement of mankind and but a vicious substitute for the reign of God and nature. From evil flows evil and it can only be cured by a return to nature and a life in harmony with nature.[1]

[1] *Cf.* Maine, *Ancient Law*, ed. 1861, pp. 53–7, 70–2 ; Pearson, *Fragments of Zeno*, pp. 11–12 ; Cornford, *Transition from Religion*

The educated Romans, in so far as they were susceptible of philosophic speculations, accepted the Stoic doctrines ; later on the Roman lawyers incorporated it as *ius naturale* into their legal system, not, however, without materially changing some of its tenets. It was in the Hellenic world that Stoic philosophy became an integral part of ethical and religious thought, and with the influx of Greeks into Christianity Stoic concepts took place among the formative elements of patristic and scholastic theology.

2.—THE PRIMITIVE CHURCH

JEWISH ethical monotheism and Stoic philosophy, both saturated either with social reform or communistic ideals, formed the mental atmosphere into which Christianity was born. As a religion of the lowly and hungry it came into the world, endowed with the sentiment that communism was capable of raising economic life to a higher moral level. The hindrance to salvation was not poverty, but riches. " Blessed be ye poor, for yours is the kingdom of God. . . . How hardly shall they that have riches enter into the kingdom of God " (Luke vi. 20 ; xviii. 24). It may fairly be doubted whether positive communistic institutions really existed amongst the primitive Christian communities, as one might infer from Acts iv. 32, but there cannot be any doubt that common possessions were looked upon by many of the first Christians as an ideal to be aimed at.[1]

Under the overpowering influence of the teachings of Christ the members of the first communities were " of one heart and of one soul, neither said any of them that aught of the things which he possessed was his own, but they had all things common " (Acts iv. 32). In this moral exaltation sacrifice was easy and renunciation of worldly possession a spiritual joy. Or as S. Cyprian says, " When at the first beginnings of the Church the mind flourished with great virtues, when the soul of the believers

---

to *Philosophy*, 1911 ; Voigt, *Ius Naturale*, 1857 ; Barth, *Die Stoa*, 1906 ; D. G. Ritchie, *Natural Rights*, 1895.

[1] Compare, however, Gibbon, *Roman Empire*, c. 15 (ed. Bury, II. 47) ; also Latimer, *Sermons*, First Before Edward VI.

burned with a glow of faith yet new, then they had all things common, they imitated the divine law, the equity of God the Father." [1] Barnabas enjoins the Christian, " to communicate in all things with thy neighbour ; thou shalt not call things thine own ; for if ye are partakers in common of things that are incorruptible how much should ye be of those things which are perishable." [2] Clement of Alexandria teaches, " All things are common and not for the rich to appropriate an undue share. That expression therefore, ' I possess and possess it in abundance, why should I not enjoy ? ' is suitable neither to man nor to society. . . . God has given to us the liberty of use, but only so far as necessary, and He has determined that the use should be common." [3] Tertullian argues with the Romans, " We are brethren in our family property, which with you mostly dissolves brotherhood. We, therefore, who are united in mind and soul, doubt not about having our possessions in common. With us all things are shared promiscuously, except the wives. In that alone do we part fellowship, in which alone others (Greek and Roman pagans) exercise it." [4] S. John Chrysostom preaches, " Consider the time of the Apostles. I say not the chief men, but the believers themselves generally. All, it is written, were of one heart, neither said any of them that aught of the things which he possessed was his own. There were no such words as ' mine ' and ' thine.' This is friendship. . . . It is only impossible (to-day) because we have not the will, for possible it is. If it were not possible neither would Christ have commanded it nor have discoursed so much upon love." [5]

The corollary of these beliefs was the condemnation of wealth and the exaltation of poverty. It found epigrammatic expression in the sentence, *dives aut iniquus aut iniqui heres.* " To grow rich without an injustice is impossible. But what if he succeeded

---

[1] S. Cyprian, *Of Works and Alms* c. 25.
[2] Barnabas, *Epistles*, 19.
[3] Clement of Alexandria, *Paed.* II. 13.
[4] Tertullian, *Apol.* I. 39.
[5] S. John Chrysostom, *Homilies*, 1 Thessal. *Hom.* 2.

to his father's inheritance ? Then he receives what had been gained by injustice." [1]

The communistic ideal is evidently compatible with Christianity, provided that the methods employed for its realisation are strictly ethical and religious, and not political, seditious, or revolutionary ; they must be confined to self-reform through a moral and religious life. Therefore, it was possible for S. Paul, without offending the communistic sentiments of the believers, to exhort the Roman community to be subject to the civil authorities and obedient to their laws (Romans xiii.).

3.—CHRISTIAN THEOLOGY AND NATURAL LAW

To the teachers of primitive and mediaeval Christianity *ius naturale* must have been particularly congenial. It appeared to them to be a pagan version of the Scriptural truths of the innocence of the original man in the Garden of Eden, his Fall and the consequent corruption of man's heart, and the inferior nature of civilisation and human laws, as well as a confirmation that even Nature dictates certain commandments in conformity with divine law.[2] And they found authority for its validity in S. Paul, who argues, "For when the Gentiles, which have not the law, do by nature the things contained in the law, these . . . are a law unto themselves, which show the work of the law written in their hearts, their conscience also bearing witness " (Romans ii. 14, 15). Here the law of nature is expressly recognised. To that argument of S. Paul the Church Fathers, Schoolmen, and theologians always refer as the authority for the incorporation of *ius naturale* into their theological systems. But the *ius naturale* of the Roman lawyers lost in the process of assimilation

[1] The same, *Homilies*, 1 Tim. *Hom.* 12. Compare Pöhlmann, *Sociale Frage in der antiken Welt*, vol. 2 ; also Laurent, *Histoire du droit des Gens*, IV. 102, *seq.*

[2] William of Ockham : " *Omne ius naturale in Scripturis divinis explicite et implicite continetur* " (*Dialogus* in Goldast, *Monarchia*, II.), p. 934 ; Richard Hooker : " The Scripture is fraught even with Laws of Nature, insomuch as Gratian defining natural right . . . that which the Books of the Law and the Gospel do contain " (*Ecclesiastical Polity*, book 1, c. 12).

to the body of Roman law much of the communistic ardour which
it had in the age of Vergil, Josephus, and Seneca.   In Roman
Law it was combined with *ius gentium*, which had grown out of
the international relations and commercial transactions of the
ancient world and therefore could not but be unfavourable to the
social conceptions of the state of nature : the Law of Nations
legalised dominion and servitude and private possessions.
According to the Institutes *ius naturale* is that which nature
teaches animals and man ; from it originates the joining together
of male and female ; from it also procreation and education of the
offspring.[1]   Likewise, all men are born free ; and air, water,
public and religious buildings are common possession.[2]   Indeed,
in Roman Law, *ius naturale* lost its old meaning and became a
rudimentary organ, while in the patristic and scholastic literature
it is in full vigour.   This is due to the Greek Fathers, then to S.
Augustine, but particularly to S. Isidore of Seville (*d.* 636), who
transmitted not only the body of Roman learning to the Church,
but also the primitive Christian spirit.   According to him,
" *ius naturale* is common to all nations and it contains everything
that is known to man by natural instinct and not by constitutions
and man-made law, and that is : the joining together of man
and woman, procreation and education of children, *communis
omnium possessio, et omnium una libertas*, the acquisition of things
which may be captured in the air, on the earth, and in the water,
restitution of loaned and entrusted goods, finally, self-defence
by force against violence." [3]   This definition of *ius naturale*
contains, first, the usual characteristics as given in the Institutes ;
secondly, the doctrines concerning the state of nature (communism
and universal equal liberty) ;   thirdly, the essence of the law
of nations.   It forms an integral part of the *Corpus Iuris
Canonici ;* [4] the Schoolmen always refer to it ; indeed, this definition appears to them as authoritative as the reference of S. Paul
to natural law.   The canonic lawyers and commentators who

[1] *Inst.*, 1. 1, §§ 2, 3.
[2] *Ib.*, l. 3, § 1.   *Cf.* Voigt, *Ius Naturale*, 1857, vol. 1, § 57.
[3] Isidore, *Etym.*, l. v., c. 4 (ed. Migne, *tom.* 82).
[4] *Decr. Grat.*, prima pars, dist. 1, c. 7.

direct their keenest shafts against commercialism speak with evident delight of S. Isidore's additions and declare that *dulcissima rerum possessio communis* and that *meum et tuum ex iniquitate procedunt*.[1] Only from the division of things discord came, *sic inter mortales facta divisio est.* Also William of Ockham refers to the delectable words of S. Isidore.[2]

On the other hand, they meet with great difficulties when attempting to reconcile economic and political equality, or the state of nature, with acquisition of things, restitution of loans and deposits, the use of force and violence, which are foreign to the concept of the state of nature and which evidently presuppose private property, discord, and enmity. S. Isidore, of course, erroneously joined *ius naturale* to *ius gentium* ; and a modern critic, despite his reverence for great and good men and their learning, would simply draw a line between those two legal concepts and show that *ius gentium* was much more akin to civil than to natural law. But the mental attitude of the Schoolmen was different. Revering authority above everything they saw in S. Isidore's definition of *ius naturale* one of those incompatibilities and contradictions which were but superficially so, and therefore called for subtle distinctions and interpretations to reconcile them.

The discovery of America and her tribal organisations added new strength to the system of *ius naturale,* and the rather romantic descriptions of natural society that followed upon the acquaintance with the American tribes are to some extent due to the preconceived notions which sprang from the concept of the state of nature. To Amerigo Vespucci, Sir Thomas More, Sahagun (a Franciscan missionary in Mexico), Hugo Grotius, Joseph Acosta, and many other scholars and travellers, the American tribes and communities appeared as striking demonstrations of the truths of natural law.[3]

The influence exercised by that system of thought in the

---

[1] *Decr. Grat.*, sec. pars, causa 12, qu. 1, c. 2, gloss. *a.*

[2] William of Ockham, *Dialogus* (in Goldast *Monarchia* II.), p. 932.

[3] Compare particularly John Locke, *On Civil Government*, II., c. 8, §§ 102, 108.

development of English, and generally, European social and political speculations could hardly be over-estimated. School-men, theologians, statesmen, lawyers, revolutionists, and poets based their reasonings and wove their imaginings on it, and even as late as in the first half of the nineteenth century, despite Burke and Bentham who opposed it, British Socialists, poor-law and social reformers were thinking in the terms of that system. From Alexander of Hales, Duns Scotus, and Ockham to Locke, Bolingbroke, Abraham Tucker and Paley ; from Bracton to Blackstone ; from Wycliffe and John Ball to Hodgskin, Feargus O'Connor, and Cardinal Manning, social and political philosophy was swayed by doctrines of natural rights. And yet, during all those centuries the concept of *ius naturale* was practically always passing through divers changes and interpretations which all but obliterated its original traits. It was, evidently, a useful hypothesis, and had to be maintained by interpretations and commentaries, which were merely adaptations of the theory to the profound mental and social transformations which English, and generally, European society was continually undergoing.

II

THE ENGLISH SCHOOLMEN

I.—DISSOLUTION OF THE MANORIAL SYSTEM

NATURAL and canonical law, as it moulded the speculations of the early Middle Ages, was in conformity with the customs and views of an agrarian, martial, and clerical society, whose units consisted of manorial demesnes, village communities, abbeys and monasteries, with towns as their appendages. Land formed the chief source of wealth, while trade and commerce were the exception and were despised as base callings ; movable capital played a negligible part, and private property in the sense of absolute individual control over wealth was little known. This natural society reached its culmination in the Crusades, the zenith of pure mediaeval spirit.

In the age of the Crusades the germs of the new social organisation had already made their appearance. Cities and towns, such as Venice, Genoa, Cologne, Augsburg, Nuremberg arose, founding their prosperity on commerce, money-changing, trade, and handicrafts. The Crusades themselves, with their need of money and their effects on the intercourse between West and East, promoted the new movement in which movable capital was destined to come into conflict with, and finally to overwhelm, the institutions and customs of feudal and clerical society.[1] The towns gradually emancipated themselves from manorial and episcopal control ; their social and economic needs and conditions became too differentiated and complicated to fit in with the communistic and anti-commercial tendencies of natural and canonical law. The growth of town economy, in its reaction on the mediaeval agrarian organisation, loosened the

---

[1] Compare H. v. Eicken, *Mittelalterliche Weltanschauung*, p. 778, sqq.

bonds between lord and vassal, manor and abbeys and village, and finally broke up the old relations. Concurrently with those events great religious and moral teachers and reformers arose, and a momentous spiritual and social ferment set in which led to (a) heated discussions on property and poverty (b) social upheavals, (c) changes in the doctrine of *ius naturale*, (d) rise of natural and moral philosophy, and (e) the formation of national Churches and States.

2.—THEOLOGICAL CONTEST ABOUT POVERTY

Social philosophy formed throughout the Middle Ages a part of theology, and the disputes concerning property, communism, and poverty were fought out by theologians. The most scholarly and influential among them were the Franciscans and the Dominicans, who from the thirteenth to the fifteenth century supplied the Church with great teachers. No member of any other Order or of the secular clergy was equal in learning and acuteness of thought to Alexander of Hales, S. Thomas Aquinas, Roger Bacon, Duns Scotus, and William of Ockham. The Dominicans were conservative and conciliatory, while the Minorites, impelled by the primitive Christian fervour of their saintly founder, were the guardians of the poor, the counsellors of the people, and the defenders of the nation against all usurping domination ; a happy people and a good king, ruling in conformity with natural and divine law, were their social and political ideals. The controversies and struggles concerning property and poverty as well as the relation between Church and State, which filled the thirteenth and, in a more intense degree, the fourteenth century, were led by Minorites and Dominicans ; and their stage was Western and Central Europe.

S. Francis of Assisi took for his rules of conduct the Scriptural texts, Matthew x. 9–10 ; xvi. 24 ; xix. 21, which command absolute poverty for the true followers of Christ. These rules were evidently a protest against the new commercial civilisation of Italy and an appeal to the pious to return to primitive Christianity, to the spirit of the Sermon on the Mount. The followers of Jesus should live a life of self-abnegation, no ties should bind

them to the secular conditions of society ; they should embrace
poverty, practise charity, and derive their living from service,
labour, and mendicancy. His doctrine of *paupertas evangelica*
was uncompromising and unworldly, and although it applied to
the Order only, it could not but influence the views of its adherents
concerning property in general ; they held in the spirit of natural
and canonical law that property had its origin in iniquity.

Different in character and teaching was the greatest of the
Dominicans, S. Thomas Aquinas. He was essentially a man of
compromise, a great conciliator, who attempted to bring natural
and canonical law into a certain harmony with the requirements
of a society divided into rich and poor, agriculturists and merchants, proprietors and propertyless. He distinguished between
the ideal and the possible, relegating communism to the region
of the ideal and reducing it in practice to generous almsgiving
and care for the propertyless. He sanctioned private property
and its conditions as necessary for the peaceful existence of
society. As long as man lived *in statu innocentiae* there was no
danger that community of goods would lead to discord and
strife. Indeed, many good men held everything in common.
But after the state of innocence had vanished and separate
dominions multiplied, the division of possessions became necessary
for the sake of a secure social life.[1] The division of possessions
led to the division of society into rich and poor, but by natural
and divine law it is incumbent upon the rich to give the
whole of their superfluous wealth to the poor : *Res quas aliqui
superabundanter habent, ex naturali iure debentur pauperum
sustentationi.*[2] In the meaning of Aquinas the poor are not
merely the destitute and paupers, but the wage-workers, the
labouring poor, whose only source of living is their daily work.
In times of need they must be given relief so as not to allow
them to sink into destitution. Still, in the writings of the
" doctor angelicus " opinions are to be found which are in
complete harmony with the most uncompromising tenets of

[1] S. Thomas Aquinas, *Summa* 1, qu. 98, art. 1, ad 3.
[2] *Ib.*, 2, 2, qu. 66, art. 7.

ius naturale : *In exterioribus divitiis non potest unus homo superabundare nisi alter deficiat.*[1]

The practical nature of the social teaching of the Dominicans held the Order together, while the sublimity of the Franciscan rules precluded their realisation and, therefore, gave rise to dissensions and splits.   In the main, the divisions were represented by two parties, one adhering to the *usus moderatus*, the other to the *usus pauper*.   According to the first common property and common use were permitted to the Order, whose members were thus joint possessors of wealth, while according to the other practice the Order had to live in absolute poverty, without any common property, for *habere aliquid minuat de perfectione*.   Over a hundred Franciscans of the extreme wing perished at the stake in the defence of absolute poverty against the decision of Pope John XXII., who was in favour of the *usus moderatus*.   Of the English Franciscans Alexander of Hales and Duns Scotus appear to have adhered to the *usus moderatus*, while William of Ockham was one of the foremost upholders of the *usus pauper*.   He, in the capacity of the English Provincial, supported the Minister General of the Minorites, Michael of Cesena, and charged the Pope with heresy.   In 1328 he and his friends were cast into prison at Avignon, but rescued by emissaries of Emperor Lewis of Bavaria, who brought them to Munich, where Ockham composed his chief works.

3.—HALES, DUNS SCOTUS, AND OCKHAM

Alexander of Hales (de Ales, *d.* 1245), the elder contemporary and theological precursor of S. Thomas Aquinas, points out the contradiction involved in S. Isidore's definition of *ius naturale* and asks how common possessions and the rights accruing from acquisition and occupancy can be reconciled with the equity and goodness which are the basis of *ius naturale*.   And he solves the question by showing that what was equitable and good *in statu naturali* was no more so *in statu naturae corruptae*.   In the first

[1] S. Thomas Aquinas, *Summa* 2, 2, qu. 118, art. 1, ad 2.   Compare Adam Smith, *Wealth of Nations*, book 5, part 2, " The affluence of the few supposes the indigence of the many."

state communism was just, equitable and good, in the other
private property. It was quite true, he says in the words of S.
Augustine, that it was only *iure imperatoris* and not *iure divino*
that a person may say *haec villa est mea, meus est iste servus, mea
est ista domus*. The corruption of man's nature made it necessary
for civil government to introduce private property. Alexander
of Hales is however of opinion that the right of private property
could not apply to those things which belong to the whole community, and that it was not permitted to appropriate common
fields and ways : *platea aliqua, vel campus communitatis ; in
talibus non licet appropriare sibi*. In the same manner he solves
the contradiction between the doctrine of *ius naturale* that all
men are born free and equal, and the existence of dominion and
servitude which is sanctioned by S. Paul (Rom. xiii). In the
state of nature or *ante peccatum* universal liberty and equality
prevailed, while servitude came *post peccatum*, partly by God's
dispensation, which is always just though occult, partly as a
punishment of the wicked, finally, as the universal effect of
sin.[1]

Duns Scotus (*d.* 1308 at Cologne) looked upon property from
the point of view of his Order. Voluntary poverty was his ideal ;
to divest oneself of all earthly goods and use them in common
with all who strive after a perfect Christian life. The right of
private property sprang neither from natural nor divine law,
but from civil law, and was the effect of the Fall of man, when
covetousness took hold of man's heart and caused him to occupy
more than he needed.[2] The principle of natural law concerning
communism fell into desuetude, because the corruption of man
by sin no longer allowed communism to continue undisturbed.
The weak and peaceful were in danger of being wronged or were
actually offered violence by the strong and rapacious. The
common possessions were divided, but not by divine or natural
law, since such law could not cease to exist even after the original
state had disappeared ; thus it must have been civil government
that established the division of possessions. Private property

[1] Alexander de Ales, *Summa* 3, qu. 27.
[2] Duns Scotus, *Quaestiones super sententias* 4, dist. 15, qu. 2.

once instituted, led to changes of ownership. Civil laws were
enacted to regulate the transfer of property by selling and
buying, loan and hire, grant and gift. Gain or profit on such
transactions is only permitted as a compensation for the sacrifice
of a certain advantage, but not as a means of enriching oneself.
Trade and commerce are useful to society and therefore lawful.
It is however wrongful and vile to engross and forestall ; persons
who are what the French call *regrattiers* are a danger to society.[1]

William of Ockham (*d.* 1347 at Munich) was the last English
Schoolman of European stature. His philosophical and political
front faces modern times, but his armour is mediaeval. Hence
the heaviness and hesitation in his gait. His starting point is
the Franciscan doctrine of *paupertas evangelica.* This doctrine
led him to a life-long struggle with the Papacy, and he used it in
his attempts to destroy the secular power of the Church, its claim
to the supremacy over the nation.   In this contest he incidentally
brought out his views on property and government, some of which
are strikingly modern.

His problem was, If common possessions and universal liberty
are *iure naturali et divino,* and if natural and divine law is
eternal and immutable, how did private property and servitude
arise ?   And how was it possible for S. Isidore to include institutions of private property in the definition of *ius naturale ?*

His solution is ingenious. He distinguishes three kinds of
natural law, evidently corresponding to the three moral stages of
man : *ante lapsum, post lapsum,* and the setting in of iniquity
and corruption.   Ockham puts these stages in a slightly different
order—*post lapsum, ante lapsum,* state of iniquity, but as to his
reasonings and conclusions it makes no difference in which order
we regard the first two stages. And his reasonings and conclusions are as follows : In the state of *ante lapsum* man lived
according to natural equity, without constitutions and customs ;
everything was held in common and all men were free. S.
Isidore, in defining *ius naturale* as *communis omnium possessio
et omnium una libertas,* had this stage in view. In the state
post lapsum right reason aided man and gave him command-

---

[1] Comp. Carl Werner, *Duns Scotus*, p. 585.

C

ments, as for instance, Do not commit adultery, do not tell lies,[1] live in common and be free. The third stage was that which followed *propter iniquitatem ;* in this stage private property and civil dominion—economic and political inequality—were introduced. *Ex iure naturali omnia sunt communia . . . et si post lapsum omnes homines secundum rationem viverent, omnia deberent esse communia, nihil proprium ; proprietas enim propter iniquitatem inducta est.* Also dominion and servitude sprang from the same cause. They were introduced by *ius gentium et civile.* How, then, could the third stage of man's history partake of the character of *ius naturale ?*

The answer to this question is the most original part in Ockham's system and distinguishes it from the *Summae* of his predecessors. He asserts that the institutions of private property and civil government are only natural and rational if they were introduced in the interest and with the consent of the governed. Only in proportion to the consent of the subjects are these institutions just and equitable, and therefore *iure naturali.*[2] Or to speak the language of the moral philosophers, the successors of the Schoolmen : private property and civil government are just and legitimate if they are the effect of, and in conformity with, the social and political contract.

All that applies to society in general, while the strict practice of *paupertas evangelica* applies to those who desire to follow Christ. Such poverty is superior to communism, charity, and almsgiving. Christ and His apostles were absolutely propertyless. Evangelical poverty means abdication of all temporals. The secular Church is as inferior to Christ's conduct as the Pope is to the Holy Scriptures.

The tide of the Reformation and Moral Philosophy was coming in. Ockham was its European herald.

---

[1] Also Sir Thomas More regards lying as against nature. *Treatise on Passions, Works,* p. 1384.

[2] William of Ockham, *Dialogus* (Goldast, *Monarchia* II.), pp.932–34.

III

EARLY ENGLISH COMMUNISM

I.—THE PEASANTS' REVOLT

THE new social forces began to make themselves felt in England
in the reign of Henry II. Like islands from a receding sea the
towns were emerging from their feudal surroundings, gaining an
independent economic and legal existence. By the middle of
the thirteenth century dozens of towns were already noted for
trading and manufacturing activities, for their gilds and courts.
The towns offered remunerative markets for foodstuff and raw
material, and in proportion as agricultural produce grew in value
and could be exchanged for money land was enclosed and the
village community encroached upon. The Statutes of Merton
(1235), and Westminster (1285), bear evidence of the incipient
stage of the new economy. Since the middle of the twelfth century the village community was losing its ancient status,[1] and
villeinage was turning into serfdom. This legal deterioration
of the peasantry was taking place at an age in which the economic
conditions of the peasantry were either improving or capable
of improvement. For, as joint-possessors of the communal lands,
the peasants could sell their produce in town and as labourers
could command money-wages for their work. The contrast
between a deteriorating legal status and improving economic
conditions grew sharper from the effects of the Black Death and
the Statute of Labourers, the first raising the value of labour
to a higher level than ever, while the other sought to check the
economic tendencies which were favourable to the labouring
population.

It is hardly possible to do historical justice to this period if

[1] A. Réville, *Soulèvement des travailleurs en Angleterre*, Introd.,
Petit-Dutaillis, p. xxxviii.

we look upon the serf in relation to the lord only and disregard his relation to, and his standing in, the village community. The peasants of the later mediaeval times were not mere serfs, but also respected members dwelling among their people, or as Locke would say, " tenants in common," [1] who regulated their affairs by collective customs, rights and responsibilities. They were not atomised, propertyless proletarians, but partners of agrarian co-operative associations, imbued with traditions of their ancient liberties and with sentiments of communal life, and looking upon enclosures as private appropriations of what was common, and on the lords as usurpers,—indeed, the verb " to enclose " means to create private property. They felt very keenly the encroachments upon their common rights and, when the Revolt broke out, they demanded the return of their old charters of liberty and the restoration of their rights of common, pasture, and piscary ; [2] they destroyed hedges and fences.[3] True, they did not formulate any communist programme, for they were not suffering from a system of private property, but from encroachments upon their common rights, and against those encroachments they rebelled. It was a rebellion of obsolescent communistic associations [4] against the tightening legal and commercial grip of lords and abbots. Theoretically, it was a rebellion of *ius naturale* against *ius civile*, or friar against lawyer.

In the fourteenth century, the English peasantry were not without teachers and prophets. An age that saw Langland's ethical writings, the Wycliffite Bible translation, and Chaucer's poetry, must have been an age of a mentally active commonalty. The men who prepared the minds of the people for such gifts were Minorites, " poor priests," and other friars who toured the country, or former friars and monks, who, impelled by Franciscan doctrines, or swayed by a zeal for religious reform, found no

[1] John Locke, *On Civil Government*, II., c. 5.
[2] Walsingham, *Gesta Abbatum*, III., pp. 308, 311, 306.
[3] A. Réville, p. xli.
[4] Compare, however, Trevelyan, *Age of Wycliffe*, 1909, p. 197, and Oman, *Great Revolt of* 1381, pp. 51–2, where contrary views are expressed.

room in the Church for their ideals and aims. Some of them preached communism as the economic frame of society nearest to godliness, and all of them sympathised with the oppressed labouring population, and desired to see a communal and demo-cratic peasantry, freed from the encroachments of commercialised temporal and spiritual lords. It was an age of agitation, brought about by an alliance of an intellectual proletariat with the dis-satisfied labouring masses.[1] From Oxford as the intellectual and spiritual centre the light was spread by the friars to the open fields.[2] The burden of their sermons was undoubtedly the social ethics of Primitive Christianity, and of patristic and Minorite doctrines. All of them must have known S. Isidore's definition of natural law.

> " They preach of Plato and prove it by Seneca,
> That all things under heaven ought to be in common."

So writes Langland,[3] who condemns such preaching to the lewd, for Moses taught, Thou shalt not covet thy neighbour's things. The author of *Piers Ploughman* was anti-communistic ; he anticipated Protestantism far more consistently than Wycliffe, inasmuch as he was more individualistic. With great care he avoided all references in favour of communism, as may be seen from the following passage :

> Water, air, fire, and wit—these four
> The heavenly Father gave to all in common.[4]

The four elements were, of course, water, air, fire and earth. Instead of earth Langland puts wit, apparently with the purpose of not lending his authority to agrarian communism. Still, the protests of Langland against communism may serve as evidence of the widespread communistic agitation. How widespread it was among the intellectuals may be gauged by a curious variant in one of the manuscripts of Britton. Here is a case of a cleric

[1] Thomas Wright, *Pol. Poems and Songs*, I., Introd., p. lx.
[2] G. A. Little, *Gray friars of Oxford*, pp. 63–4.
[3] *Piers Ploughman*, B. xx. 273–76, quoted by Trevelyan, p. 198. For other proofs of communistic teachings of friars, compare Little, p. 84.
[4] *Piers Ploughman*, B. vii. 52–3.

playing a trick upon a lawyer.   In Bracton's *De legibus* (i. 31)
it is said, " All men, even serfs, are free by natural law, but civil
right or the law of nations detracts from natural right, and
men may be serfs under the law of nations."   Britton, probably
enlarging upon Bracton, declares, in his Norman French, that
originally all men were free and held all things in common and
lived according to the law of nature, but in ancient times (*en
grant antiquité*) freedom was changed into bondage.[1]   In the
Manuscript F. of Britton, copied late in the fourteenth century,
the words " *en grant antiquité* " are changed into " *en grant
iniquité.*"   It is Ockham's " *propter iniquitatem.*"   Such were
the sentiments of the time.

2.—JOHN WYCLIFFE

What Ockham strove to accomplish for Western and Central
Europe his disciple, John Wycliffe (*d.* 1384), set himself to do for
England.   The stage was of smaller dimensions, the degree of
economic development less advanced, and the mental capacities
of the actor were less extensive.   Wycliffe was, however, no mere
epigonus of his revered master.[2]   To the armoury of scholastic
speculation on communism he added new arguments—the feudal
concepts of possession and lordship.   His sources of knowledge
were the same as those of his predecessors—namely, the Scriptures, the Fathers, the Corpus Iuris Canonici, and Aristotle.   He
collects his materials with the view of solving the vital problems
of his country and his age, and weaves them into a certain
whole, the cohesive forces of which are an intensely ethical conception of Christianity and an overpowering interest in the
welfare of England.   In Wycliffe we touch English soil of the
fourteenth and fifteenth century.   The dissolution of feudalism
gave rise to two great questions : first, How to establish a central,
national authority to take the place of the feudal, decentralised
order ;   and, secondly, How to protect the peasantry.   In
his attempts to formulate an answer Wycliffe met with two

---

[1] Britton, ed. Nichols, I. 32 (31).
[2] Netter of Walden. *Fasc. Ziz.*, Shirley's Introd., p. liii.

difficulties. Mediaeval theology, dominated partly by *ius naturale* and partly by Hildebrandian traditions, regarded civil dominion as tainted with iniquity. This taint had to be removed if England were to emerge from the chaos consequent upon the decay of the feudal order. The second difficulty was the growing helplessness of the village community and the dispossession of the peasantry. It was no small matter for a theologian and scholastic like Wycliffe to set his face against the exhortations of the prophet Samuel concerning kingship, or against S. Augustine's view that Empire had its origin in fratricide,[1] or, finally, against a fundamental doctrine of natural and divine law. No less difficult was the defence of the village community in the teeth of powerful social forces which were undermining it. In the midst of such mental perplexities the strong lead given by his famous countryman, William of Ockham, must have greatly comforted him. And he decided for kingship and for communism; in short, a social reform monarchy. A good king using his authority to protect the peasant communities was his ideal.

Like all his predecessors Wycliffe assumes that society at its origin lived in a state of innocence and communism; natural law governed its conduct. Absence of private property and civil government was thus the distinguishing feature of the state of nature. After the Fall of man *ius naturale* became insufficient; man's moral fibre weakened and needed an artificial support. Therefore, God set up civil dominion and entrusted it with the mission of fostering love among men. The best form of such dominion is government by Judges, as among the Israelites of old. Wherever such government is impossible kingship is the next best. Civil government is thus of divine origin, though it smacks of venial sin: *Dominium civile . . . sapit tamen veniale peccatum.*[2] But if it is combined with communism it may approach to the perfect state, to the state of innocence and fatherly rule.[3] In this way it becomes natural. Wycliffe's

[1] S. Augustine, *Civ. dei*, l. 15, c. 5, referred to in Willmann's *Geschichte des Idealismus*, II., p. 309.
[2] John Wycliffe, *De ecclesia*, c. 14, p. 321.
[3] *Civ. dom.* I., c. 14, p. 99.

mental bent is strongly towards justification of kingship, indeed,
not only justification, but sanctification of kingship, and endowing
it with the supremacy over the Church. His dictum, *Deus
debet obedire diabolo*,[1] may perhaps be interpreted as directed
against Pope Gregory VII., who in the epistle to Bishop Herman
of Metz (1081) declares, as a matter of fact, that kings and dukes
derived their principle from the prince of evil, while the Church
was of divine origin,[2] therefore, kings must obey the Church.
In his rather bold and too finely pointed epigram, Wycliffe
essentially replies, the Church must obey the king. With regard
to private property, however, he is, theoretically, a decided
opponent. The division of possessions arose *ratione peccati* and
the taint of sin was still attached to it.

And now comes the specific addition of Wycliffe—the feudal
aspect of dominion and property. God is the supreme lord.
In the Scriptures, the only infallible source of knowledge, God is
called Lord. He is master of all things. He is the over-lord.
In contradistinction to men who do not know how to bestow gifts,
He grants His fiefs to the righteous only on condition of service.
And He grants them directly, there being neither ecclesiastical
nor lay intermediary between God and man. The kings are His
bailiffs and all the possessors His vassals. As He grants His gifts
to the righteous only, nobody can hold dominion or worldly
goods who is in mortal sin or who is not in grace. *Nullus est
dominus civilis, nullus est episcopus, nullus est prelatus, dum est
in peccato mortali*.[3] Moreover, the possessions of the unrighteous
were acquired by rapine, theft, robbery, and usurpation.[4] For
only to those who are in grace everything is given, and they are
the lords of the earth and the fulness thereof.[5] Now, all men
ought to be righteous and in grace and, therefore, ought to be lords
of the earth and the fulness thereof. But how could multitudes
of men be lords of everything if not by holding everything in

---

[1] *Fasc. Ziz.*, p. 278.
[2] *Gregorii VII. Opera*, ed. Migne, tom. 147–8 epistola 21.
[3] *Fasc. Ziz.*, p. 280.
[4] *Civ. dom.* I., c. 5, p. 34, c. 14, p. 101.
[5] *Ib.*, c. 6, p. 41.

common ? *Ergo omnia debent esse communia.*[1] Only through communism can the multitudes, if righteous, be lords of everything and fulfil the supreme condition of lordship—service to one another. Communism does not infringe upon Christianity. The apostles held everything in common (Acts iv. 32). Communism is as superior to private property as universal truths are to particular truths ; Christ loves the human species as a whole more than particular men. It is true that Aristotle reasons against Plato's doctrines concerning community of goods,[2] but his reasonings hold good only as regards community of wives. His objection that communism weakened the Commonwealth, inasmuch as people cared more for their own than for common goods, amounts really to the statement that there are sinful people. It must, however, be denied that communism weakened the Commonwealth. For, the greater the number of people holding possession the greater their interest in the welfare of the Commonwealth. Community of interests leads to unity, and unity is strength. Communism, then, leads to the strengthening and not to the weakening of the Commonwealth. Possessions in common being thus morally best will be best cared for. Indeed, civil dominion combined with common possessions is natural and spiritual, while dominion based on private property is artificial and corruptible.[3]

Such are the views of Wycliffe concerning monarchy and property. It is evident that he makes his communism conditional upon a high moral state of society, upon the constant effort of man to check sinfulness and to attain to that degree of grace which would render him worthy of receiving the earth as a fief at the hands of the over-lord. His doctrines preclude all sedition, rebellion, violence, and even party and faction fights, as a means to realising communism, since civil government is of divine origin, and rebellion against it is *ipso facto* treason against the supreme lord, which is punished by the forfeiture of grace and escheat of possessions.

[1] *Civ. dom.* I., c. 14, p. 96. Compare Poole, *Mediaeval Thought,* c. x.
[2] Aristotle, *Politics,* II. 1.
[3] *Civ. dom.* I., c. 14, pp. 99–100.

However, the combination of righteousness as the condition
of possession with the feudal principle as the basis of dominion
gave rise to a difficulty which could not easily be set aside.   And
it was this—What if the holders of political and economic
dominion are in mortal sin ?   Would not, under such circumstances, rebellion be in accordance with the intention of God ?
It was a problem which theological communists of a revolutionary
and democratic temper might not have been inclined to answer
in a feudal sense.   And this was actually the case with John Ball.

3.—JOHN BALL

Wycliffe's attitude towards the Peasants' Revolt was similar.
to, though less violent than, that of Martin Luther towards the
German Bauernkrieg (1525) ; and John Hus would, in all
probability, have taken up the same attitude towards the Taborite
wars in Bohemia, had he lived to witness them.   The chief
leaders of the Reformation brought their reforming zeal to
bear upon ecclesiastical and national affairs and left social
grievances to be removed by the operation of ethical endeavour.
The times were however out of joint, and the Reformation
movement was in all three countries accompanied by social
upheavals.   The three reformers had their revolutionary
counterparts in John Ball (d. 1381), Andrew Prokop, and Thomas
Münzer respectively, who, as priests, started from the same
theological premisses as the reformers, but were launched on
revolutionary careers by their democratic conception of mediaeval
communism.   Legend or tradition makes Ball a disciple of
Wycliffe, Münzer a disciple of Luther, while Prokop was actually
a professed adherent of Hus.   The simultaneous occurrence of
strong movements for national and ecclesiastical reform and of
violent social upheavals in England, Bohemia, and Germany, and
the rise of similar minds as Wycliffe, Hus, and Luther on the one
hand, and of Ball, Prokop, and Münzer on the other, are worthy
of notice, indicating as they undoubtedly do a certain regularity
of historical movements.   In point of time England preceded
Bohemia and Germany, while in point of intensity and thorough-
ness Bohemia and Germany outstripped England.

The question as to whether Ball was really the disciple of Wycliffe, as Netter of Walden states,[1] is quite immaterial. The social thoughts and sentiments which Ball disseminated among the peasantry were truisms in mediaeval theology. The doctrines concerning the natural state he could have learned from patristic and scholastic as well as legal literature, and the denunciations of the wealth and corruption of the Church were quite in keeping with the general tenets of the Franciscans, the complaints of the peasantry and the townspeople. The same applies to Walsingham[2] and Knighton;[3] as far as Ball's social doctrines are concerned there is neither external nor internal evidence that they had any special connection with Wycliffe. Many years prior to the Peasants' Revolt Ball was occupied in inflaming the peasantry against the lords temporal and spiritual, adding to the social ferment that was rapidly growing since the Black Death and the Statute of Labourers.

According to Knighton, Ball was a most famous preacher among laymen and disseminated the word of God " in an insipid manner, mixing tares with the wheat." His speeches were indeed similar to those of Thomas Münzer. Liberty and equality, democracy and communism formed their chief theme. Ball looked back to the origins of society and asked :—

> " When Adam dalf and Eve span
> Who was then a gentilman ? "

In consonance with the theological doctrines of *ius naturale* he went on to discourse upon the natural state. At the beginning men were created equal by nature ; servitude was introduced by unjust oppression of worthless men, contrary to the will of God. For, if it had pleased God to create serfs He would have constituted who should be serf and who lord. The people have now been given the opportunity of breaking the servile yoke they have borne for a long time ; if they chose they could enjoy the liberty so long desired by them. Therefore, they should take good courage and like wise husbandmen should cultivate their

---

[1] *Fasc. Ziz.*, p. 273.   [2] Walsingham, *Historia Angl.*, II., pp. 32–3.
[3] Knighton, *Chronicon*, II., p. 131.

soil and extirpate and cut off the noxious weeds that choke the fruits of the earth. They should fell the great lords, judges, lawyers, and remove everybody from the land who was injurious to the community. Then they would have peace for the present and security for the future ; for when the mighty ones are cut off all men would enjoy equal freedom, and all have the same nobility and rank.[1]

The sample which Froissart handed down of the speeches of Ball contains both democracy and communism :—

" My good people,—Things cannot go well in England, nor ever will, until all goods are held in common, and until there will be neither serfs nor gentlemen, and we shall all be equal. For what reason have they, whom we call lords, got the best of us ? How did they deserve it ? Why do they keep us in bondage ? If we all descended from one father and one mother, Adam and Eve, how can they assert or prove that they are more masters than ourselves ? Except perhaps that they make us work and produce for them to spend ! They are clothed in velvets and in coats garnished with ermine and fur, while we wear coarse linen. They have wine, spices, and good bread, while we get rye-bread, offal, straw, and water. They have residences, handsome manors, and we the trouble and the work, and must brave the rain and the wind in the fields. And it is from us and our labour that they get the means to support their pomp ; yet we are called serfs and are promptly beaten if we fail to do their bidding." [2]

In abandoning ethical propaganda for political and revolutionary agitation, Ball went outside the bounds of the communistic and equalitarian doctrines of mediaeval theology. This was his real guilt. After the defeat of the insurrection his career came to a violent end. Less fortunate than Prokop and Münzer, who fell in battle, Ball died on the gallows at St. Albans.

[1] Walsingham, *Hist. Angl.*, II. 32–3.
[2] Froissart, *Collection des Chroniques*, VIII., c. 106.

problems of his time.   More's capacity for unravelling economic
questions is amply testified to by the mission he undertook at the
instance of the London mercers to settle certain litigious cases
between them and the Hanseatic merchants of the Steelyard, as
well as by his participation in the embassy sent by King Henry
VIII. to Antwerp for the purpose of adjusting the commercial
relations between England and the Low Countries.[1]

No less important was More's acquaintance with the accounts of
the discovery of America and the influence they exercised on his
imagination.   " In a little tract of four leaves . . . entitled
Mundus novus, Vespucci gives an account of his second
voyage, on which he started from Lisbon, May 14, 1501. . . .
The voyage was past the Canary Islands to Cape Verde.   In
those regions—the voyager names them very vaguely—' the
people live according to nature, and may be called Epicureans
rather than Stoics. . . .   Property they have none, but all
things are in common.   They live without a king, without any
sovereignty, and every one is his own master.' . . .   In the
later treatise referred to by More, in which an account is given
of the first four voyages of Vespucci (*quattuor Americi Vesputii
Navigationes*) it is said, ' Gold, pearls, jewels and all other such
like things, which in this Europe of ours we count riches, they
think nothing of, nay, they utterly despise them.' " [2]

More did not in the least doubt the moral excellence of a population which was said to live in the state of nature, since as a
student of patrology and jurisprudence he was familiar with
ius naturale.   In a letter to his friend, John Colet, Dean of St.
Paul's, he is full of praise of the virtues of rural life ; " in the
country, as opposed to town life, the face of the earth is smiling
and the sight of the sky is a delight ; one sees nothing there but
the bounteous gifts of nature and the sacred vestiges of innocence." [3]   The state of nature appeared to him as the *status
innocentiae*, and how closely that state is bound up with com-

---

[1] Thomas More, *Utopia*, ed. Lupton, 1895, pp. 72, 79.   (All
references given below to More's *Utopia* apply to this edition.)

[2] J. H. Lupton, Introd. to his edition of *Utopia*, p. xxxviii.

[3] Th. Stapleton, *Tres Thomæ*, Cologne, 1612, p. 164.

D

munism we know from the patristic and scholastic writings. In his *Utopia* he also refers several times to the law of nature and life according to nature.[1]

The influence of rising rationalism must also be noticed. More, writing to Gunnell, the domestic tutor of his children, on the importance and aim of education, tells him, " that from learning they ought to derive the most sublime lessons—piety towards God, benevolence towards men, modesty of heart, and Christian humility. . . . These I look upon as true and genuine fruits of learning ; and as I acknowledge that all learned do not attain to them, so I maintain that those who begin to study with this intention may easily obtain this happy result." More, like Hooker after him, was, however, too good a Christian to put reason and philosophy in the place of the fear of God and the divine commandments.[2] His view of the relation between reason and faith he expressed in the *Utopia*, of whose scholars he said that " they join to the arguments of philosophy certain principles of religion without which they think reason of itself weak and imperfect " (p. 188).

4.—THE *UTOPIA* : CHARACTER AND PUBLICATION

More's *Utopia* is the application of the ethics and politics of the Church Fathers and the philosophy of Humanism to the greatest secular problem—the organisation of human society, and in particular to the social England of the age of transition from feudalism to commercialism, from rural economy to money economy, from associated and regulated activities to individual enterprise. It is mediaeval in so far as it regards communism as more favourable to virtue than private property ; and it is differentiated from the early communist doctrines by the fact that, while the Church Fathers and schoolmen reasoned from abstract morality or a Scriptural text and deplored the vices of mankind which they regarded as the effects of the disappearance of the natural and divine state, More's point of departure was that

---

[1] More, *Utopia*, pp. 155, 190, 192.
[2] Compare Hooker, *Ecclesiastical Polity*, book 3, c. 8.

of a Catholic and patriotic statesman, who, after an examination into the actual conditions of his country, looked for a remedy to social reform.

The book is divided into two parts, the first exposing the actual social conditions of England, the second presenting a model communist society. The first is thus given to social criticism, embracing economics, politics, and criminology ; the second is a social reconstruction.

Its form is partly dialogue and partly narrative. Its scene is Antwerp and some unknown country in South America. The *dramatis personae* are : Raphael Hythloday, Peter Aegidius or Giles, and More himself. Raphael is represented as a keen sea-farer who is supposed to have accompanied Amerigo Vespucci on his voyages ; he is a scholar of a perfect Humanist type, thoroughly familiar with Greek literature and philosophy ; he desires neither wealth nor power, and is a thoroughgoing defender of communism. On his voyages he cares nought for mythical monsters and fantastic apparitions, but inquires into the social organisation of the discovered countries, for " to find citizens ruled by good and wholesome laws is an exceedingly rare and hard thing " (p. 33) ; furthermore, he is convinced that, " where possessions are private, where money is the measure of all things, it is hard and almost impossible that the commonwealth should have just government and enjoy prosperity " (p. 104). He is the discoverer of Utopia, on the advantages of which he discourses.

The second figure is Peter Giles, an enlightened merchant, a good Christian and citizen in the usual meaning of the word, knowing how to take care of himself and family ; he is satisfied with the laws of his country and does not believe " that there is better order in that new land than there is in the countries we know," and he thinks " that our commonwealth is more ancient than theirs " (p. 111), and, therefore, more likely to possess a larger measure of social experience than Utopia.

More himself intervenes sometimes in the course of Raphael's narrative. He appears to agree in every detail with the social criticism, but not always with the possibilities of communism.

He generally enters on the scene when communism seems to offer some difficulties and is, therefore, open to objections, or where the ideal is too high for the realities of life so that a compromise between the ideal and the actual might be more practicable.

On the whole, it may be said that Raphael represents the most uncompromising aspects of communism ; he also dominates the stage. Peter Giles defends the present order, but there seems to be so little in favour of it that his part is very subordinate. More is critical, seeing both the shortcomings of the existing society and the difficulties of integral communism ; he is not a communist, but a social reformer, favouring a gradual amelioration of society and the application of all that is practicable in communism. His real attitude towards the communistic ideal is expressed in the closing sentences of *Utopia* : " In the meantime, though I cannot agree to all things that he (Raphael) said . . . I must needs express and grant that there are many things in the Utopian commonwealth which in our country I rather wish than hope for " (308–9).

As Erasmus relates in his letter to Hutten mentioned above, More first composed the second part of *Utopia* in his leisure hours while employed on his mission at Antwerp ; soon after he added the first part, which he wrote down as an improvisation, " so well stored was his mind and so great his skill in composition." He wrote it in Latin and published it at the end of 1516 in Louvain under the title *De optimo reipublicae statu, deque nova insula Utopia*. Within less than two years of its first appearance in print it was republished in Basle (1518), then in Paris (1520), and from time to time new editions have been issued in Great Britain, Germany, France, and America. The first English translation was made and published by Raphe Robynson, a London goldsmith, in 1551. But the German, Italian, and French editions preceded the English translation, and are still often reprinted, so that More's *Utopia* is one of the best known books in the literature of the world.

5.—THE *UTOPIA :* SOCIAL CRITICISM

(a) *Rich and Poor.*—There is no trace of equity or justice in any country which gives great rewards and fees to gentlemen, goldsmiths (bankers), usurers, and such like who do nothing or are merely the flatterers or devisers of vain pleasures of the rich, and on the other hand makes no provision for the poor ploughmen, colliers, labourers, carters, ironsmiths, carpenters, and other workers, without whom no commonwealth could exist. The lot of the working people is even harder than that of the beasts of burden ; poverty is the recompense of their toil when they are strong enough to be in employment, and destitution and misery when old age or illness renders them incapable of work. And the laws are against them. Keeping all this in mind it is impossible not to perceive that what we call a commonwealth to-day is but a conspiracy of the rich to procure their own well-being. Money and pride are the roots of all evil. All crime would die if money perished ; indeed, poverty itself, which only seems to arise from lack of money, would disappear if money disappeared. The rich undoubtedly perceive all this and would be prepared to change the constitution of society, but Pride, the queen of all mischief, hinders them ; she measures her own felicity by other people's misery (pp. 300–6). Another source of mischief, peculiar to England, are the enclosures and the conversion of arable land into pasture. The sheep, once so meek and tame, have become wild and devouring ; they consume and destroy the peasant and his land. Where the finest wool is grown there gentlemen and abbots leave no soil for tillage ; they are no more satisfied with the revenue, leisure, and pleasure that husbandry used to afford, but desire untold wealth ; insatiable covetousness causes them to depopulate the country and fill it with sheep ; and they do so by fraud and violence, legal or illegal. The decrease of tillage has for its effect a dearth of victuals ; and the rise in the price of wool makes it impossible for the poor clothmaker to continue his employment. The wealth of the country is being engrossed by a small number of persons.

(b) *Crime and Punishment.*—The covetousness of a few has

greatly injured the well-being of this island. The great dearth of victuals causes men to restrict their household, to curtail hospitality and dismiss servants. The nobles disband their retainers—those idle and boisterous fellows who have been used to live on the labour of others. The enclosers restrict employment and render many useful labourers idle. Hence theft, robbery, vagabondage, and all manner of crime increase. The unemployed must either beg or steal, and despite all severity of punishment crime does not diminish. The nation brings up thieves and vagabonds and then punishes them. Is this justice? Great and horrible punishments are meted out to thieves, while provision ought to have been made to enable them to get their living, so that no man should be driven to the extreme necessity, first to steal and then to be hanged for it (pp. 44–58).

(c) *Reform or Revolution.*—But is there any use in proposing reform to kings? Or, in other words, may a communist enter a non-communist government? Raphael replies, No, while More does not exclude the possibility of promoting the welfare of the realm by advising kings, " for you must not leave a ship in a tempest because you cannot rule the storm ; nor must you tender advice derived from new ideals which no king, except a king-philosopher—who, however, needs no advice—would accept, but you must handle the matter subtly and diplomatically so that if you are not able to achieve the best you may at least prevent the worst ; for it is not possible for all things to be well, unless all men are good, which cannot be expected for a good many years yet " (pp. 99–100). But the revolutionary Raphael replies : Princes and governments do mainly care for warlike matters— for conquests, territorial expansion, great armies, and full treasuries. And their counsellors aid them in those schemes, therefore they are tolerated ; they flatter the royal self-conceit, praise the princely wisdom, and oppress and tax the people for the sake of aggrandisement of the princes. What could a social philosopher achieve in the teeth of such royal councils? He would simply be made a laughing-stock of, or worse, he would become either as bad as the government, or the people would think him so, and thus learn to despise communist philosophy.

Would a king listen to the advice of a counsellor who told him that the people gave him the crown not for his own sake but for the welfare of all ? Or would he perceive the truth that his kingdom, small though it be, is already too big to be ruled by one man ? No, it is no good to be subtle in such matters (pp. 80–95). All attempt at palliating evil by craftiness and reform measures must lead to nought. The only remedy is a radical change of the whole social system. Plato acted rightly in refusing to make laws for a country where private property reigns supreme. Such countries may multiply laws until no lawyer could count them, and yet they will never enjoy prosperity, peace, and happiness. For, as long as private property exists the greatest and best part of the nation will be condemned to over-work, poverty and misery. Palliative laws may cure one part of the disease, but will at the same time aggravate the sore of another part, so that the help afforded to one will cause harm to another, for nothing can be given to Peter without taking from Paul. To this harangue in favour of catastrophic communism More replies that communism, in withdrawing the incentive of personal gain and thus the motive of industry, might lead to the neglect of work and to general impoverishment, and when the pressure of poverty is felt and there is no law to defend the means of production and life, will not there of necessity be continual strife, enmity, and bloodshed ? (pp. 100–11). To this question, in support of which More could have quoted Aristotle and theo-logical *ius naturale*, Raphael gives no direct reply, but refers More to the example of the Utopians. At first sight it might seem that Raphael's reply involves a *petitio principi*, in reality, how-ever, it is based on the philosophy of Humanism, which is that trained reason aided by religion and good laws will make man virtuous dutiful, and active. Raphael also points out that More's objection is taken from social conditions based on private property which never admits good laws and is at cross-purposes with religion and right reason, while the minds of the Utopians have been trained by a communist system of life (p. 100).

6.—THE *UTOPIA:* SOCIAL RECONSTRUCTION

(*a*) *The Republic and its founder.*—Utopus, a king-philosopher, conquered a rugged and rainless peninsula called Abraxa and changes it into a prosperous island which henceforth bears his name and merits to be called Eutopia, the abode of felicity (pp. 118, xciii.). The inhabitants, originally poor, rude, and rent by religious dissensions, are brought to a state of perfection in humanity, manners, virtue, learning, and material prosperity that surpasses anything that would be found among the other nations of the earth (pp. 132–4). The means that Utopus applied were communism and education, the latter in its broader sense as understood by the rationalists ; it includes not only schooling proper, but the training and experiences which the surroundings, occupations, customs, and laws afford. The island of Utopia consists of fifty-four shires, with a spacious and magnificent city in each as the centre of administration, public education, scholar- ship, handicrafts, markets, store-houses, and foreign commerce ; the hospitals are on the outskirts of the cities. The inhabitants have all the same language, manners and laws, and this similarity promotes peace and harmony. None of the shires contains less than twenty miles of land, and none has any desire to extend its boundaries, for the people regard themselves as mere tillers of the soil rather than its proprietors. In the centre of the republic is the capital city, Amaurote, the seat of the National Assembly (pp. 119–20).

(*b*) *The Constitution.*—The Republic is a democratic federation of autonomous shires. The laws are few, yet sufficient ; the in- habitants know them well and do not suffer subtle and crafty interpretations (p. 234). The Central Government is a Senate or Council consisting of 162 members, three members for each shire, who meet annually at Amaurote to discuss the common affairs of the nation (p. 119). The Senate has sometimes to settle unsolved questions of the local bodies (p. 138) ; they also keep account of the demand and supply of the commodities, so that nothing shall lack in the Commonweal (pp. 169–70). The real management of the country is, however, in the hands of the governments of the shires. Each shire consists of 6,000 families or farms; each family of not less than forty members and two bondmen is under the rule of a *pater-* and *materfamilias*. Every thirty families elect annually their Phylarch or Syphogrant or head bailiff; every ten Phylarchies or 300 families elect their Chief Phylarchs or Tranibors. The Phylarchs of the shires, 200 in number, elect by ballot the Prince or Chief Magistrate of the shire. The Phylarchs are elected annually; the Chief Phylarchs likewise, but are generally re-elected; the Chief Magistrate is elected for life, removable only on suspicion of striving after tyranny. The Chief Phylarchs and the Chief Magistrate form the Council of the Shire; they meet, as a rule, every third day and invite two of the Phylarchs to their meetings. Public affairs cannot, under the penalty of death, be discussed outside the Council or the election house of the Phylarch (pp. 135–138).

(c) *Trades and Occupations.*—Agriculture is the basis of the Commonweal. There is no person, male or female, who has no expert knowledge of it. Agricultural instruction, theoretical and practical, is compulsory. Every year a certain number of townspeople change places with farmers, so that city and village should keep in touch with each other. Besides husbandry every inhabitant learns one of the handicrafts necessary for the work of the Commonweal—clothmaking, building, smithing, and carpentering; as a rule, everybody is brought up in his father's trade. There is no other trade besides those mentioned, the life in Utopia being simple and knowing no luxury.

(d) *Duty and hours of labour.*—The chief function of the Phylarch is to see that the citizens shall perform their duty of labour. Idlers are expelled from the republic. The hours of labour are six per diem. Where all labour there is no overwork for anyone. Only illness, old age, and devotion to study and science give exemption from labour (pp. 141–6). Any craftsman or farmer who by devotion to learning in his leisure hours shows that he could be more useful to the community by study is promoted to the order of the scholars (pp. 146–8).

(e) *The bondmen.*—All toilsome and unclean work of the Commonweal is done by the bondmen, who are either prisoners duly convicted of heinous offences which in other countries are punished with death, or poor labourers from foreign lands. The first are treated with severity, while the latter are gently treated, and are allowed to leave whenever they like and are not sent away empty-handed (pp. 161, 221–2).

(f) *Family and social life.*—Monogamy is strictly enforced, and adultery is punished with most grievous bondage. Also ante-nuptial chastity is strongly insisted upon. Matrimony is in their eyes so solemn and holy an institution that man and woman who are about to enter it should know all the circumstances. They have therefore a custom that a virtuous matron shows the woman naked to the wooer, and a wise man exhibits the wooer naked to the woman. The Utopians are given the opportunity of taking their meals in common. For this purpose there are in the residences of the Phylarchs large halls where wholesome food is prepared. Every meal begins with reading something that refers to good manners and virtue. During the meals the elders hold conversation on serious, but not unpleasant subjects, and the younger members are encouraged to express their opinions. The dinners are short, the suppers somewhat longer, and these are followed by music, games, and all kinds of harmless entertainments. At eight o'clock they all go to bed to rise at four. The morning and, generally, the leisure hours are devoted to public lectures, study, and play (pp. 160–6).

(g) *War.*—The Utopians regard war as gross and cruel injustice. Yet they undergo the discipline of war in order to be able to defend themselves or to help their friends to repel invasion or to deliver any people from tyranny (pp. 243–4). They likewise declare war upon any nation who, possessing vacant land in abundance, prohibit the immigration of the surplus population of Utopia who desire to cultivate it and to form a colony there ; such a prohibition they regard as a violation of the law of nature (p. 155).

(h) *Education and learning.*—The constitution of the Commonweal chiefly aims at saving time from the necessary labours and giving it to the free cultivation of the mind. Herein they suppose the happiness of this life to consist (p. 152). Education of the children is general and compulsory. They study music, logic, arithmetic, and geometry (p. 184), astronomy, and physical geography (p. 187). Children who show special aptitude for learning are exempted from bodily labour and are allowed to devote themselves to study ; they form the Order of the Learned.

(*i*) *Moral philosophy.*—Good and evil, virtue and happiness, soul and body, immortality and God's kindness to man are much discussed by the Utopians. Their principles are :—the soul is immortal and created for happiness by God's kindness ; virtue is rewarded and vice punished after this life. These purely religious truths, which are beyond reasoning, they think meet to prove by arguments from reason. The chief discussion, however, turns upon happiness. They think that it consists of pleasure as differentiated from lust, for it is only good and honest pleasure which they believe to produce happiness. They are opposed to the Stoics, who attribute happiness to a virtue that implies self-torture and abnegation. Life according to nature and reason they interpret as meaning a life that produces joy by good actions to others and to oneself (pp. 187–92). They distinguish between true and false pleasures. True pleasures are those which give intelligence to the mind, satisfaction to moral conscience, or which arise from the contemplation of truth and art, listening to good music, recollection of good deeds in the past, and hope of future happiness. False pleasures arise from vainglory, titles, fineries, so-called precious metals and stones, gambling, hunting, and all cruel pastimes that cause pain to beast or man.

(*j*) *Religion.*—The Utopians enjoy complete freedom of religious worship. By this means Utopus healed the wounds caused to the nation by religious dissensions. It enabled them to discuss their religious differences, carefully to weigh each other's arguments, and to arrive at a certain unity as to the essence of religion. The great majority worship under various forms one sovereign spiritual power, the Creator and Ruler of the universe, the initial and final cause of all things. Atheists, however, are not regarded as good citizens.

(*k*) *Summing up.*—Utopia is the only commonwealth which

deserves that name.   It is in reality a common weal and public wealth.   In all other places they speak of common wealth while everybody is trying to secure his own private wealth at the expense of his neighbour.   In Utopia, where nothing is private, everybody cares for the common affairs.   In other countries where nobody is secure against poverty and hunger, though the national wealth may be very considerable, everybody is compelled to make provision for himself and disregard the common interests of all.   Conversely, where all things are common, nobody has reason to fear lest he should starve, so long as the public storehouses are well supplied with commodities.   Therefore it is the interest of everybody to care for the community.   In such a republic everybody is rich, though nobody possesses anything.   This form of a republic will endure for ever, for by destroying pride and money the Utopians have uprooted the main causes of ambition, sedition, and all those vices which in other countries lead to internecine struggles, civil wars, and finally to the destruction or decay of nation and Empire (pp. 267–307).

7.—RISE OF INDIVIDUALISM

In 1549, fourteen years after the execution of More, half of the English peasantry were in insurrection.   They rose up in arms to vindicate their natural right to the soil and to the fruits it yielded to their labour.   It was the last great protest, the final struggle on a national scale, against the destruction of the village communities.   Their defeat marks the turning point in the history of English mediaeval communism.

Robert Crowley, vicar, printer, archdeacon, and zealous Protestant, writing in 1550 on the prevalent spirit of sedition and its causes, puts the case very clearly both of the peasantry and the masters of the land and money :—

" The great farmers, graziers, rich butchers, lawyers, merchants, gentlemen, lords, and I cannot say who more," says the peasant, " men that have no name because they are doers of all things where gain is to be had . . . they take our houses over our heads, buy our lands out of our hands, raise our rents, levy great (yea, unreasonable) fines, they enclose our commons . . . and to go to the cities we have no hope, for we hear that these unsatiable beasts have there all in their hands."

The lord replies :—

" The peasant knaves . . . will have no gentlemen, they will have all men like themselves, they will have all things in common. . . . They will appoint what rent we shall take for our grounds. They will cast down our parks and lay our pastures open. We will teach them to know their betters ; and because they would have all commune, we will leave them nothing." [1]

Bishop Latimer's sermons of that period are no less outspoken concerning the conflicts between the agricultural population and the lords of the land, and are imbued with great love for the people.

That conflict must have exhibited strong communistic tendencies, since both Crowley and Latimer are at pains to repudiate communism and only ask of the lords of the land to exercise Christian charity and patriotic virtue towards the peasantry as the stay of the nation. Crowley says, " I do not agitate the people to make all things common . . . but the possessioners must consider themselves stewards rather than lords over their possessions." [2] And Latimer, in his fifth sermon on the Lord's Prayer, on the verse " Give us this day our daily bread," exhorts the people to remember that the word " our " does not mean communism. And he adds :—

" Here I have occasion to speak of the proprieties of things ; for I fear if I should leave it so some of you would report me wrongfully, and affirm that all things should be common. I say not so. . . . If all things were common there could be no theft and so this commandment ' Thou shalt not steal,' were in vain. The laws of the realm make *meum* and *tuum*, mine and thine. If I have things by those laws then I have them. But this you must not forget that S. Paul says, ' Relieve the necessity of those which have need.' Things are not so common

[1] Robert Crowley, *Select Works*, pp. 133–43.
[2] *Ibid.*, pp. 156 *sqq.*

that we ought to distribute them unto the poor . . . but we ought to help one another."

Latimer uses the same argument as Langland ; moreover, his learning is wide enough to include the opinion of S. Augustine that property has been established by civil law. He reminds the people that in the time of the apostles the believers did distribute their property among the poorer brethren and had all things in common, but he interprets this as an exceptional measure.

On the whole, with the rise of Protestantism the clear Scriptural text of the Ten Commandments prevailed over the communistic traditions of Primitive Christianity, monastic orders, and scholastic *ius naturale*. The work begun by the author of *Piers Ploughman* was accomplished by Bishop Latimer. Communism lost its sanction in Church and State, and took refuge with the extreme wing of Nonconformity, revolutionary rationalism, and working class organisations, while society at large moved towards individualism, whose first manifestation was the Elizabethan Age—an age of pioneers, men of keen initiative. Its great interpreters, Spenser and Shakespeare, were both anti-communist and anti-democratic. Spenser, in his *Faery Queen*, matches Artegall, the champion of true justice and skilled in righteous lore, against the communist Giant, who, standing on a rock near the sea, is telling the vast crowd that, with the huge pair of scales held in his hands, he would weigh equally all the world, for he saw that all was unequal and that the elements of Nature as well as the men in society were encroaching upon each other's share. He undertook to mend these things—

> " In sort as they were formèd anciently
>   And all things would reduce unto equality."

The people liked to hear him discourse upon this subject and

> " Therefore the vulgar did about him flock,
>   And cluster thick unto his leasings vain,
>   Like foolish flies about a honey-crock,
>   In hope by him great benefit to gain,
>   And uncontrollèd freedom to obtain."

Artegall, seeing the mischief the Giant was causing, upbraided him for misleading the people since " All change is perilous, and all chance unsound." Upon which the Giant replies :—

> " Were it not good that wrong were then surceast,
> And from the most that some were given to the least !
>
> Therefore I will throw down these mountains high,
> And make them level with the lowly plain ;
> These tow'ring rocks, which reach unto the sky,
> I will thrust down into the deepest main,
> And, as they were, them equalize again.
> Tyrants that make men subject to their law,
> I will suppress, that they no more will reign,
> And lordlings curb, that commons overawe ;
> And all the wealth of rich men to the poor will draw."

Artegall succeeds in throwing the Giant into the sea, whereupon the people rise to revenge the blood of their leader and saviour.

> " For certain loss of so great expectation ;
> For well they hopèd to have got great good,
> And wondrous riches by his innovation."
>
> *(Faery Queen,* book 5, canto 2.)

Shakespeare deals in a similar manner with Jack Cade and the lower orders generally. Caliban, the slave or personification of Labour, is a spiritless braggart, an easy prey to ignorant adventurers ; Gonzalo, an inefficient, though noble-hearted statesman and humanist, whose description of Utopia turns out to be " merry fooling " (*Tempest,* Act 2, sc. 1). It was the spirit of the age. The labouring population was defeated and communism discredited. Its place was taken by Government action and social reform—the Elizabethan Poor Law Reform, which was much more than mere relief of destitution, for it aimed at prevention of destitution and promoting the efficiency of the productive capacities of the labouring classes.

CIVIL WAR AND GLORIOUS REVOLUTION

I.—RISE OF SCIENCE : NEW ATLANTIS

THE reigns of Henry VIII., Edward VI., and Mary were anything but favourable to the growth of modern civilisation. The painful birth of the Reformation out of a welter of violent religious fluctuations and baffling cross-purposes, the confiscations and cruelties and futilities of the rulers, the debasement of the coinage, the conspiracies attendant upon absolutism, impeded thought and enterprise, and kept down the energies of the nation. With the accession of Elizabeth, the triumph of the Reformation, the sack of Antwerp by the Spaniards, and the destruction of the Armada, the pent-up forces of all that was alive in England sped forth with the freshness and vigour of youth and ushered in the English Renascence—the prologue of modern England. The spirit of invention and discovery, of experiment and enterprise, the desire for sea-power and political freedom increasingly took hold of the English mind. Mediaevalism was expiring ; Francis Bacon came to bury scholasticism and heralded the advent of the Kingdom of Science, of practical work and production of wealth. His *Novum Organum* is sober positivism ; his *Nova Atlantis* is idealised scientific practice.

The *New Atlantis*, as far as its form is concerned, was undoubtedly suggested to Bacon by More's *Utopia* ; but with this the similarity ends. Bacon looks for the happiness of mankind chiefly to applied natural philosophy and productive work, More to social reform and religious ethics. These two conceptions are still at war with each other, yet the happiness of man on earth depends on the combination of both.

In New Atlantis, an island in the South Seas, a wise lawgiver established a happy and prosperous kingdom on the basis of

applied science. Its centre is Solomon's House or College of
Six Days, situated in the capital, Bensalem, and it aims at
gaining " knowledge of causes and secret motions of things, and
the enlarging of the bounds of human empire to the effecting of
all things possible." [1] It contains preparations and instruments
for all kinds of physical and technological experiments ; deep
caves for the investigation of the innermost of the earth, high
towers for the study of the air and its phenomena ; laboratories
for the experimental production of organic and inorganic matter
as well as for the study of medicine ; agronomical stations ;
shops for mechanical arts and manufacturing processes ; furnaces
for the production of all degrees of heat ; halls for demonstrations in light and sound.   " We have also engine-houses, where
are prepared engines and instruments for all sorts of motions.
. . .   We imitate the flight of the birds, and have ships and
boats for going under water."   This college of science and tech-
nology sends also missions to foreign countries to study the progress of the world, it convenes meetings and conferences to
discuss past achievements and new experiments ; it has its
theorists who " raise the experimental discoveries into observations, axioms, and aphorisms."   The inhabitants of this happy
scientific Utopia adore the inventors and discoverers.   " Upon
every invention of value we erect a statue to its originator and
give him a liberal and honourable reward."   Their religious
service consists of praising God for His marvellous works, and of
imploring His aid and blessing for the illumination of their labours
and turning them into good and holy uses.   Their ethics appear
to be the result of scientific training and self-respect ; chastity
is regarded as an economy of force, and self-respect the bridle
of vice.

New Atlantis is, in short, a model of scientific organisation of
production, a commonwealth which knows how to honour
inventors, discoverers, technologists, and scientists, the real
creators of economic value.   From the laboratories of the College
of Six Days, through the multiple activities of applied science
and the marvellous development of the productive forces, came

[1] Lord Bacon's *Essays*, etc. (Bohn's Library, ed. 1907), p. 297.

E

the solution of the social problem.   They banished poverty by
making the production of wealth easy.

Looked at from this point of view the *New Atlantis* is one of
the most important contributions to the history of social science.
But it is essentially materialistic, inasmuch as it presupposes
human happiness to be the result of a general diffusion of wealth.
It anticipates, however, the speculations of some of the acutest
minds of the nineteenth century.

2.—RATIONALISM AND SOCIAL CONTRACT

The bounds which Humanism had set between the spheres of
faith and reason were removed in the seventeenth century.
Reason encroached upon the kingdom of faith, and in moments
of revolutionary exaltation it was adored.   During the Civil
War the True Levellers worshipped reason, though in a less spectacular manner than the Jacobins were to do in the French Civil
War.   Philosophers like Locke and Leibnitz argued for religion
on account of its conformity with the dictates of reason.   Theological authority faded away before the glaring light of reason
and the law of nature.   Moral philosophy, which was in the
century of Waynflete, More, and Hooker an auxiliary to theology,
gained the upper hand.   Mr. Worldly Wiseman had the audacity
to advise Christian not to continue his tedious and health-destroy-
ing pilgrimage to the holy mountain, but to go to the village of
Morality where dwelled a gentleman, Mr. Legality.   In the eyes
of austere Bunyan moral philosophy was pagan or heretic.   It
is none the less a historical fact that the transition from mediaevalism to modern times was everywhere marked by a subordination of theology to moral philosophy.   As soon as faith failed to
supply adequate motives for social discipline and public peace,
another basis of morality was sought and, for a time, found in
philosophic speculation.   Francis Bacon had a fine glimmer of
this crisis in human thought when he said, " Moral philosophy
took with the pagans (*ethnicis*) the place of theology," [1] or rather
mythology.   So it was also in Christian Europe.   Instead of the
folios of *Summae theologicae* which every great Schoolman felt

[1] Francis Bacon, *Novum Organum*, I. 79.

bound to write, treatises on jurisprudence and moral philosophy appeared, dealing with ethics, law, particularly natural law, then with politics and economics. It thus embraced the science of morality, law, government, and wealth. Economics was originally the least and the last branch of the tree of knowledge of good and evil, but was destined to become, with the Industrial Revolution, the first and most important. The period which separates Hugo Grotius from Adam Smith clearly shows this development.

The soul of moral philosophy was *ius naturale,* which is, as we know, pure ethics in a pseudo-historic guise. Its most pronounced characteristic was the doctrine concerning the absence of private property and civil government in the original state of man. Mediaeval communistic and political thought rested on it. The final outcome of these mediaeval speculations was that personal monarchy had a divine origin and was therefore legitimate, while private property was tainted with sin. Modern English civilisation was now going to make a new use of natural law. Its material and mental conditions now demanded a reversal of the scholastic conclusions, declaring personal monarchy to be a usurpation, and private property legitimate and sacred. This task was carried out by moral philosophers, mostly Protestant jurists and political thinkers. And they did it by making the social contract and the labour value theory an integral part of moral philosophy.

The idea of contract was in the older *ius naturale* only in its incipient stage. For tribal society knew nothing of contract, its social relations having been regulated by authority and tradition. Mediaeval society had only the germ of it; apart from the relations between overlord, lord, and vassal which were supposed to rest on agreement, the great mass of the population were born into a certain status and died in it, without ever having had any chance of ordering their conditions and relations by negotiation or discussion. It was different in towns and cities. Their inhabitants settled there individually and formed corporations, gilds, clubs, and other organisations by voluntary agreements. With the growing complexity of trade and commerce, the transactions between the inhabitants became numerous and they settled them by contracts. And in the same proportion as town life began to dominate the life of the nation, and the political centre of gravity moved from the manor to the city, the *status* gave way to the *contractus*.[1] Custom, tradition, authority ceased to form the cohesive and vital force of society, and the concept of agreement, compact, and contract took their place.

We have previously noticed the striking arguments of William of Ockham as to private property and civil government having had their origin in the consent of those whose interests demanded such a change. Consent means, of course, agreement, or express or tacit contract. Richard Hooker argues also in the same manner with regard to civil dominion :—

" There being no impossibility in Nature considered by itself, but that men might have lived without any public regiment. Howbeit, the corruption of our nature being presupposed, we may not deny but that the Law of Nature doth now require of necessity some kind of regiment," for envy, strife, contention, and violence grew among men. " To take away all such griev-ances, injuries, and wrongs, there was no way but by growing into composition and agreement amongst themselves, by ordain-ing some kind of government public, and by yielding themselves subject thereunto . . . and they gave their common consent all to be ordered by some whom they should agree upon. . . . So that, in a word, all public regiment seemeth eventually to have arisen from deliberate advice, consultation, and composition between men, judging it convenient and behoveful."[2] Hooker does not apply his contract theory to property ; his view appears to be that, civil government once constituted, civil laws regulate the economic relations between men. He is, however, decidedly of opinion that the contract between subjects and sovereign may be revoked, provided there is " universal consent " for such a step. Universal consent is, however, a difficult condition to fulfil, revolutions being generally initiated by minorities. It must also be noticed that he is not quite consistent, for he some-

---

[1] Compare Maine, *Ancient Law*, ed. 1885, pp. 168–70.
[2] Richard Hooker, *Ecclesiastical Polity*, Book I, c. 10.

times ascribes the origin of civil dominion to divine appointment. Still, the contract theory dominates his reasonings.

Independently of each other moral philosophers of Western Europe and Italy put similar constructions upon *ius naturale*, the most famous among them being Hugo Grotius, who also exercised considerable influence on English political thought. Following the Church Fathers and scholastics, he assumes an idyllic state of nature, the Fall of man, the introduction of civil society, and private property. Communism was general in the natural state as well as absence of human government, but after the Fall of man vice crept in, and made a change in the social conditions a necessity. By an express or tacit agreement men abandoned the communistic mode of life and introduced private property, first with regard to movables, then immovables, and laws of property were enacted.[1] By contract they likewise constituted civil society, and by virtue of an agreement a supreme authority was set up. Grotius is, however, not quite clear with regard to the lawfulness of resistance of the people to constituted authority. He appears to be of opinion that, as a rule, non-resistance was best, yet he thinks resistance lawful if it could be achieved without endangering civil society itself, and without destroying the lives of innocent people. He is further of opinion that all depended on the tenour of the original agreement ; if the people subjected themselves unconditionally to their sovereign resistance was unlawful ; if, however, the submission was conditional resistance was lawful. But who is to decide on the tenour of the original agreement ? Grotius thinks that the decision lay with the people who happened to raise such questions. This, of course, means that the people was sovereign and had, therefore, the right to dethrone the monarch.[2] For a sober and conservative logician, like Sir Robert Filmer, it was under these conditions an easy matter to detect and expose the illogical attitude of Grotius.[3]

[1] Hugo Grotius, *De iure belli et pacis* (1625), l. 2, c. 2.

[2] *Ibid.*, l. 1, cs. 3 and 4 ; l. 2, c. 2.

[3] Sir Robert Filmer, *Observations*, on Hobbes, Milton, and Grotius, 1652, pp. 38-50.

John Selden, though inclined to favour the hypothesis that communism never existed, appears rather impressed by the communist verses of the Roman poets, whom he quotes, and arrives at the conclusion that " neither law natural nor divine . . . has expressly commanded or prohibited, but permitted both private property and common possessions." Yet he assumes that private property arose by consent of the whole body of mankind. By virtue of a compact men gave up their common interests, and ancient rights to their common possessions, and made that compact binding on their posterity.[1]

It must have been in the first quarter of the seventeenth century that a short pamphlet entitled " A Paradox " appeared, in which the state of nature is defended on ethical grounds. It attempts to prove that the inhabitants of Madagascar, or St. Lawrence, were, in things temporal, the happiest people on earth. For they knew not the " inordinate desire for riches, which is the root of all mischief—a raging famished beast that will not be satisfied, a bottomless gulf that cannot be filled." Those inhabitants set no value on gold ; their life was simple and free from the sorrows of civil society.[2]

The first attack on the communist and idyllic element of *ius naturale* came from Thomas Hobbes. He admits that in the state of nature everybody had a right to everything, " that is to say, to do whatever he listeth and to whom he listeth, to possess, use, and enjoy all things he will and can . . . and for this cause it is rightly said, *Natura dedit omnia omnibus;* " but considering the passions, rivalries, and the lust of glory, such a state was anything but idyllic. It led to perpetual strife, discord, and war, to a *bellum omnium contra omnes*, in which the strongest or craftiest prevailed, and therefore the natural rights were of no use whatsoever.[3] Laws of nature such as equity, mercy, modesty, without the terror inspired by some power to cause them to be observed, were rendered nugatory by the

---

[1] John Selden, *Mare Clausum*, l. i, c. 4.

[2] *A Paradox, Harl. Misc.*, vol. I., pp. 263–9.

[3] Thomas Hobbes, *Elements of Law*, ed. Toennies, I., c. 14 ; II., c. i, *et seq.*

natural passions, partiality, pride, revenge, etc.[1] Not right, but brute force ruled. Man had only the choice between natural liberty plus destructive war and subjection to authority plus security and peace. He chose the latter, since life and the preservation thereof were fundamental laws of nature.[2] Men entered into an agreement with each other to surrender their sovereignty and transfer it unconditionally to one man or an assembly of men. Thus arose civil dominion out of an inchoate and warring demos. The transfer of sovereignty having been unconditional, all must obey the sovereign's laws. " Though a monarch, a sovereign, may in his passion pursue aims contrary to the law of nature, no subject has a right to make war on him, because having authorised all his actions, and in bestowing the sovereign power, made them their own."[3] With the transfer of the natural rights to the sovereign the state of nature was at an end, and the artificial state, the Leviathan, omnipotent by the power, the sword, of concentrated sovereignty, orders the mode of property, religion, justice, and all the affairs of the organism of the Commonwealth. " The inequality that is now to be seen has been introduced by civil law . . . The constitution of ' mine ' and ' thine ' and ' his,' in one word, ' propriety,' belongs in all kinds of commonwealth to the sovereign power . . . Propriety consists in the right of a subject to exclude all other subjects from the use of the things which he possesses."[4]

We see that, apart from the principle of contract which all the moral philosophers accept, there prevails among them much difference of opinion as to its mode of application. Ockham applied it both to civil dominion and property, Hooker to the rise of civil society and civil government, but not to property. Hobbes knows only one contract, viz., between the afflicted and distracted people themselves to surrender, without any condition whatsoever, their sovereignty to one man or several men who henceforth form the civil power. The contract theory of Hobbes was exceedingly distasteful to a nation which drastically revoked their agreement with King Charles I. It was indeed a counter-

[1] Thomas Hobbes, *Leviathan*, c. 17. [2] *Ibid.*, c. 14. [3] *Ibid.*, c. 16·
[4] *Ibid.*, c. 15, c. 16.

revolutionary blast, a plea for absolute monarchy. The nation preferred Milton's *Tenure of Kings and Magistrates*, and, later, Sydney's *Discourse on Government*, which popularised Hooker's views on the social and political contract.

It was, however, John Locke who summed up the political and economic speculations of the revolutionary period. In his *Two Treatises on Civil Government* (1689) he popularised Hooker's reasonings on the social and political contract, but in a more rationalist and less theological manner. The great difference between Hooker and Locke is this—the first, still very near the scholastic period, fully admits that the transition from the natural to the civil state was due to the corruption of man, while Locke, in the midst of the rationalist wave, evidently dislikes the theological interpretation, and still more so the anti-idyllic theory of Hobbes, which so little tallies with Locke's belief in the inherent goodness and the power of reason of man. Still, the loss of the natural state had to be accounted for. After much hesitation Locke finally admits that the natural state had its " inconveniences," particularly in the administration of justice, and, therefore, the natural men entered into an agreement to form a civil government,[1] which, of course, was from the beginning responsible to the people. In his contract theory there is, however, nothing original ; it is all rationalised Hooker. His real contribution, and a very considerable one, is his theory concerning property.

We have seen the efforts of Ockham to demonstrate the compatibility of private property with *ius naturale*, and thus to remove the taint of sin from the division and appropriation of things. Locke makes a similar effort. His main proposition is that private property is natural and existed even in the state of nature ; it is on this account just and good. He therefore rejects altogether the theory that property had its origin in a contract, as Ockham and Grotius assumed, for this theory implies that in the state of nature there was no property. Even more important than the main proposition of Locke is his labour argument, by which he supports it. The doctrine that

[1] John Locke, *On Civil Government*, II., c. 7, § 90.

labour is the title to property and the source of value was destined to be made into the main weapon of socialism, although Locke himself used it in a contrary sense, trying to prove the legitimacy and justice of private property. He argues :—

" I shall endeavour to show how men might come to have property in several parts of that which God gave to mankind in common, and that without an express contract of all the commoners." He then goes on to say that while God gave the earth and the fulness thereof to mankind in common, He gave it for use, and, therefore, there must needs have been a means of appropriating the natural products before they could be of use to any particular man. When " the wild Indian, who knows no enclosures, and is still tenant in common," gathered eatable things and prepared them for his use, they belonged to him, and became his exclusive property. And this for two reasons :— first, man was originally free and independent ; his body belonged only to him and to nobody else ; his labour power was a part of his person, and when he removed a thing from the state of nature and made it useful, he mixed with it his labour and joined to it something that was unquestionably his own, and thereby made it his property. Secondly, the things in their natural state are generally of very little value. It was human labour which made them valuable. Nine-tenths of the value of things were created and added to them by labour. And as labour, the creator of value, was a part of man, and man was his own master and the proprietor of his person, he really took what was his own. " Labour is the title to property " ; by it a " man does, as it were, enclose the common." And only so much of land and things that he could work, and thus render useful (valuable), was rightly his own. The original meaning of value or the intrinsic value of a thing was its usefulness. In the state of nature, before the *amor sceleratus habendi* had set in, nobody appropriated more than he needed and could make useful. So there was then private property. In this respect the difference between the natural and civil state consisted only in the degree of appropriation.[1]

[1] John Locke, *On Civil Government*, II., c. 5.

Locke's doctrines concerning monarchy and property form the complete reverse of Wycliffe's.   The latter aimed at sanctioning personal monarchy and defending communism, while the former attempted to condemn personal monarchy and sanction individual property.   Both, the theologian as well as the political philosopher, interpreted the movements of their times.

We shall see later how Locke's labour theory of property and value was used by socialist critics, particularly after the labour value theory had been expanded and established by Adam Smith and David Ricardo.   Meanwhile, we must return to the communists and social reformers of the seventeenth century.

3.—SOCIAL-REVOLUTIONARY THEORIES IN THE CIVIL WAR

In the shock of the struggle between Parliament and Monarchy, the flood-gates of revolutionary ideas opened, and a stream of religious heresies, rationalist and radical philosophy, communist theories, and social reform schemes spread over the land.   The main element of this flood of ideas was *ius naturale* in one form or another.   A careful observer, though zealous opponent of these movements, has left us a fairly correct summary of them. He complains :—

" Instead of legal rights, and the laws and customs of this nation the sectaries talk of, and plead for, natural rights and liberties, such as men have from Adam by birth, and in many of their pamphlets they still speak of being governed by right reason, so that look now as they do in matters of religion and conscience fly from the Scriptures and from supernatural truths revealed there, that a man may not be questioned for going against them, but only for errors against the light of nature and right reason, so they do also in civil government and things of the world go from the laws and constitutions of kingdoms, and will be governed by rules according to nature and right reason. . . .   And as we are delivered of God by the hand of nature into this world, every one with a natural innate freedom and propriety, even so are we to live, every one equally and alike to enjoy his birthright and privilege."[1]

[1] Thomas Edwards, *Gangræna*, 1646, Part III., pp. 16A and

This period is also instructive for the attempt then made to determine the time of the transition of England from the natural to the civil state. That critical time was assumed to have been the Norman Conquest. Before the Conquest the Anglo-Saxons, the descendants of the Germanic tribes, so gloriously described by Tacitus, were supposed to have lived in a democratic and communal manner or in natural equality, and this natural state was destroyed by the Romanised conquerors, who divided the lands and introduced new and alien laws. This anti-Normanic agitation was partly nationalist and patriotic, and partly revolutionary and communist. The representative of the first was a certain John Hare, who published three pamphlets on the matter, the first of which was written in 1642, but published in 1647. He is strongly pro-German and anti-French. The English, he believes, had a most honourable and happy origin, viz., from Germany, but their liberties were afterwards shut up by the Normans under the name and notion of franchises ; the heraldry and the names of the nobility were nothing but inventories of foreign villages, and the royal title reminded them always of the conquest by the sword ; in short, an Englishman could not move without hearing " the chains of captivity rattle." Among other reforms Hare proposes " That all the Norman nobility repudiate their names and titles brought over from Normandy, assuming others more consistent with the honour of this nation, and disdain all right of possession here as heirs and successors to any pretended conqueror."[1] The king did not govern by law of nature and the inferences from *salus publica*, but by right of conquest;[2] whereas the honour of Englishmen consisted of living under laws of their own choosing and under princes to whose rule they consented.

The leader of the political Levellers, John Lilburne, agitates

16D. Owing, probably, to a printer's oversight, there are between the numbered pages 16 and 17 fully sixteen pages without any number at all. In order, however, to facilitate the reference to them, I add to page 16 the letters A, B, C, D, etc., so as to cover the unnumbered pages.

[1] John Hare, *Anti-Normanism, Harl. Misc.*, Vol. 8, pp. 96, 104.
[2] The same, *Plain English, Harl. Misc.*, Vol. 9, p. 94.

the people with the argument that " the greatest mischief of all and the oppressing bondage of England ever since the Norman yoke is a law called the common law. The laws of this nation are unworthy of a free people, and deserve from first to last to be considered, debated, and reduced to an agreement with common equity and right reason, which ought to be the form and life of every government."[1]

And Gerrard Winstanley, the fiery soul of the little body of men called Diggers, appeals to Oliver Cromwell to cast out the " Conquerors and to recover our land and liberties . . . for when the Norman power had conquered our forefathers he took the free use of our English ground from them and made them his servants."[2]   In another Digger pamphlet it is said, " We do protest against all arbitrary courts, terms, lawyers, impropriators, lords of manors, patents, privileges, customs, tolls, monopolisers, incroachers, enhancers . . . against the whole Norman power, as being too intolerable a burden any longer to bear. . . . We protest against any coming to Westminster Terms, but will endeavour to have our controversies ended by two, three, or twelve men of our neighbourhood, as before the Norman Conquest."[3]   In short, the whole communist movement of the years from 1648 to 1652 assumes the Norman Conquest to have marked the Fall of the Englishman and his transfer from the natural to the civil state.

4.—THE DIGGERS OR TRUE LEVELLERS

The Digger movement, although small in the number of its adherents, was an agrarian revolt on a surprisingly extensive theoretical basis. It was as if all the Peasant Wars of the past had suddenly become articulate. It aimed at making the earth the common treasury of all. The whole substance of mediaeval communism reappeared, but in a rationalist and sectarian setting. The logical theology of the Schoolmen was superseded by a mysti-

[1] John Lilburne, *Just Man's Justification*, pp. 11–15.
[2] Gerrard Winstanley, *Law of Freedom* (1652), p. 3.
[3] *Declaration of the Well-Affected in the County of Buckinghamshire* (1649).

cal religion, the axis of which was Reason; and for the Fall of mankind from the natural state was substituted the conquest of the democratic and communal Englishmen by the property-struck and iron-handed Norman. Quite in the style of Pope Gregory VII., the first manifesto of the Diggers denounces kingship as having its patent from the devil and from murder.[1] William the Conqueror is the personification of that kingship. "And all our nobility and gentry came from the outlandish Norman bastard." They all originated from cruel murder, theft, and conquest.[2] The earth and the fulness thereof were given to men in common; it was plain that every man had a right and property in the creation, "so that for any to enclose them from its kind, to his own exclusive use, is tantamount to the impoverishment and enslavement of his fellow-men."[3] The pattern of a right commonwealth was to be found in the Scriptures, partly in the agrarian legislation of the Israelites and partly in the Gospel. "And all that believed were together, and had all things common" (Acts ii. 44).

These two pamphlets were preparatory to the propaganda by deed. A few months after, viz., on April 1, 1649,[4] a few men, led by William Everard (late of the army) and Gerrard Winstanley, took to digging and manuring land on St. George's Hill, in the parish of Walton, and later at Cobham, in Surrey, in order to encourage the people to go and do likewise and form communities, or to " restore the creation to its former condition . . . and ancient community of enjoying the fruits of the earth." On April 16, an information of their doings was given to the Council of State, who on the same day ordered Lord Fairfax to disperse the Diggers. Four days later Everard and Winstanley appeared before Lord Fairfax at Whitehall. Everard, as spokesman, said that all the liberties of the people were

---

[1] *Light Shining in Buckinghamshire*, 1648, p. 3. In Thomason's Collection of Tracts, where most of the Diggers' pamphlets are to be found. A special catalogue of that collection is in the British Museum Reading Room.   [2] *Ibid.*, p. 9.

[3] *More Light Shining in Buckinghamshire*, pp. 2–15.

[4] *A New Year's Gift to Parliament*, p. 44.

lost through the coming of William the Conqueror, and that ever since the people of God lived under oppression and tyranny. The remedy was to dig and plough up the commons, parks, and other untilled lands. The Diggers did not intend to interfere with any man's property, or to break down the pales of the enclosures, but only to cultivate those lands that were common and untilled. When people would see the blessings of it they would come in and join the community.

The reporter of this interview adds that Everard and Winstanley stood before the Lord General with their hats on, and when asked the reason of their behaviour they replied, he was but their fellow-creature.[1]

As a movement the Diggers were unsuccessful. Although they sent missionaries to other counties of England,[2] and gained a small following in Buckinghamshire and Northamptonshire, the peasantry were against them. The settlements at Walton and Cobham were destroyed by the people ; they pulled down the few huts, cut the spades and hoes to pieces, and maltreated the Diggers. " The enemy were so mad that they tumbled the earth up and down, and would suffer no corn to grow."[3] The movement lasted only for about twelve months, but it left numerous manifestoes and pamphlets of considerable power, mostly written by Gerrard Winstanley, with whose two chief works, *New Law of Righteousness*, and *Law of Freedom*, we shall deal presently. As regards the Digger movement itself, the most characteristic manifesto is that entitled, *The True Levellers' Standard Advanced* (April 26, 1649), signed by fifteen Diggers, headed by William Everard. This declaration of their principles asserts (pp. 6–13) :

" In the beginning of time the great Creator, Reason, made the earth to be a common treasury to preserve beasts, birds, fishes, and man, the lord who was to govern this Creation. . . . The rules of Creation were, Not to enclose any part into any particular hand, but all as one man, working together, and

---

[1] *Declaration of the Levellers*, April 23, 1649, p. 3.
[2] *A Perfect Diurnal*.
[3] *A New Year's Gift*, p. 45.

feeding together as sons of one father, members of one family, not lording over another, but all looking upon each other as equals in the Creation. . . . But since human flesh began to delight itself in the things of the Creation more than in the spirit of Reason and Righteousness . . . and selfish imagination ruling as king in the room of Reason therein, and working with covetousness, did set up one man to teach, to rule over another ; and thereby the spirit was killed and man was brought into bondage. . . . Hereupon the earth was hedged into enclosures by the teachers and rulers, and the others were made servants and slaves. And the earth which was made to be a common storehouse for all is bought and sold and kept within the hands of the few." The Diggers declare that they are resolved to remove from the Creation the curse and bondage of Civil Property, not by the force of arms, but " by labouring the earth in righteousness together, to earn our bread by the sweat of our brows, neither giving hire nor taking hire . . . and lay the foundation of making the earth a common treasury for all, both rich and poor, that every one that is born in the land may be fed by the earth his mother that brought him forth, according to the Reason that rules in the Creation."

All the other manifestoes and pamphlets of the Diggers are in a similar strain, so that if we know one we know them all. The struggle is essentially against private property in land, civil law, and tyranny or oligarchy in matters of government, and for a rationalist and Christianised *ius naturale*. The Diggers looked on Jesus as the first True Leveller.

The rhymes left by the Diggers are of small poetic value. " The Diggers' Song " was evidently written in the autumn, 1649, when they met with the enmity of the people and opposition of the clergy and authorities. A few verses will suffice to learn the spirit of it :—

" Ye noble Diggers all, stand up now, stand up now,
    You noble Diggers, stand up now ;
The waste land to maintain, seeing cavaliers by name
Your diggings do disdain and persons all defame.
    Stand up now, stand up now.

    *   *   *   *

" The lawyers they conjoin, stand up now, stand up now,
    The lawyers they conjoin, stand up now ;
To arrest you they advise, and such fury they devise,
The devil in them lies, and has blinded both their eyes.
    Stand up now, stand up now.

" The clergy they come in, stand up now, stand up now,
    The clergy they come in, stand up now ;
The clergy they come in, and say it is a sin
That we should now begin, our freedom to win.
    Stand up now, stand up now.

            *   *   *   *

" To conquer then by love, come in now, come in now,
    To conquer then by love, come in now ;
To conquer then by love, as it does you behove,
For He is King above, no Power is like to Love,
    Glory here, Diggers all ! "[1]

In a long " Christmas Carol " the Diggers declare that the
titles of the lords of the manors originated with the Norman
Conquest, which in consequence of the execution of Charles I.
had lost all value, and therefore fell to the common people.
The Civil War, however, had shown that even after much bloodshed the people could have no hope in Government :—

            " Therefore let me advise
            All those who freedom prise,
            To till each heath and plain,
            For this will freedom gain,
            Heriots and fines this will expell
            A bondage great—men know full well.

            " Freedom is not won
            Neither by sword nor gun ;
            Though we have eight years stay'd,
            And have our moneys pay'd ;
            The Clubs and Diamonds cast away,
            The Hearts and Spades must win the day."[2]

And in " A Digger's Ballad," a communistic song written by

[1] C. H. Firth, *Clarke Papers*, II., p. 221.
[2] *The Diggers' Mirth*, 1650.

Robert Coster, only the last of the nine stanzas shows some merit :—

> " The glorious state which I do relate
> Unspeakable glory shall yield,
> The corn will be green and the flowers seen,
> Our storehouses they will be filled.
> The birds will rejoice with a merry voice
> All things shall yield sweet increase.
> Then let us all sing and joy in our King,
> Who causes all sorrows to cease."[1]

5.—WINSTANLEY'S IDEAL COMMONWEALTH

Gerrard Winstanley, the fiery soul of the Digger movement, was a peaceful John Ball. His own writings, as well as the Digger manifestoes, which he drafted or inspired, exhibit familiarity with mediaeval communism. In the history of English social thought he is the first sectarian communist. He was devoted to mysticism and had visions. Of his life little is known. He was born at Wigan, Lancashire, on October 10, 1609.[2] A few biographical data were supplied by Winstanley himself in the introductory epistle published in his *Watchword to the City of London* (1649). He lived for a time in the City of London as a freeman, possessed " estate and trade," and was " beaten out of both " partly through business failure or, as he says, " by the cheating sons in the thieving art of buying and selling," and partly through the disturbances of the Civil War, " by the burden of and for the soldiery in the beginning of the war." His friends assisted him to retire to the country, probably to the Chiltern Hills, where he evidently found leisure enough for contemplation and reading. The progress of the Civil War, the final defeat of the King, and the feverish mental activity which set in and which manifested itself in the numerous pamphlets dealing with natural law, social and sectarian speculations on religion and ethics, mightily stirred the mind of Winstanley. He interpreted this upheaval to be a levelling of the political mountains as a preliminary to the advent of the great reformation, the radical

---

[1] Robert Coster, *A Mite Cast into the Common Treasury*, 1650.
[2] L. H. Berens, *Digger Movement*, p. 41.

F

change of the spiritual and social conditions of England. " The Spirit of the whole Creation (who is God) is about the Reformation of the World, and he will go forward in his work. . . . The great searching of heart in these days is to find out where true Freedom lies, that the Commonwealth of England might be established in peace." [1]

He at first wrote four pamphlets, *The Mystery of God*, *The Breaking of the Day of God*, *The Saints' Paradise*, and *Truth lifting up its Head*, all in 1648, interpreting Biblical and theological subjects in a spirit of mysticism and religious philosophy. Then he commenced to see visions which led him to communism, and to fierce attacks on kingship and private property. Winstanley has left us a description of his mental state at that time. [2] " As I was in a trance not long since, divers matters were presented to my sight, which must not be related here. Likewise I heard these words : ' Work together : Eat bread together : Declare this all abroad.' Likewise I heard these words : ' Whosoever it is that labours in the earth, for any person or persons that lift up themselves as lords and rulers over others, and that doth not look upon himself as equal to others in the Creation, the hand of the Lord shall be upon the labourer. I the Lord have spoke it and I will do it. Declare this abroad.' " This mental experience gave him a mission. He " was filled with abundance of quiet peace and sacred joy . . . and much pressed in spirit to declare all abroad."

The first communist treatise which he published under his name was *New Law of Righteousness*. We find in it the usual mediaeval communist interpretation of the creation and fall of man. At the beginning man was created perfect, then he fell from his estate through following self-love, covetousness, and carnal lust. Appropriation of land followed, likewise buying and selling, " mine " and " thine," civil laws to uphold property, and hereby restraining men from seeking nourishment from their mother earth. This was all the work of the unrighteous or first

---

[1] Gerrard Winstanley, *Law of Freedom*, pp. 4, 17.
[2] The same, *New Law of Righteousness*, January, 1649, quoted extensively by Berens, p. 73.

Adam, who dammed up the wells of universal liberty and brought the Creation under the curse of bondage, sorrow, and tears. For as long as there were lords who called the lands theirs and rulers who upheld this particular property, the common people would not be free. Only by making the earth a common treasury, as it was in the beginning, could the first Adam, or covetousness, pride, and envy be got rid of, Still, nothing was to be taken from the rich. " If the rich hold fast to this propriety of mine and thine, let them labour their own lands. And let the common people who say the earth is ours, not mine, let them labour together and eat bread together up on the commons, mountains, and hills." It was with Winstanley a struggle of common against enclosure, or collective possession and co-operative work against private property and hired labour. The ultimate remedy was the abolition of private property and civil government.

The society which was to take the place of the civil one is described by Winstanley in his *Law of Freedom* (1652). This ideal commonwealth rests on the following principles and laws :—

" Government is a wise and free ordering of the earth and of the manners of mankind by observation of particular laws and rules, so that all the inhabitants may live peaceably in plenty and freedom in the land where they are bred " (p. 25). This government acts according to the law of nature which is supported by reason so as not to allow the propensities of the flesh to deflect the natural law from its rational course (p. 30). The function of governing is entrusted to a Parliament chosen annually. It is the real court of equity. Its duties are four-fold :—

" First, as a tender father, a parliament is to empower officers and give orders for the free planting and reaping of the Commonwealth's land, that all who have been oppressed and kept back from the free use thereof by conquerors, kings, and their tyrant laws, may now be set at liberty to plant in freedom for food and raiment, and are to be a protection to them who labour the earth, and a punisher of them who are idle. But some may say, What is that I call Commonwealth's land ? I answer, All that land which has been withheld from the inhabitants by the conqueror or tyrant kings and is now recovered out of the hands of that oppression by the joint assistance of the persons and purses of the communers of the land. It is their birthright to them and to their posterity, and ought not to be converted into particular hands again by the laws of a free commonwealth. In particular, this land is all abbey lands . . . Crown lands, bishops' lands, with all parks, forests, chases, now of late recovered out of the hands of the kingly tyrants. . . .

" Secondly, to abolish all old laws and customs which have been the strength of the oppressor, and to prepare and then to enact new laws for the ease and freedom of the people. . . .

" Thirdly, to see all those burdens removed actually, which have hindered the oppressed people from the enjoyment of their birthright. If their common lands be under the oppression of lords of manors, they are to see the land freed from that slavery. If the commonwealth's land be sold by hasty counsel of subtle, covetous, and ignorant officers . . . then a parliament is to examine what authority any had to sell or buy the land without a general consent of the people. . . . They are to declare that the bargain is unrighteous, and that the buyers and sellers are enemies to the peace and freedom of the commonwealth.

" Fourthly, if there be occasion to raise an army to wage war, either against an invasion of a foreign enemy, or against an insurrection at home, it is the work of a parliament to manage that business for the preservation of common peace " (pp. 50–56).

The land having been restored to the nation it is given over to the farmers to till it in common. " There shall be no buying and selling of the earth, nor of the fruits thereof." For, when mankind began to buy and sell, they fell from the state of innocence, and began to oppress each other and discontents and wars arose (p. 12).

"The earth is to be planted and the fruits reaped and carried into barns and storehouses by the assistance of every family. If any man or family want corn or other provisions, they may go to the storehouse and fetch without money. If they want a horse to ride, they may go into the fields in summer or to the common stables in winter, and receive one from the keepers and when the journey is performed, bring him back. . . . There shall be storehouses in all places in the country and in the towns to which all the fruits of the soil and the works of the tradesmen shall be brought and thence delivered again to the families and to every one who want them ; or else be transported by ships to other countries in exchange for those things which our land will not or cannot produce. All the labours of husbandmen and tradesmen within the country shall be upon the common stock. And as every one works to advance the common stock, so every one shall have free use of any commodity in the storehouse for his pleasure and comfortable livelihood, without buying or selling or restraint from anybody. . . . For as particular families and tradesmen do make several works more than they can make use of and do carry their particular works to the storehouses, so it is all reason and equity that they should go to other storehouses to fetch any other commodity which they want and cannot make " (pp. 74-5).

In order that these laws and regulations be carried out and to check the covetous, proud, and idle, there must be officers to regulate the irrational conduct of such men.

All officers of the Commonwealth to be chosen annually. " Choose such as are men of peaceable disposition ; likewise who suffered under kingly oppression, for they will be fellow-feelers of others' bondage ; likewise who have adventured the loss of their estates and lives to redeem the land from bondage and who have remained constant ; likewise men of courage who are not afraid to speak the truth ; likewise who are above forty years of age, for these are most likely to be experienced men. . . . And if you choose men thus principled who are poor men, as times go, for the Conqueror's power has made many a righteous man a poor man, then allow them a yearly maintenance from the common stock, until such time as a Commonwealth's Freedom is established, for then there will be no need of such allowance " (pp. 37-9).

Each parish shall choose a number of peacemakers to manage the affairs of the parish, to prevent trouble and to preserve the common peace. They shall settle any matters of offence between man and man.   If the peacemakers are unable to bring about a reconciliation of the parties, then he shall command them to appear at the Judge's Court.   Each parish shall also choose a number of overseers to preserve peace ; to see that the young people receive proper instruction in some labour, trade, or service in the common storehouses ; to see that the products of labour shall be delivered up to the storehouses and shops, and that all who serve in the storehouses and shops do their duty.   All old men above sixty years of age are general overseers (pp. 40–6). There shall also be chosen a taskmaster, whose office it is " to take those into his supervision who are sentenced to lose their freedom, to set them to work and to see that they do it."

Education must be general and compulsory.   After the child is weaned the parents shall teach it a civil and humble behaviour towards all men.   Then it shall be sent to school to learn to read the laws of the Commonwealth, the arts and languages.   But there shall be no special class of children brought up to book-learning only.   " For then through idleness they spend their time to find out policies to advance themselves to be lords and masters over their labouring brethren, which occasions all trouble in the world.   Therefore it is necessary and profitable for the Commonwealth that all children be trained to labour and to learning."

Inventions were to be promoted by all means.   " Let no young wit be crushed in his invention."   Experimenting should be encouraged.   " And let every one who finds out an invention have a deserved honour given to him."   Knowledge and experiment should take the place of believing and imagining (pp. 68–76).

Such a Commonwealth did not mean idleness, community of women, or anarchy.   It meant labour as a duty of every member of the Commonwealth, purity in sexual relations, and observance of the laws.   Under common management would be the soil, workshops, and storehouses ; labour would be exchanged for labour, without the intermediary of money.   Family life must be private and strictly monogamous.   " Every man's house, furniture, and the provisions which he fetches from the storehouses are proper to himself, likewise the wife to her husband and the husband to his wife " (p. 24).[1]

6.—THE SOCIAL REFORMERS

The years from the beginning of the Civil War to the end of the seventeenth century produced also several social reformers. As we are concerned only with those reformers whose schemes contain socialistic elements, we must confine ourselves to the pamphlets of Samuel Hartlib, Peter Chamberlen, Peter Cornelius Plockhoy, and John Bellers. The most important of them is that of Chamberlen, whose social criticism is closely related to communism, inasmuch as he makes use of the proposition that the labour of the poor, *i.e.*, the wage-workers, is the source of all wealth. John Bellers, a member of the Society of Friends, whom Robert Owen as well as Karl Marx greatly admired, represents a combination of Hartlib, Plockhoy, and Chamberlen, making, however, a serious contribution to social-economic speculation by proposing to make labour—time, and not money, the standard of value.

In point of time, but by no means of thought and originality, Hartlib comes first. He was a German Protestant refugee from Poland, a man of much learning and some influence with his English friends on account of his endeavours to promote education and agriculture. He wrote, in 1641, a small treatise, *A Description of the Famous Kingdom of Macaria*, reminiscent of readings in Sir Thomas More's *Utopia* and Francis Bacon's *New Atlantis*. The name Macaria actually occurs in More's Commonwealth: " The laws of the Macarians are not far distant from those of Utopia."[2] The main characteristic of the constitution of Macaria is that the government, consisting of departments of agriculture, fishing, home trade, foreign trade, and colonisation, manage the economic affairs of the commonwealth. No man may hold more land than he can improve ; the death duties amount to the twentieth part of the goods left, and are

[1] *Cf.* Bernstein, *Sozialismus und Demokratie*, 1905. Gooch, *Democratic Ideas*, 1898.

[2] More, *Utopia*, ed. Lupton (1895), p. 95.

used for the improvement of agriculture, highways, and bridges ;
the home trade is so regulated as to correspond to the needs
of the people ; crown lands are so carefully tilled and cultivated
that they yield considerable revenues and lighten the burden of
taxation.[1]

Of considerably higher historical value is Peter Chamberlen's
Poor Man's Advocate (1649). It combines " Nature, Reason,
and Religion " with the doctrine of labour as creator of wealth,
and makes use of these theories to advocate the justice of the
claims of the working classes. Chamberlen argues that the
wealth and strength of all countries were the poor (labouring
poor, or the propertyless workmen), for they did all the necessary
works of society and formed the main body of the armies. They
had the same right to the earth as the rich. Moreover, they
provided for the rich. The latter must, therefore, regard
themselves merely as stewards whose main duty it was to care
for the poor and enable them to produce wealth. The end of
wealth was not enjoyment for the rich, but to banish poverty
from the land. And that was also in conformity with religion,
which commands to love our fellow-man. " For if we love not
our brother whom we have seen, how can we love God Whom we
have not seen ? " And the same commandment was the basic
principle of organised society. There could be no peaceful and
healthy social life as long as the many were poor. In order
to get rid of poverty Chamberlen proposes to nationalise (*a*) the
estates of the King, bishops, deans and chapters, and delinquents ;
(*b*) the commons, wastes, heaths, woods, forests, etc. ; (*c*) the
mines, which are not worked ; (*d*) parish charities ; (*e*) unearned
increment[2] of agriculture, trade, and manufactures, arising from
improvements and inventions and colonisation ; (*f*) treasures
found in sea and land. Finally, he proposes the establishment
of a national bank, like those of Amsterdam and Venice,
likewise of academies for higher learning in arts and sciences
in order " to prevent youth from going abroad, in the

---

[1] *Harl. Misc.*, I., pp. 580–5.

[2] Chamberlen does not use this term, but the sense of his proposal
amounts to that.

blossom of their years, to be corrupted there in religion and manners."

This national stock of wealth should be organised by the Commonwealth with a view to employment of the poor. The land was to be cultivated on a co-operative basis ; still, if any farmer desired to work individually, a certain number of enclosed acres should be let to him on an annual rental of £5. The government of the Commonwealth should procure implements and raw material for the farmers and handicraftsmen and generally assume those duties which employers performed.

In creating this national stock the former owner's claims should be considered, except of those who legally forfeited their rights. The revenue that would accrue to the Commonwealth from those enterprises would be used for the needs of the government. It might be objected that only unworthy and ignorant men were poor, or by the improvement of their social condition the poor might become untractable, insolent, and idle. To these and similar objections, Chamberlen replies : " Let no man say that men were poor because they were unworthy. Some of the greatest philosophers, also Christ and the apostles, were poor. Besides, the poor would not be so poor, if the rich were honest, so as to let the poor have their own ; the riches of the rich are oftentimes but trophies of their dishonesty, of having robbed the poor, or cozened the Commonwealth " (p. 12).

And as to idleness it might be said that, if wealth made idleness to be a reason why the poor should be kept poor, then it was also a reason why rich men should not be rich, since " Edel "-man (gentleman) is idle-man. There was no necessity in " Nature, Reason, and Religion why they that are rich should continue so, and they that are poor should always remain so. Is aught of thine taken from thee ? O, envious man ! The demands of the poor are but food and raiment, and to be disposed into such an order that they and their posterity should not lack the necessaries of life nor be exposed to slavish labour." Finally, as regards insolence there was no greater incitement to insolence than poverty face to face with flaunting wealth.

The reforms, if carried out, would bring the poor into a condition of regular employment, instruction, and good, orderly government, such as they had never known before. Such conditions would engender love for the country, obedience to the laws, and stability of government. The new order would act as a good Samaritan and pour oil and wine into the wounds of the nation.

Far less revolutionary was the proposal of Peter Cornelius van Zurik-Zee, or Plockhoy (sometimes written Plockboy), in his pamphlet, *A Way to Make the Poor in these and other Nations Happy* (1659). He was a Dutchman, who lived for some time in England, evidently attracted by the social ferment of the Civil War and Commonwealth period. The reforms he proposed aimed at the establishment of " Little Commonwealths." They amounted essentially to the formation of co-operative societies for trade and commerce on a voluntary basis. His main idea was that co-operative production was cheaper than individualised enterprise, and could therefore more efficiently compete in the markets. Wholesale buying of raw material, co-operative work and common householding would result in a decrease of the prime cost of the commodities, in lessening the household expenses, and therefore in a greater ability to undersell the competitors. These " Little Commonwealths " should establish the most efficient schools and educational institutions, so as to induce the rich to send their children to those schools and thereby to spread the knowledge of co-operative enterprise. Also, the most skilled surgeons and physicians were to be engaged, who would treat the poor free of charge, and by this means advertise the blessings of co-operative labour. The regulations of the " Little Commonwealths " were to aim at uprooting covetousness, excesses, lying and deceit and all other vices that sprang from riches and poverty. In the schools the children were to be taught no particular form of religion, but to read the writings of the saints, study arts, sciences, languages, " and learn to follow those that have the spirit of God, doing miracles as the prophets."

Plockhoy's idea of combining voluntary social reform, philan-

thropy, and business was particularly congenial to the Society of
Friends, a prominent English member of which was John Bellers
(1655–1725). In his pamphlet, *Proposals for Raising a Colledge of Industry of all Useful Trades and Husbandry* (1696),
he aimed at affording the poor co-operative and remunerative
work, the rich a fair rate of interest, the youth good education.
All social revolutionary enthusiasm, all millennial vision had
vanished, and prosaic business enterprise began to dominate
the life of the nation. The sobering process had set in with the
Restoration, and went on at an accelerating rate after the
Glorious Revolution. Bellers saw that " What sap is to the
tree, profit is to business," or, if social reform was to succeed,
it had to be put on a business footing. He did not denounce
the rich, but spoke of their pity for their poor, among whom
" crime, misery, idleness, and lewdness " prevailed. He believed
that there were many rich who would like to see the poor reformed
in manners and better provided for, and who, therefore, would
be willing to contribute money for the establishment of co-operative agricultural colonies.

Each agricultural colony was to consist of 300 persons who
would be so selected as to be able to perform all the labours
necessary for farming. The cost of establishing such a colony,
inclusive of acquiring land, he estimated at £18,000, which could
be raised by shares. In all trading centres of the country
co-operative workshops for arts and crafts should be established.
The advantages of co-operative labour, by eliminating competition and waste, would be considerable, and would ensure
a remunerative rate of interest to the shareholders. But the
main benefit would be moral, such colleges of industries affording
the best opportunity of educating the children of the poor
to useful work, industrious habits, and good manners. Bellers
does not attach undue importance to learning, for " though
learning is useful, yet a virtuous, industrious education tends
more to happiness here and hereafter." The life in those agriculture and trade colonies would be communistic. " The poor
thus in college will be a community like the example of primitive
Christianity that lived in common, and the power that did attend

it bespeak their excellency ; but considering the constitution of mankind that have estates (but it is not so with the poor), it was none of the least miracles of that age." In these colleges or fellowships the standard of value of all necessaries would be labour, and not money. Bellers evidently means labour-time, and thus anticipates Robert Owen and John Gray, who in the years from 1820 to 1850 advocated labour-time notes as a means of exchange instead of money tokens. Bellers goes on to say that " though money has its conveniences, it being a pledge among men for want of credit, yet it is not without mischiefs, and called by our Saviour the Mammon of Unrighteousness. When the rich lose their money they can't employ the poor, though they have still the lands and hands to provide victuals, which are the true riches of the nation and not money. Money in the body politic is what a crutch is to the natural body, crippled ; but when the body is sound, the crutch is troublesome. So when the particular interest is made a public interest, in such a college, money will be of little use there." A college thus constituted " cannot so easily be undone, for if plundered, twelve months' time will recruit again ; like the grass new mowed the next year supplies again, labour bringing a supply as the soil does. When men work together they assist one another, but when scattered are useless, if not preying upon another." Bellers reminds the rich that they had no other way of living but by the labour of others, as the landlord by the labour of the tenants, and the merchants and tradesmen by the labour of the mechanics, unless they turned levellers and took to work together with the poor (p. 35). Labour being the monies of the rich (p. 10) it behoved them to see the poor work under the most advantageous conditions, both for the creation of wealth and the moral elevation of the poor.

Bellers was only one of a long and honourable series of Poor Law reformers, who, in the years from the Restoration to the reign of Queen Anne, were dealing with the question of utilising the labour power of the poor for the welfare of the nation. Some of the greatest men of that age, viz., Sir Josiah Child, Sir Matthew Hale, John Locke, Dr. Davenant, and Daniel

Defoe, devoted much attention to that problem,[1] but in none of them was the spirit of social criticism so reminiscent of the Commonwealth period as in Bellers.

As a reaction against all those proposals for raising the material, intellectual, and moral condition of the poor must be regarded Bernard Mandeville's *Fable of the Bees* and *On Charity and Charity Schools*, in which he pleaded for letting the poor alone, for " in a free nation, where slaves are not allowed, the surest wealth consists in a multitude of labouring poor . . . ignorant as well as poor." Their wants should be relieved, but it were folly to cure them.[2]

[1] Compare Sir Frederick M. Eden, *State of the Poor*, 1797, I. 184–264.

[2] Mandeville, *Fable of the Bees*, etc., edition 1724, pp. 328 and 280

VI

THE ANTI-COMMUNIST PERIOD

I.—EVE OF THE ECONOMIC REVOLUTION

LOOKING at England of the seventeenth century, with her mighty ferment and titanic clash of forces, her intellectual and spiritual giants who filled the national arena, her immortals who illumined the path of human history, it is exceedingly difficult to believe that we are dealing with a numerically small nation—a country of something over one million families only. And they overthrew personal monarchy, established the sovereignty of Parliament, produced Harvey, Milton, Hobbes, Petty, Locke, Newton, Cromwell, and Marlborough, and a host of lesser stars who, in any other age or country, might be counted as of first magnitude.

Gregory King, a political arithmetician of no mean value, left us, in his *Natural and Political Observations* (1694), a statistical view of England in 1688. The population of England and Wales consisted of five and a half million souls, or 1,360,000 families. The national income amounted to £43,500,000 ; the annual increase of wealth to £1,800,000. How narrow the circle of life then was, may be gauged from the remark of King that Lichfield was " a large town in the Midlands of nearly 3,000 souls." The number of families of the various classes and groups of the nation were then as follows : Nobility and gentry 16,586, officials 10,000, oversea traders 12,000, home traders 2,000, law 8,000, clergy 10,000, yeomanry 48,000, farmers 150,000, liberal professions 16,000, small traders and shopkeepers 40,000, handicraftsmen and mechanics 60,000, officers in army and navy 9,000, seamen 50,000, workmen and servants 364,000, cottars and paupers 400,000, soldiers 35,000. The income of the nobility and gentry was between £2,800 and £180 per family, oversea traders £400, home traders £200, yeomanry between £84 and £50, shopkeepers £45, handicraftsmen and mechanics £40, workmen, labourers and servants £15, cottars and paupers £6 10s. According to King, all families whose income was above £40 belonged to the productive classes, and increased the national income, while the labourers and workmen were non-productive, and decreased the national wealth, for their earnings had to be supplemented by parish relief in order to allow them to meet the cost of living. King appears to have looked upon society from the point of view of distribution ; statistics and not economics was his proper field. There is still another important feature in his statistical view of the nation, viz. that the size of each family depended on its income ; the number of the members of each family was large or small in proportion to the large or small income ; he computes for instance, the number of the members of a noble family to have been between sixteen and forty, of a merchant family eight, of a yeoman family between five and seven, of a workman's family between three and four. In short, the means of subsistence determined the size of the family. This view is confirmed by Adam Smith, who declares : " Poverty, though it does not prevent the generation, is extremely unfavourable to the rearing of children. . . . It is not uncommon in the Highlands of Scotland for a mother who has borne twenty children not to have two alive. . . . Every species of animals naturally multiplies in proportion to the means of subsistence, and no species can ever multiply beyond it. But in civilised society it is only among the inferior ranks of people that the scantiness of subsistence can set limits to the further multiplication of the human species ; and it can do so in no other way than by destroying a great part of the children which their marriages produce."[1]

English society as it emerged from the Glorious Revolution consisted of a population fifty per cent. of whom were relatively well-to-do. But the bulk of the national income fell to the agricultural proprietors. Of the 43·5 millions sterling only 2·4 millions fell to the great merchants, a similar sum to the craftsmen, and 1·8 millions to the small traders and shopkeepers.

[1] Adam Smith, *Wealth of Nations*, book 1, chap. 8.

Agriculture was the main occupation of the nation, while the industries played a relatively small part and were chiefly in the hands of small masters and mainly dependent upon the skill of handicraftsmen and artificers using human power. Even in the larger factories the skilled workman, and not the mechanical contrivance, was the dominant labour factor. The handicrafts-man, the artificer, the mechanic appeared as the creator of wealth. This was the period when Sir William Petty and John Locke formulated their labour value theories.

From 1688 to about 1750 the progress of agriculture, trade, commerce, and population was slow and even halting. It by no means corresponded with the great exertions of the statesmen, diplomats, and generals of the nation. As regards home politics and economics, the period was altogether counter-revolutionary and conservative. The stream of life flowed quietly and cautiously, avoiding rapids and eddies, and though it was some-times caught by the whirlpool of speculation, like the South-Sea Bubble, or by the delusions of the decadence-mongers, the popula-tion lived, on the whole, peacefully and enjoyed a certain amount of contentment. Poor Law rates were comparatively small, oscillating between £600,000 and £800,000 sterling annually, the inconsiderable number of enclosures hardly touched the yeomanry and farmers, the harvests were good, the cost of living was low, and, therefore, the real wage satisfactory. Philosophers and essayists busied themselves with ethics and natural religion, believing in a rational government of mankind and expecting virtue to be rewarded. Addison's prose, Pope's *Essay on Man*, Richardson's novels are the mirrors of the age, while Swift and Fielding are the rebels. The doctrines of natural law were made to tally with and to strengthen the constitution and the institu-tions of England. Pope, Burke, Blackstone, Robert Wallace, Adam Smith and Abraham Tucker's populariser, Paley, either use and interpret natural law in a conservative sense or draw its social-revolutionary teeth.

2.—POPE, BOLINGBROKE, AND BURKE

Inspired by Henry St. John, Lord Bolingbroke, who, in his retirement from public life, inquired into the system of *ius naturale* from an ethical-religious point of view, Pope sought to reconcile the state natural and civil, to teach man that happiness, the great aim and end of life, did not depend on equality of goods and station, but on virtue, on the rule of reason over passion, on the harmony between self-love and social, on the identification of individual with social interests. The state of nature was undoubtedly a state of innocence, in which the whole creation was united in peace. But man's passion got somehow the upper hand and ordered society became a necessity. Then nature spoke to man to take instruction from the ants' republic and the realm of bees, "how those in common all their wealth bestow, and anarchy without confusion know." Thus arose paternal government and common possessions. " True faith, true policy, united ran, that was but love of God, and this of man." Then came force and conquest, ambition, lucre, and lust, and destroyed the paternal and social state. In the reign of self-love, conflict and rebellion made all life impossible, until " forced into virtue thus, by self-defence, even kings learned justice and benevolence." Men learned to restrain each other, and join order to liberty. They ceased to fight about constitutions and religions, but desired good order and right behaviour :

"Order is Heaven's first law ; and this confessed,
Some are, and must be, greater than the rest,
More rich, more wise." [1]

Although Pope's description of the state of nature and social equality is, in comparison with the apology for the existing order, the more poetical, Edmund Burke thought that Bolingbroke was not satisfied with it. " Pope cannot bear every truth. He has a timidity which hinders the full exertion of his faculties, almost as effectually as bigotry cramps those of the general herd of mankind." [2] And when, in 1754, Bolingbroke's *Philosophical*

[1] Pope, *Essay on Man* (1734), epistle 3, c. 4–6 ; epistle 4, c. 2.
[2] Burke, *Vindication of Natural Society*, ed. 1905, p. 41.

G

Works were published, in which natural religion and the simple teachings of Jesus are defended against artificial religion, revelation, and Christian theology, Burke set himself the task of finishing, once for all, with natural law. For this purpose he wrote his pamphlet, *A Vindication of Natural Society* (1756), which was supposed to have been left, in manuscript, by Lord Bolingbroke. It is a disturbing essay. Burke intended it as a *reductio ad absurdum* of Bolingbroke's doctrines, as an incisive condemnation of the dangerous tenets of natural law, yet its tone is so serious and its criticism of civil society so keen that it has often been taken as a genuine justification of the state of nature. Also, the bad reputation of its author among revolutionary writers has contributed to the misunderstanding of its purpose. It has been thought that Burke, having found his critique of civilisation inconvenient, " burked " its true character.[1]

The author exhibits a wide knowledge of the literature of natural law, but his main sources are Pope's *Essay on Man* and Bolingbroke's *Works*. The luminous features of the state of nature stand out against the dark and dismal background of civil society. Peace fled, and war transformed the world into an Aceldama. " Leviathan or civil power overflowed the earth with a deluge of blood, as if he were made to disport and play therein." And the cause of all that slaughter was the division of mankind into nations, created by artificial society, natural liberty was lost, and coercion made dungeons, whips, chains, racks, and gibbets a necessity. And there was no essential difference between despotism, oligarchy, and democracy. Everywhere the people, in an artificial or civil society, were sacrificed to the passions of the few. " In proportion as we have deviated from the plain rule of nature, and turned our reason against itself, in that proportion have we increased the follies and miseries of mankind." The same happened in law and religion. Laws multiplied and confusion increased, until it could be discovered no longer what things were held in property and what in common. The professors of artificial law had always walked hand in

---

[1] I may add that I was of the same opinion myself, until a study of the whole period convinced me of my error.

hand with the professors of artificial theology. " As their end in confounding the reason of man, and abridging his natural freedom, is exactly the same, they have adjusted the means to that end in a way entirely similar." It might be said that in a state of nature the strong could rob the weak, but then the weak had at least full liberty to defend himself, or make reprisal by surprise or cunning, or by any other means in which he thought to have a superior advantage ; in political society, however, the poor man could not defend himself, since the only weapon he was allowed to use was money, and if he tried to avenge himself the whole force of that society would be directed against him. " The most obvious division of society is into rich and poor ; and it is no less obvious that the number of the former bears a great disproportion to those of the latter. The whole business of the poor is to administer to the idleness, folly, and luxury of the rich ; and that of the rich, in return, is to find the best methods of confirming the slavery and increasing the burden of the poor. In a state of nature it is an invariable law that a man's acquisitions are in proportion to his labours. In a state of artificial society it is a law, as constant and invariable, that those who labour most enjoy the fewest things ; and those who labour not at all, have the greatest number of enjoyments. . . . I suppose that there are in Great Britain upwards of a hundred thousand people employed in lead, tin, iron, copper, and coal mines ; these unhappy wretches scarce ever see the light of the sun ; there they work at a severe and dismal task, without the least prospect of being delivered from it. . . . A hundred thousand more, at least, are tortured without remission by the suffocating smoke, intense fires and constant drudgery necessary in refining and managing the produce of those mines. If any man informed us that two hundred thousand innocent persons were condemned to so intolerable slavery, how we should pity the unhappy sufferers, and how great would be our just indignation against those who inflicted so cruel and ignominious a punishment ! " All those miseries came upon men in consequence of having abandoned the laws of nature and reason.

Burke's argument is clear. By laying open the foundations of society, as Pope and Bolingbroke did, by contrasting natural with political society to the disadvantage of the latter, the poor, *i.e.* the great majority of the nation, might shake the whole fabric of the existing order. It was no use replying that the theorists and poets of *ius naturale* confined themselves to religion and abstract ethics. The masses, once awakened to their grievances and wrongs, would not stop there. In short, the popularisation of the doctrines of natural law might lead to a social upheaval. English history, since the days of John Ball, confirmed those misgivings. And Burke lived long enough to witness the French Revolution—that great experiment in *ius naturale*.

3.—ROBERT WALLACE

As a preacher in the royal chapel at Edinburgh and a man of liberal culture and learning, Robert Wallace devoted his leisure to the study of problems of population, scientific progress, and Utopian constitutions. Some of the results of his researches and speculations he published in a series of essays under the collective title *Various Prospects* (1761), which deal also with the ideal of perfect government, its great advantages and obstacles. He was the first social-economic student who expressed the opinion that a communist republic, while it would at first banish poverty and promote the welfare of the people, would eventually come to grief from over-population.

Wallace's point of departure is the glaring disproportion between the capacities of man and nature on the one hand and the miserable and backward condition of the masses in particular and society in general. Mankind, evidently, did not take advantage of the opportunities offered to it. How little care did society take either of the souls or bodies of men! Great numbers of the poor were but slaves and beasts of burden to the rich. Ignorance, toil, a scanty and unwholesome diet were their share. Yet all these unhappy mortals were as much qualified by nature as the most fortunate of their kind, for a more agreeable life and nobler enjoyments. Society as a whole made very little progress. Even the most civilised nations knew little of the mysteries of nature. No experiments were made to discover the essence of life. The advance in morality was hardly perceptible ; lust of wealth and power set man against man, nation against nation. Even the increase of population fell far short of the necessities for an adequate cultivation of the earth and the pursuit of useful arts, and yet the sexual appetites and human fertility were enormous.

It would appear that these evils and shortcomings could not be removed as long as private property and individual work prevailed, for without united efforts and harmonious endeavours neither agriculture nor arts and sciences would be cultivated. The great inequality which private property involved must necessarily lead to overwork and idleness, and both were unfavourable to acquisition of knowledge and self-culture. In order, therefore, to enable man to lift human affairs to a higher level new maxims of property and education must be introduced. The best models for such society were presented by Plato's *Republic* and Sir Thomas More's *Utopia*, and they essentially consisted of common possessions, co-operative labour, agriculture as the chief occupation, and education as the main care of society. The advantages which joint labour and the simple life of all the members of society might offer, were sufficiently known. Only such a society could provide for the improvement of the happiness of mankind.

The introduction of such government was, however, a difficult task now, for the minority who possessed wealth and power would use all means to prevent it. No amount of preaching and moralising could persuade them to acquiesce in a change of private property into common possessions. Such a transformation could only take place in times of a general revolution, when mental exaltation, love of equality, and a spirit of sacrifice took hold of all ; if in times like these a great legislator arose he might lead the nation to perfect government. Or it could be established by the example of small communist colonies formed by men of exceptional abilities ; the advantages reaped by them might stir up their neighbours to imitate their constitution and thus gradually spread the ideas of a communist and equitable constitution. There was nothing in the human mind which was averse from such a mode of life. There would be room enough in a communist society for any one to distinguish himself and satisfy his ambition and desire for distinction, by excelling in his work or by invention or discoveries. The love of liberty implanted in man's heart could find no higher satisfaction than in a society of the free and equal. The love of ease and pleasure would not be disappointed in a society where labour was moderate and more in the nature of healthy exercise than of toil. Idleness, one of the sources of poverty and decay, could not exist to any appreciable extent in a society where labour constituted the main basis ; public opinion would soon brand it as one of the worst vices. The equitable distribution of labour and its produce would remove the main cause of envy, jealousy, discord, hardship, and intrigue. Finally, general and careful training of the mind and body would steadily be directed towards developing those propensities, abilities, and forces of mankind which were favourable to, and suppressing those passions which were destructive of, communist life.

Such government was not only the happiest, but the most worthy of man. Poverty, ignorance, vice, could thus effectually be removed, and education, knowledge, health, and security afforded to everybody.

But there frowned one tremendous rock ahead on which the communist ship would be dashed to pieces. Under a perfect government the inconveniences of having a family would be entirely removed ; children would be so well taken care of and everything become so favourable to populousness that the earth would be overstocked with the human species and become unable to support it. The increase of mankind would outstrip the fertility of the soil. And these facts constituted the primary determinants in social affairs. To them all other things must be adjusted. A limited earth, a limited degree of its fertility, and the continued increase of mankind were the primary determinants. Poverty, war, vice, in short, the evils which we were complaining of were but the means of adjusting society to its primary determinants. The speculations of the social philosophers who framed a perfect constitution were only useful in so far as they might suggest some particular reform, but as a whole they were doomed to remain charming fiction, serving to enlarge our views and amuse our fancies.

Needless to say that Robert Wallace is the forerunner of Thomas Robert Malthus.

4.—BLACKSTONE, ADAM SMITH, AND PALEY

In his *Commentaries on the Laws of England* (book 2, chap. 1), Sir William Blackstone has left a summary of the critical attitude of *ius naturale* towards private property as well as of the wisdom of civil law in promoting order and ownership. The whole chapter, although by no means original, is curious ; the idea is still lurking therein that private property was more in the nature of a politic expedient than a right principle. Blackstone declares that, while people were pleased and charmed with the right of property, they were fearful of some defect of their title. It was none the less necessary to examine more deeply into the rudiments and grounds of the institutions of property. In the beginning of the world the all-bountiful Creator had given to man dominion over the earth and the fulness thereof. This gift was the only true and solid foundation of man's dominion over external things. As long as the population was insignificant in numbers all things were common, and every man took from the public stock to his own use such things as he required. In the same state of primeval simplicity lived also the American nations when they were discovered by Europeans ; and the Europeans themselves had once lived under similar conditions, or, as tradition related, in the golden age of the poets. By the law of nature and reason, he who first began to use a thing acquired a kind of transient property that lasted so long as he used it and no longer. Thus the soil was held in common, and no part of it was a permanent property of any man in particular, yet whoever was in occupation of any particular spot of it acquired for the time a sort of ownership. But when mankind increased in number, craftiness, and ambition, it became necessary to change occupation into ownership, otherwise innumerable disturbances might have arisen. In order, therefore, to secure peace private property was introduced, first in movables, partly by possession, but principally by the bodily labour bestowed upon them by the possessor ; then, in the soil, which was vested in the sovereign of the State or in his representatives, *i.e*, the lords of the manors. " And thus the legislature of England has universally promoted the grand order of civil society, the peace and security of individuals, by steadily pursuing that wise and orderly maxim of assigning to everything capable of ownership a legal and determinable owner."

After the great legal authority came the great economist to prove the necessity of private property. With Adam Smith it was not peace and security but the productivity of labour and the increase of wealth which justified private property. The most considerable improvements in the productive powers of labour were made after the appropriation of land and accumulation of stock. As professor of moral philosophy Smith knew all the phases through which natural law had passed. In his time the laws of nature, natural order, and natural liberty, came to signify freedom of trade and commerce from the regulations and interferences of Mercantilism, freedom for the natural promptings of the economic man. With the physiocrats, he assumed the existence of a natural order of things, which, if not interfered with by State laws and subtle regulations, would result in the happiness of mankind.[1] He never misses the opportunity of pointing out that civilisation or the improvement of society was not the product of human foresight and calculation, but of the natural propensities of economically active men.[2] *Laissez faire* did not mean licence or anarchic confusion, but a settled confidence in the laws inherent in nature and man, and distrust of State-made laws. But Smith was also fully cognisant of the communist interpretation of natural law. " In the original state of things," he declares, " which preceded both the appropriation of land and the accumulation of stock, the whole produce of labour belongs to the labourer. Had this state continued, the

[1] Adam Smith, *Wealth of Nations*, book 3, chap. 1 ; book 4, chap. 9.

[2] *Ibid.* Introduction ; book 1, chap. 2.

wages of labour would have augmented with all those improvements in its productive powers to which the division of labour gives occasion." , For " the produce of labour constitutes the natural recompense or wages of labour. . . . But this original state of things . . could not last beyond the first introduction of the appropriation of land and the accumulation of stock. It was at an end, therefore, long before the most considerable improvements were made in the productive powers of labour, and it would be of no purpose to trace further what might have been its effects upon the recompense or wages of labour." [1]

It was, then, under the system of private property that improvements in the production of commodities were introduced and it was no use speculating upon a dead past. Besides, the poorest labourer in a civilised society enjoyed a greater share of the necessaries and conveniences of life than any member in a natural society, though the distribution of labour and its produce was very unequal in the former, and equitable in the latter society.[2] Private property was thus justified by the increase and improvements in the production of wealth. And were it not for the passions, such as envy, malice, or resentment, society could exist with some tolerable degree of security, even if there were no civil government to protect life and property from the injustice of those passions. " But avarice and ambition in the rich, in the poor the hatred of labour and the love of present ease and enjoyment, are the passions which prompt them to invade property. . . . Wherever there is great property, there is great inequality. For one rich man there must be at least five hundred poor, and the affluence of the few supposes the indigence of the many. The affluence of the rich excites the indignation of the poor, who are often both driven by want and prompted by envy to invade his possessions It is only under the shelter of the civil magistrate that the owner of that valuable property, acquired by the labour of many years or perhaps many successive generations, can sleep a single night in security.

[1] Adam Smith, *Wealth of Nations*, book 1, chap. 8.
[2] *Ibid.* Introduction.

. . . The acquisition of valuable and extensive property necessarily requires the establishment of civil government." [1] It was thus through the inequality engendered by the increase and appropriation of wealth that the civil state became a necessity. And the civil state itself was justified by the protection it afforded to private property as the basis of the production of wealth. Lest it should be inferred that Adam Smith was prepared to sacrifice everything to the growth of wealth we must point out that his attitude towards the working classes was full of humanity. Like most philosophers who were familiar with the doctrines of *ius naturale* he was favourable to the claims of labour, and he urged the employers to listen to the " dictates of reason and humanity " and to consider the health and welfare of their work-people.

Archdeacon Paley was greatly preoccupied with the theoretical problems of the origin and justification of private property. " There is a difficulty in explaining, consistently with the law of nature, the origin of property in land, for the land was once, no doubt, common." Altogether, the whole system of economic life under private property appeared to him unnatural. In his famous chapter " On Property " he gave rein to his sentiments in the following parable : " If you should see a flock of pigeons in a field ; and if (instead of each picking where and what it liked, taking just as much as it wanted, and no more) you should see ninety-nine of them gathering all they got into one heap, reserving nothing for themselves but the chaff and the refuse, keeping this heap for one, and that the weakest, perhaps worst, pigeon of the flock ; sitting round and looking on all the winter, whilst this one was devouring and throwing about and wasting it ; and if one pigeon more hardy or hungry than the rest touched a grain of the hoard, all the others instantly flying upon it and tearing it to pieces ; if you should see this, you would see nothing more than what is every day practised and established among men." [2] That was human society on the basis of property.

[1] Adam Smith, *Wealth of Nations*, book 5, chap. 1 (part 2).
[2] William Paley, *Moral and Pol. Philosophy*, 1785, book 3, part 1, chaps. 1-4.

Did it not appear paradoxical and unnatural? Yet it existed and people did not mind it. There must, therefore, have been some very important advantages which counterbalanced those miseries and imbecilities and kept the world going. What were they? (1) Private property increased the produce of the earth. (2) It preserved the produce of the earth to maturity. (3) It prevented contests. (4) It improved the conveniences of life. Upon these accounts it may be pronounced that, with a few exceptions, even the poorest and the worst provided were, under the system of private property, better provided with the necessaries of life than any of the people who lived in societies where most things were held in common. The earth and the fulness thereof were given to mankind for use, and the system of private property made a better use of them than communism did. Paley, in effect, says the same as Adam Smith—the justification of private property lay in the improvements of production, accumulation of stock, and the growth of wealth or the necessaries and conveniences of life.

At the time when Smith and Paley were writing, the economic revolution was beginning to unchain or call into being productive forces which were destined to surpass the greatest economic achievements of the past.

PART II

1760 - 1834

I

THE ECONOMIC REVOLUTION

I.—INVENTIONS : ENCLOSURES

THE last half of the eighteenth century will ever be memorable in the history of England in particular and of mankind in general. What philosophers and scientists had dreamt, handicraftsmen and legislators had feared, came to pass. Invention after invention penetrated the enclosed dominions of arts and crafts, and transferred human skill and deftness of hand to passive and lifeless matter, changing it into a multitudinous host of ceaselessly active forces and all-powerful creators of riches beyond the dreams of the political economists.

> " . . . I exult to see
>   An intellectual mastery exercised
>   O'er the blind elements . . . almost a soul
>   Imparted to brute matter. I rejoice,
>   Measuring the force of those gigantic powers
>   That, by the thinking mind, have been compelled
>   To serve the will of feeble-bodied Man."
>   (Wordsworth, *Excursion*, book 8.)

In the wake of the triumphant march of the iron giants the social and political face of England changed. Ancient cities and boroughs lost their glamour ; insignificant hamlets rose to splendour ; a resettlement of the population went on apace.

> " . . . . At social Industry's command,
>   How quick, how vast an increase ! From the germ
>   Of some poor hamlet, rapidly produced
>   Here a huge town, continuous and compact,
>   Hiding the face of the earth for leagues—and there,
>   Where not a habitation stood before,
>   Abodes of men irregularly massed
>   Like trees in forests—spread through spacious tracts,
>   O'er which the smoke of unremitting fires
>   Hangs permanent, and plentiful as wreaths
>   Of vapour glittering in the morning sun."   (*Ibid.*)

95

The long and amazing series of inventions, particularly the improvement of the steam engine, inspired also the imagination of Erasmus Darwin, the poet-thinker, who saw in his mind the steam engine applied to sea and land and air transport, and " as the specific levity of air is too great for the support of great burdens by balloons there seems no probable method of flying conveniently but by the power of steam or some other explosive material, which another half century may probably discover." [1]

At the same time a wide net of canals, connecting the shipping, manufacturing, and commercial centres of the kingdom, were built.

> " So with strong arm immortal Brindley leads
> His long canals, and parts the velvet meads ;
> Winding in lucid lines, the watery mass
> Mines the firm rock, or loads the deep morass,
> Feeds the long vale, the nodding woodland laves,
> And Plenty, Arts, and Commerce freight the waves." [2]

Simultaneously with these revolutionary changes in manufacture and commerce a no less revolutionary transformation took place in agriculture. While in the period from 1710 to 1760 the process of enclosing farms and lands was slow and imperceptible, amounting altogether to about one-third of a million acres, its pace was enormously accelerated in the following sixty years, when no less than 5,700,000 acres were withdrawn from the common-field-system or small cultivators. The traditional regulations and tangled customs of the village community, which impeded production and nursed inefficiency, were swept away like cobwebs, and the new agriculture, carried on with improved methods and tools as well as scientific experiment, began to cope with the rapidly growing home demand. Wide tracts of waste land were brought under the plough, and the experiments in stock-raising yielded results as remarkable as those of the mechanical inventions. The economic superiority of enclosed or private agriculture over the open-field or communal agriculture was so striking that nobody denied it. Rents and prices rose, and the wealth of the landowners multiplied.

[1] Erasmus Darwin, *Botanic Garden*, ed. 1799, I., p. 31, note.
[2] *Ibid.*, canto III. 351–7.

Rapid as the changes were in England, they lacked the suddenness and catastrophic character which they exhibited in Scotland. The transition in England took centuries—in Scotland decades. Sir Walter Scott witnessed the sunset of mediaevalism of his country and with all the power of his mind attempted to bring it again to life in his poetry and romance. Instead of a preface, which he was afraid the reader would skip, he wrote an epilogue to his *Waverley*, explaining his innermost thought : " There is no European nation which, within the course of half a century, or little more, has undergone so complete a change as this kingdom of Scotland. The effects of the insurrection of 1745, the destruction of the patriarchal power of the Highland chiefs, the abolition of the heritable jurisdictions of the Lowland nobility and barons . . . commenced this innovation. The gradual influx of wealth, and extension of commerce, have since united to render the present people of Scotland a class of beings as different from their grandfathers as the existing English are from those of Queen Elizabeth's time."

It was this suddenness that produced so many Scottish social reformers, particularly land reformers. From 1775 onwards the pioneers of land reform have been Scotsmen.

2.—SOCIAL EFFECTS

In the midst of this economic revolution the statistician, Patrick Colquhoun, wrote : " An era has arrived in the affairs of the British Empire, discovering resources which have excited the wonder, the astonishment, and perhaps the envy of the civilised world " ; and spoke of " the accumulation of property, extensive beyond all credibility and (during a war of unexampled expense) rapid in its growth beyond what the most sanguine mind could have conceived." [1] Looked at from the angle of vision of production and wealth the exultation of Colquhoun, an adorer of Adam Smith, was justified. In 1688, as we know from Gregory King, the national income amounted to £43,500,000 ; in 1770,

[1] P. Colquhoun, *Resources of the British Empire*, 1814, pp. 49, 110.

H

Arthur Young [1] estimated the national income at £119,500,000 ; according to Colquhoun it amounted, in 1812, to £430,000,000.

Profound and comprehensive changes in the economics of society could not come to fruition without shaking the social structure to its foundations. " Domestic handicraftsmen and small farmers alike were overwhelmed ; industry, both manufacturing and agricultural, was re-organised on the new commercial lines which seemed best adapted for the greatest possible production at the least possible cost. The completion of the work of enclosure destroyed the inherited traditions of the peasantry, their ideals, their customs and habits, their ancestral solutions of the problems of life—all, in fact, that made up the native homebred civilisation of rural England." [2]   The economic revolution resulted in the concentration of land and manufacture in fewer hands, in production on a large scale at the expense of the small independent producers ; it collected large numbers of propertyless people as wage-earners or proletarians into factories, mines, and fields.   Out of heterogeneous masses of labourers, artizans, domestic craftsmen, coming from different surroundings, with different habits and feelings, a working class gradually arose, compact and militant.   The social stratification, built up by centuries of a stirring history, broke into a jumble of fragments which in stress and turmoil changed positions. The rise of new classes, the submerging of old social strata, and the re-valuation of traditional worth in society, rendered a long and painful process of re-organisation and readjustment an urgent political necessity.   The transformation was, however, so new and unprecedented a phenomenon that none of the contemporary statesmen and political students saw it whole or perceived the wide ramification of its effects.   They were still thinking in old political terms, busying themselves with parliamentary franchise, poor laws, foreign and colonial affairs while the social confusion was being aggravated by the powerful effects of the French Revolution and Napoleonic Wars.

[1] A. Young, *Tour Through the North of England*, 1771, IV., p. 393.
[2] R. A. Prothero, *English Farming*, 1912, p. 407. *Cf.* also Robert Southey, *Letters from England*, 1807, III., pp. 114-9, and Sir Walter Scott, *Familiar Letters*, II., p. 78.

3.—AGGRAVATION BY NAPOLEONIC WARS

England as the pioneer of the transition from the agrarian to the manufacturing state suffered more than any other nation which, in the course of the nineteenth century, followed her on the same path of development. The experience necessary to mitigate the miseries and pains attendant upon such a readjustment of society was wanting, and the empirical, go-ahead, not to say, recklessly daring nature of the English mind was not apt to pause and inquire into the operation of the new economic phase the nation was entering upon. While crossing an uncharted sea England was caught by the tornado of the French upheaval. She was involved in a long war which emptied her treasury and withdrew the attention of her best minds from home affairs at a time when every ounce of gold and silver, when every thought, was necessary to help her in overcoming the difficulties of the economic transition. The terrible decade 1810–20, the Luddites, the Spenceans, the Blanketeers, the conspiracies, Peterloo, and Cato Street, were largely due to the errors, perhaps inevitable errors, committed in the years from 1790 to 1800. One-sixth of the expenditure raised for war purposes might have been sufficient to lay the foundation of a healthy social reform, to provide for old age [1] and illness of the factory workers, to regulate child labour, to assist the small farmers and handicraftsmen, to protect agricultural labour, and generally to render the social readjustment less fortuitous and, therefore, less painful. We need not accept as wholly true all the alleged horrors that are so often ascribed to the rise of the

---

[1] Dr. Priestley advocated, in 1787, the establishment of an old age and sickness fund by means of deductions from the wages. He argued that, " since the labour of the husbandman or manufacturer is the only source of all gain or property in any country, even that of the gentleman, it is their own labour that, more circuitously and ineffectually, now maintains them in their wretched and dependent state, whereas upon this plan, their own labour (and probably much increased) will be more immediately employed for their own advantage " (*An Account of a Society for Encouraging the Industrious Poor*, Birmingham, 1787, p. 15).

factory system. Communist and Tory prejudices, particularly those of Charles Hall, Robert Southey, and Robert Owen, go some way to account for the gloomy impressions which that period still evokes. The most cogent proof against their accusations is to be found in the rapid growth of the population and the decrease of the rate of mortality, which set in with the development of the industrial revolution. Such facts cannot be gainsaid ; they are irrefragable evidence of growing prosperity. Up to 1806 wages were high, employment was plentiful. The displacement and depreciation of labour by machinery began about that time. Still, such a catastrophic change as the economic revolution implied was bound to shake society, to produce widespread discontent, and to create problems, perils, and crises which only far-seeing statesmanship and recognition of causes and effects might have mitigated or forestalled. Peace, watchfulness, and social reform were necessary. Instead of which came war, repression of the discontented elements, suspension of the Habeas Corpus Act, high treason trials, indiscriminate poor relief, and Malthus's population theory as a salve to the agitated conscience of the nation. And the drain of precious metals caused by the payment of subsidies and war expenditure as well as by the needs of expanding agriculture and trade, led, in 1797, to the suspension of specie payment and issue of a paper currency, giving rise to a high gold agio, high prices, fluctuations of trade, Socialist and Radical schemes of paper money and paper notes. For want of coin of the realm manufacturers paid their employees with money tokens, and the delusion was created that paper could completely displace precious metals as a circulating medium, and that gold as legal tender (established in 1816) was merely the invention of Lord Liverpool, Sir Robert Peel, and the Jews. Finally, the enormous national debt and the Funding System, to which the wars had given rise, caused much perturbation among reformers.

All these chaotic events, while playing havoc with men's fortunes and lives, combined to create problems which occupied two generations of social philosophers, economists, and poets, and produced a period of intense thinking and glowing emotion.

II

COMMUNIST AND DEMOCRATIC FERMENT

I.—PHASES OF THOUGHT

FROM a sociological point of view, the period from 1760 to 1825 exhibits four phases. The first phase was purely parliamentary and constitutional; its protagonists, Wilkes and "Junius," fought against the oligarchy and the remnants of personal monarchy; this phase is outside the plan of our work. The second phase was mainly agrarian; the effects of the rapid rate of enclosing farms and commons as well as of the improvements in agriculture turned the attention of revolutionary minds towards agrarian reform; its writers were Spence, Ogilvie, and Paine. The third phase was caused by enthusiasm for the French Revolution on the part of English intellectuals and London artizans, whose minds had been prepared by the theories which were current in the antecedent two phases; its writers were William Godwin, the youthful Coleridge, Southey, Wordsworth, and John Thelwall. The fourth phase was that of the industrial revolution proper, the first critical writer of which was Charles Hall, followed by Robert Owen and his school, and the anti-capitalist critics, Ravenstone, Hodgskin, and several anonymous writers; the poet of this phase was Shelley.

The common basis of all those writers consisted mainly of natural law as they found it in Locke's *On Civil Government*. This small treatise became their Bible, particularly after its theories had been consecrated by the success of the American Revolution, and had come back to England from France endowed with the fiery soul of Rousseau. The purely constitutional reformers took from Locke the theories of the social and political compact and of original society whose members were supposed to have been free and equal. The agrarian reformers appealed to Locke for the truth of their first principle that the land was originally held in common. The communists and socialist, or anti-capitalist writers, based themselves, in addition to those self-evident truths, on Locke's theory that labour was the real title to property, or, as Adam Smith puts it, " the produce of labour constitutes the natural recompense or wages of labour." The industrial revolution had shown, however, that the produce of labour belonged, not to the labourer, but to the capitalist. This experience, joined to Adam Smith's emphasis on labour being the source of wealth and the standard of value, and Ricardo's apparently irrefragable logic of the theory of labour value and the inverse ratio of wages and profit, gave to Locke's argument on labour and property a social-revolutionary turn, and converted it into a weapon against the social system which was emerging from the economic revolution.

We shall have occasion to point out the cardinal error that underlay those reasonings ; meanwhile, let us see the logical conclusions at which the communists, socialists, and anti-capitalist critics arrived. They were as follows :—

(1) Common possession was natural and therefore just and equitable ; (2) Labour was the only title to property or wealth ; (3) Nature, including human nature, was governed by inherent, divine, and rational laws.

Hence it followed :—

(1) That private property was unnatural and pernicious, and ought to be abolished ; (2) That all deductions from the produce of labour, in the shape of rent, profit, and interest, by non-labourers, constituted a violation of natural law ; (3) That all reform must be directed towards the restoration of, or be in harmony with, natural law.

This was the main current which pervaded social and political criticism in the period from 1760 to 1850. Its theorists became the teachers of the Chartists, who spread it among the masses.

However, though it formed the main current, it was not the only one on which the revolutionary writers floated their theories. We have already seen that Burke realised the danger which lurked behind the system of *ius naturale*—a system which assumed that the horde of human animals were born into the world, receiving the earth and the fulness thereof as their common inheritance, but that a few of them, endowed with cunning and strength above the rest, disliked labour and scanty fare, and therefore appropriated the earth for their own exclusive use, and made all the other human animals work for them. Burke saw the meaning of this theory, but not until 1790 did he attempt to formulate an alternative social theory. The essence of his *Reflections on the Revolution in France* (1790), written with the view of stemming the tide of revolutionary ideas that were pouring into England from Paris, was that social systems and constitutions were neither manufactured by theorists nor suddenly called into being by a vote of popular assemblies, but were an organic growth ; the past was not a stupendous error or imposture to be wiped off the national slate, but an organism grown in the course of ages and containing both living and sloughy matter, the former to be preserved and further developed, the latter to be removed. This theory of organic development of social institutions, while it gained approval among conservative publicists and jurists (Savigny), did not commend itself to the revolutionary writers. Yet the course of the French Revolution made it impossible to adhere to natural law, and thinking men were searching for a new social theory. Philosophically, the French Revolution appeared as a great experiment in *ius naturale ;* all its declarations were written in its spirit and terms, and its inspirer was Rousseau. The terroristic acts and wars into which that social earthquake degenerated had the effect of discrediting the whole system of natural law. Robespierre and Bonaparte destroyed the halo of Rousseau. A painful void was created in the minds of the poets and philosophers who had welcomed the events of 1789 to 1793 as the dawn of the rights of man. The light of nature and right reason failed. What was now to take its place as the guide of human affairs ? Some writers accepted Burke's organic theory, or Schelling's evolutionism, to which Erasmus Darwin's *Zoonomia* (translated into German in 1795–6) had probably given the impulse ; others turned to romanticism and mediaevalism, for which Sir Walter Scott found the most adequate literary forms, while the advanced English reformers found in Bentham's utilitarian philosophy a substitute and leading principle.

It was Bentham who, for a time, supplanted Locke. From the beginning of his legal career he rebelled against the abstract, unempirical, and pseudo-historical state of nature. As far back as 1780—his *Introduction to the Principles of Morals and Legislation* was printed in 1780, but published in 1789—he was convinced of the unscientific character of the theories on which jurisprudence was based. He had a historical sense, and greatly admired Montesquieu's *Esprit des Lois*.[1] Still, it was not history, but psychology, from which he took his leading principle. Following Priestley, Holbach, Helvetius, and Beccaria, he saw in utility or in the greatest happiness of the greatest number the moral test of individual and government actions. This test was accepted by political reformers and socialist writers. Happiness was thought to be the aim and end of man and human society, to which constitutions and laws should conform. Bentham himself was aggressively anti-communist and preferred security of property to equality of distribution ; he regarded private property as the only possible basis of social life, and whenever it came into conflict with equality, the latter should forthwith be abandoned.[2] But in the hands of the communists or socialists the felicific formula was converted into as effective a weapon

[1] Bentham, in his essay on the " Influence of Time and Place on Matters of Legislation," declares : " Before Montesquieu, a man who had a distant country given him to make laws for, would have made short work of it. ' Name to me the people, reach me down the Bible, and the business is done at once. The laws they have been used to shall be superseded by mine ; manners, they shall have mine, which are the best in nature ; religion, they shall have mine too, which is all of it true, and the only one that is so.' Since Montesquieu, the number of documents which a legislator would require is considerably enlarged. He would say, ' Send the people to me, or me to the people ; lay open to me the whole tenor of their life and conversation ; paint to me the face and geography of the country ; give me as close and minute a view as possible of their possible laws, their manners, and their religion.' "

[2] The same. *Works*, I., chap. 7–12, also Appendix.

against private property as natural law had been before. The founders of co-operative communities and advocates of Owenite views simply revelled in the idea of happiness, regarding it as the major premise of all social reasonings, as if it were a self-evident truth that man was born for happiness. They argued that private property was wrong, since under its sway the labouring masses, the greatest number of the nation, were condemned to misery. Nor did the institution of private property lead to security, for the produce of the exertions of labour was not secured to the labourer, but was taken from him by the land-owner, capitalist, and money-lender. With Bentham, the bar to happiness was the oligarchy, which should be removed by democratic reform. With the communist, the bar to happiness was the proprietor of the means of production, who should be discarded for the communist co-operator. The principal representatives of social reform based on happiness are Robert Owen, William Thompson, and John Gray. From about 1828 the utilitarian doctrine, as one of the principles of communism, gradually gave way to a revival of natural law. The social critic who accomplished the restoration of Locke was Thomas Hodgskin. Also the question of Poor Law reform, which at that time became increasingly urgent, contributed a good deal to the rehabilitation of natural law, the advocates of the old Poor Law arguing that men, by renouncing their community rights, reserved to themselves, or could not have abandoned, the right to existence ; the maintenance of the poor was thus guaranteed by the social compact, or by the law of nature. Theoretically, natural law formed the link of connection between the working class social reformer and the Tory who opposed the abolition of the old Poor Laws, while the same doctrine separated the socialists from the Benthamites, who worked with might and main against the old system of poor relief.

This outline of the theoretical controversies and their phases may serve as an introduction to the following chapters dealing with three groups of social critics, viz., (1) the agrarian reformers —Spence, Ogilvie, and Paine ; (2) the communists who received the strongest impulse from the French Revolution—William

Godwin, Coleridge, Southey, and the London Corresponding Society ; (3) the communists and anti-capitalist critics—Hall, Owen, Thompson, Ravenstone, Gray, Hodgskin, and several anonymous writers, whose criticisms and schemes were connected with the rise of the factory system and the unfolding of class warfare between Capital and Labour.

2.—SPENCE, OGILVIE, AND PAINE

Thomas Spence (b. June 21, 1750, d. September 1, 1814), the originator of the single-tax reform, was of Scottish origin, his father having left Aberdeen, in 1733, for Newcastle, where he followed the trade of net-making, shoe-making, and shop-keeping. Thomas, one of a family of nineteen children, was taught by his father, who appears to have been a capable educator and a man of wide reading. At first, Thomas learned the trade of his father, but on showing some talent for mental work, he was given opportunity for reading, and successively became a bookkeeper and private tutor. During his leisure hours he must have read a good deal of natural law in Locke, Grotius, Blackstone, and others, which studies gained in practical importance by a lawsuit then pending between the freemen and the corporation of Newcastle. Following the trend of the time the corporation enclosed the town moor or common, and let it for agricultural purposes. The rental was divided between the members of the corporation, to the exclusion of the freemen, whereupon the latter brought an action, demanding a share of the rent, since the town moor was common. A similar lawsuit was pending in Durham. The controversies to which these lawsuits gave rise decided the future career of the obscure schoolmaster, and turned him into a lifelong missionary for land reform on the basis of parochial partnership.

As a member of the Newcastle Philosophical Society he developed his plan in a lecture delivered on November 8, 1775, which contains all the ideas he propagated to the end of his life. Believing that the doctrines of natural law were axioms which everybody accepted, he takes it for granted that in the state of nature the earth and the fulness thereof were common and that everybody

enjoyed equal liberty.   The land was as necessary to human existence as light, air, and water ; to deprive a man of the land was to
deprive him of his life.   Jurists argued that private property in
land originated from agreement.   No agreement, however, could
bind posterity, unless it be renewed by each successive generation. Of such a renewal nobody knew or heard anything.
Besides, civil society did not arise for the purpose of rendering
the conditions of mankind worse than they were in the natural
state, but to remove the inconveniencies which had arisen from
the absence of conscious organisation.   Civil society was, indeed
an agreement between free and equal to guarantee their mutual
rights and liberties of nature against aggressions and usurpations.
From these premises it might be concluded that the earth was
still the common heritage of mankind.   Yet, the actual conditions told quite a different tale.   The land had been allowed
to be usurped by comparatively few people, who called themselves
the aristocracy, and who were actually worshipped as demi-gods
Another argument in favour of private property was labour.
It was said by Locke that labour bestowed on things was the
real title to property.   That argument held good as to manufactured goods, the manufacturer being their real creator.   But
who could seriously argue that the earth was manufactured
by the aristocracy ?   No !   It was usurpation on the one hand,
and ignorance on the other, which led to the flagrant violation
of natural law, and to the establishment of the usurpers.   An
enlightened nation, conscious of its natural rights and liberties,
could resolve to restore the land to its rightful heirs, and join
the advantages of the state of nature to those of civil society.
Public meetings all over the country would carry such a resolution. The people being sovereign would transfer the land to
the parishes, for the purpose of erecting not a complete communist republic, but a mixed state between communism and
private use—Spence called it later (1798) a state between More's
Utopia and Harrington's *Oceana*—*i.e.*, where the land belonged
to the parish, which would let it to farmers on a moderate rental.
The revenues from the rent would form the only tax, from
which the expenses of the local and central government would be

defrayed. No other taxes and duties to be levied. A complete democratic constitution in parish, borough, city, and national affairs was, as a matter of course, the only one worthy of such a commonwealth. This republic, based on justice and reason, and protected by the virtue and prosperity of large masses of farmers against all disturbers of the public peace, as well as by a well-trained citizen army against foreign aggressions, would endure for ever and ever, serving as a model and an inspiring example to all the nations of the earth. That is the substance of the lecture and the teachings of Spence, in general. He added, in 1800, a new idea to the body of his doctrines, viz. that the real struggle was not about forms of government, but for " a system of society capable of delivering us from the deadly mischief of great accumulations of wealth, which enable a few rich unfeeling monsters to starve whole nations."[1]

Spence, being an agitator rather than a scholar, published his lecture and hawked it himself in the streets of Newcastle at a halfpenny a piece. The Philosophical Society, evidently disgusted with this way of spreading the light of nature and reason, cancelled his membership. Also his reputation as a teacher suffered, for soon after this event the number of his pupils began to dwindle. Spence left for London, where he was successively a number-carrier, street bookseller, and editor of a democratic periodical, *Pig's Meat* (1793–95), consisting of extracts from various advanced writers, for which he was kept in prison from May to December, 1795. He was at the same time implicated in the conspiracies of the London Corresponding Society. In 1797 he published a pamphlet, *Rights of Infants*, in 1798 a Constitution for his Spencean Commonwealth, which consists of two parts, the first being a reprint of the French *Declaration of the Rights of Man and Citizen*, the second a codification of his agrarian proposals contained in his Newcastle lecture, adding the new provision of female suffrage. In 1800 he wrote, in the form of letters to the " Citizens " of England, *The Restorer of Society to its Natural State*, consisting of a revolutionary formulation

[1] Thomas Spence, *Restorer of Society to its Natural State*, 1801, Letter 14.

of his agrarianism and democracy. This publication brought him into conflict with the law, and he was sentenced to twelve months' imprisonment. He was his own counsel, and treated the jury to a long and laborious exposition of his theories, reading all his pamphlets and giving a history of his life and work. Shortly before his death he attempted to publish a new periodical, *The Giant Killer, or Anti-Landlord*. He had a small but very active group of adherents, who made themselves noticeable in the stormy years from 1816 to 1820 ; they were the leaders and banner-bearers of all great demonstrations of the working classes in London in those years. Even in the Chartist Movement of 1838 and 1839 the name of Spence was held dear. Francis Place, who knew him well and acquired some of his correspondence, describes him as a man of short stature, " not more than five feet high, very honest, simple, single-minded, who loved mankind, and firmly believed that a time would come when men would be virtuous, wise and happy. He was unpractical in the ways of the world to an extent hardly imaginable." [1] Spence republished his Newcastle lecture several times, in 1796, under the title *Meridian Sun of Liberty or Rights of Man*, a new edition of which was published by H. M. Hyndman in 1882.

The critical apparatus of natural law used by Spence was handled with incomparably greater skill and erudition by William Ogilvie (1736-1813) in his *Essay on the Right of Property in Land* (1781). Ogilvie, a professor of humanity at the Aberdeen University, and a successful agriculturist, was evidently distressed at the sight of the misery, ignorance, and stagnation of the labouring classes, and regarded private property in land as the source of all evil ; the monopoly in land, " by the operation of which the happiness of mankind had been for ages more invaded and restrained than by all the tyranny of kings, the imposture of priests, and the chicane of lawyers taken together, though these are supposed to be the greatest evils that afflict the societies of human kind " (§ 28–9).

[1] Place, Add. MSS. 27808, Vol. 1, Part 3 (British Museum). *Cf. Quarterly Review*, 1817 ; Mackenzie, *History of Newcastle*, 1826 ; Davenport, *Life of Thomas Spence*, 1836.

The rumblings of the French Revolution are distinctly heard in that denunciation. Yet Ogilvie was no revolutionist. " It is natural to the mind, when new ideas arise on important subjects, to open itself with fondness to the pleasing impressions which they make. Yielding to the seducing enthusiasm, the author has been led to speak with freedom of great changes, suddenly to be accomplished, as practicable in some cases, and to be desired in many. Yet he is well aware that great changes, suddenly accomplished, are always pregnant with danger and evil, and ought, on almost no occasion whatever, to be desired or brought forward by the friends of mankind. Partial reformation, gradual progressive innovation, may produce every advantage which the most important and sudden changes can promise, yet without incurring those dreadful hazards and those inevitable evils with which great and sudden changes are still attended " (Introduction).

His critical shafts are, nevertheless, exceedingly keen. The earth having been given to mankind in common, every man possessed a natural right, an inalienable birthright to an equal share in the land. This right could not be renounced by any express or tacit compact on man's entering into civil society, and therefore could still be claimed. Rude societies, like the ancient German tribes, or the Irish up to the sixteenth century, acknowledged it. In short, the first maxim of natural law was that every man had an equal share in the land. But there was a second maxim of natural law, " that every one, by whose labour any position of the soil has been rendered more fertile, has a right to the additional produce of that fertility, or to the value of it, and may transfer this right to other men. On the first of these maxims depends the freedom and prosperity of the lower ranks. On the second, the perfection of the art of agriculture and the improvement of the common stock and wealth of the community " (§ 10). Natural law was destroyed by the progress of trade and commerce or by conquest. Municipal (civil) laws took its place and confirmed and extended private property and the monopoly in land, thereby causing misery to the lower ranks of society. The interest of society was completely subordinated to the interest of the land owners, who were permitted to enjoy revenues out of all proportion to their services rendered to agriculture or society. All property ought to be the reward of industry ; all industry ought to be secure of its full reward ; the exorbitant privileges of the landholder subverted both these principles of good policy. And " whoever enjoys any revenue, not proportioned to such industry or exertion of his own or of his ancestors, is a freebooter, who has found means to cheat or rob the public, and more especially the indigent of that district in which he lives. The hereditary revenue of a great landholder . . . increases without any efforts of his . . . it is a premium given to idleness " (§ 39). The real problem was, how to abolish that monopoly and to combine the two maxims of natural law, *viz.*, equal share in the land, and right of property to the additional value produced by man's labour, so as to banish poverty and, at the same time, promote improvement of cultivation ?

Revolutionary as Ogilvie is in his critique, he becomes conservative when dealing with reform propositions. Very little remains of man's natural and inalienable right to an equal share in the land. The utmost that a propertyless citizen might claim was a farm of forty acres for which he was to pay to the landlord a rent, fixed by arbitrators, besides " certain aids and services of a feudal nature, so regulated as to produce that degree of connection and dependence which may be expedient for preserving order and subordination in the country without danger of giving rise to oppression and abuse " (§ 71, number xv.). The farm or allotment thus acquired should be perpetual. The occupier should have the right to transmit it to his heirs or assignees, but could not sublet it ; if he sold it to another man who did not reside upon it, but annexed it to some other farm, one-tenth part of the price or reserved rent should go to the community. The occupier of such a farm was not given any right in the commons, moors, woodlands, private roads, or other appendages of the manor. Ogilvie also advocated the appointment of a special board, with powers to purchase estates which were in the market and might be had for a reasonable price (twenty-five to thirty years' purchase), and divide them into small farms of a single plough only, to be let for a full reserved rent in perpetual property.

Ogilvie's *Essay* was reprinted in 1838 for the instruction of the Chartists, and the following preface appended to it :—

" The present reprint is submitted to the public at a time when the demands of the labouring classes are beginning to be heard from the deep degradation to which they have been submitted ever since the Norman Conquest. They will see here the cruelty, absurdity and tyranny of man monopolising the labour of thousands ; and they will also see the means whereby they may extricate themselves from so miserable a bondage." The editor, however, knew nothing of the life of the author, whom he calls John Ogilby, " who lived about the year 1778." He also declares that the book was then suppressed and the author bribed by the government. Still, the doctrines contained therein " are the same, unchanged and immutable, and will afford the only remedy for the existing miseries and oppressions of the labouring and useful classes of England."

A third edition was published in 1891.

Thomas Paine (1737–1809), a radical politician and moderate social reformer, who, in the present age, would have been a respected member of the Liberal Party, sketched in his *Agrarian Justice* (1795–96) a plan of social reform, based on arguments of natural law, particularly of Locke's *Civil Government*, part second. It may be regarded as the economic supplement to his *Rights of Man* (1791–2), which was written with the purpose of refuting Burke's *Reflections*. The division of society into rich and poor, he argues, was the effect of civil government or civilisation. In the natural state, such as the Indians in America still presented, there were not to be found any of those spectacles of human misery which met the eye in the great cities of Europe. On the other hand, the natural state lacked the advantages that sprang from agriculture, arts, science, and manufacture. As it was not possible for a civilised man to return to the life of an Indian and thus to escape misery, some means must be found to bring to him the advantages which he enjoyed in the natural state and join them to those of civilisation. And this could be effected by accepting the principle of natural law that every man and woman was entitled to an equal share in the land. But the land in its uncultivated state was of small value. It was cultivation and improvement which made it valuable, but at the same time made it property of the agriculturist. Still, only the improved value was the property of the cultivator, while the ground itself belonged to all. Each cultivator owed, therefore, a ground-rent to the community. The absolute right of property in land sprang from identifying the improvement of the land with land itself. This identification was, in reality, confusion, and ought to be removed, for it had been the source of evil. The community as the owner of the land must reclaim the ground-rent in the shape of a 10 per cent. death duty on estates, and turn its revenues into a national fund, out of which should be paid to every propertyless person, in compensation for the loss of his or her natural rights, the sum of £15 when arrived at the age of twenty-one years, and £10 annually as an old age pension for life. The surplus should be used for the upkeep of the blind, lame, and incapable. Paine had, in 1792, proposed a similar plan of reform. In the second part of the *Rights of Man*, he asked for the abolition of the poor laws, remission of indirect taxation, imposition of a surplus tax on the wealthy, out of which a fund should be created for the support of the poor, unemployed, and old, as well as to defray the cost of popular education.

Paine's reform plan displeased Spence, who severely criticised it in his pamphlet entitled *Rights of Infants* (1797), charging him with trying to sell the birthright of the people for a pottage of lentils.

3.—WILLIAM GODWIN

The wealth of ideas created in the simple, rude forges of the English mind in the seventeenth century flowed to France, where Cartesians and Encyclopædists endowed them with new elements and with *esprit*, logic, and grace. Then the reflux began. The apparently simple constitutional doctrines of Locke reappeared in the dazzling shape of Rousseau's *Discours sur l'inégalité* and *Contrat Social;* the empiricism of Bacon,

I

Hobbes and Locke returned in the machine-like perfection of Lamettrie's and Holbach's materialism, and English ethics was transformed by Helvetius into utilitarianism.

In the thunder and lightning of the French Revolution the English intellectuals eagerly opened their minds to the various enunciations of the Encyclopædists, and desired a systematic exposition of those theories which appeared to reveal themselves as creative fiats. The man who satisfied that desire was William Godwin. He was anything but an original social philosopher ; his mental make-up was that of a first-rate journalist, but his intellectual adventures as a nonconformist theologian and un-frocked preacher, combined with a rich vocabulary and flowing style, enabled him to recast political science for the younger generation of feverish enthusiastic intellectuals. Nothing less satisfied them than political anarchy, abolition of private pro-perty, absolute reign of reason, universal benevolence and joyful devotion to social duty and justice. And he supplied it to them in two quarto volumes for three guineas. What Burke's *Reflections* were for the upper classes, Paine's *Rights of Man* for the masses, that was Godwin's *Enquiry Concerning Polit-ical Justice* (1793) for the intellectuals. Godwin suddenly woke up one morning as the most famous social philosopher of his time. Youthful poets, like Coleridge, Southey, and Words-worth, all of them University students, looked upon their studies as a useless dust heap, but read Godwin with avidity.

Political Justice went through four editions ; the first appeared in February, 1793, the second in 1796, the third in 1798, the fourth in 1843 at the culmination of Chartism. The most characteristic is the first edition, which was written in the heat and fever of the French Revolution, and also at the time when some of the author's opinions were still in a ferment, or, as he says, " The ideas of the author became more and more perspicuous and digested as his enquiries advanced " (Preface),[1] and his enquiries advanced during the printing of the book. The second edition is more systematic, but in less revolutionary language. In the interval between the first and second edition a revolutionary

[1] Our references are throughout to the first edition.

movement made itself noticeable in London and in the industrial centres of Great Britain, initiated by the London Corresponding Society, which consisted of workmen, small traders, and intellectuals, and alarmed the Government. Mr. Pitt took at once repressive measures and some of Godwin's friends were arrested and charged with high treason. Likewise the terror in France revealed the fact that revolutions were apt to silence reason and philosophy. These circumstances induced Godwin to soften the attacks on government and property, to emphasize the evil of physical force, and to point, in the most unmistakable manner, to reason, persuasion, and argument as the sole instruments of social changes. Some critics saw in those emendations a betrayal of the cause of justice, but, in reality, Godwin remained what he had been, a peaceful revolutionist, peaceful even to the point of non-resistance, believing in the omnipotence of reason and truth (book 4, chapter 2, section 2) ; still, his unmeasured invectives against the institutions of government and property must have left on the readers of the first edition the impression that Godwin had identified himself with the Jacobins and levellers. The irritation caused by the second edition was aggravated by his pamphlet entitled *Considerations on Lord Grenville's and Mr. Pitt's Bills*," published anonymously (by a " Lover of Order ") in 1795, in which he approved of the government's repressive measures and denounced the agitators and democrats, *i.e.* his own friends.[1]

In order to understand Godwin it must always be borne in mind that he was essentially a Calvinist preacher. His materialism is inverted Calvinist theology. God is reason ; predestination necessity or determinism, Providence causation, the Kingdom of God ethical communism. His criticism is one long Nonconformist sermon, vivacious, diffuse, and sometimes powerful, but always based on abstract reasoning. He held the historical view of society as of little use compared with the philosophical view, which he considered to be " of a higher order and more essential importance " (*Political Justice*, book 2, ch. 1).

Political Justice is divided into eight books. The following

[1] Cestre, *John Thelwall*, p. 136 ; Coleridge, *Letters*, 1895, I., p. 162.

thoughts pervade the whole. The human mind in action, or human psychology, is a mechanism, a combination of phenomena, operating strictly according to the law of causation (b. 4, ch. 7). It has no innate ideas nor good or bad propensities (b. 1, ch. 3), but is endowed with the passive capacity of receiving sensations which turn into impressions, and with the active faculty of reason which turns the impression into thought, the real motor force of animal life. On thought depends volition or moral action (b. 4, ch. 7 and 8). Were the external world based on justice the impressions that the mind receives would be good, consequently the thoughts and motives good, and vice would be eradicated (b. 1, ch. 3), all the more so as the influence of reflection on man is incomparably greater than that of physical factors (b. 1, ch. 7). Reason is favourable to virtue and is potent enough to overcome error. It would thus lead man on the way of perpetual improvement and perfection ; the great series of inventions and discoveries sufficiently show the perfectibility of man. But government, originating in force and violence, darkens counsel and strengthens error, by supporting and defending all those institutions that are opposed to justice or utility or happiness. It perpetuates the alarmingly great inequality of property (b. 1, ch. 5 ; b. 8, ch. 1), and puts man in chains of authority. It thus prevents renovation and checks the operation of reason— the sole legislator. All government, no matter what its form is, is evil, while society is natural. With Thomas Paine [1], our author is of opinion that government springs from our wickedness, society from our wants (b. 2, ch. 1). But how will society keep together if government, law, and authority are abolished ? By equity and the common deliberations on general welfare, which is the law of reason. Society cannot legislate, but can interpret the inherent law of reason (b. 3, ch. 5). And this law implies those actions and conditions that contribute most to the enlargement of understanding, stimulation of virtue, and awakening of the independence of man (b. 2, ch. 2). It is the duty of every man to apply his capacities to the general welfare. The fulfilment of that duty is virtue—

[1] Thomas Paine, *Common Sense*, p. 1.

the sole source of happiness. The sum total of those actions and conditions is political justice.

Having instituted a no-government society, there still remains property to be dealt with. Indeed, the solution of the question of property is the keystone of the system of political justice. It enables man to leave artificial or complicated government-society for natural or simple society. Errors with regard to wealth preclude the attainment of freedom, virtue, and happiness. For private property leads to inequality, and this renders all mental improvement impossible. The possession of wealth produces vanity, ostentation, depravity, while poverty stunts the mind, turns man into a slave, ruins his reason and morality. The effects of the present distribution of wealth are by far more pernicious than those of government, priestcraft, and lawyers.[1] They lead men to extol selfishness, teach them to adore their oppressors, and to strive after luxuries and vice. Even the distribution which to-day is thought to be just is not consistent with justice. If a man renders greater service he receives a hundred times more than he needs. Is this really just ? No ! For nobody has a right to superfluities. If one man possesses ten loaves of bread while another has nothing, justice demands that the hungry should get from the former bread enough to satisfy his hunger. And yet we see to-day superabundance on the one hand and privation on the other, without any attempt being made to equalise distribution (b. 8, ch. 1). What magic is there in the pronoun " my " to overturn the decision of ever-lasting truth (b. 2, ch. 2). " If justice reigned a state of equality would prevail. Labour would become light as rather to assume the appearance of agreeable relaxation and gentle exercise. Every man would have a frugal, yet wholesome diet ; every man would go forth to that moderate exercise of his corporal functions that would give hilarity to the spirits. None would be made torpid with fatigue, but all would have leisure to cultivate the kindly and philanthropical affections and to let loose his faculties in the search of intellectual improvement. How rapid would be the advances of intellect, if all men were admitted into

[1] This is evidently a reminiscence from Ogilvie's *Essay*.

the field of knowledge. And the moral progress would be as great as the intellectual. The vices which are inseparably joined to the present system of property would inevitably expire in a state of society where all shared alike the bounties of nature. The narrow principle of selfishness would vanish. No man being obliged to guard his little store, or provide, with anxiety and pain, for his restless wants, each would lose his individual existence in the thought of general good. No man would be an enemy to his neighbour, for they would have no subject of contention, and of consequence philanthropy would resume the empire which reason assigns her."

But how would such a distribution of commodities be effected in any particular case? As soon as law was abolished, men would begin to inquire after equity, " which bids giving to each according to his needs." Godwin is not unmindful of the objections raised against equality, and he answers them with a series of arguments similar to those of Wallace, whose *Various Prospects* evidently impressed him (b. 8, ch. 7). He differs however from Wallace on three points. Godwin gives no outline of any Utopian scheme, but merely argues that equality, established by persuasion and the reasoned consent of all, would endure ; the only hint he gives of the form or constitution of his future society is when he declares that small societies or aggregates of men were preferable to large societies, since on a small surface the waves of popular commotion would soon subside. Secondly, Godwin does not desire economic co-operation nor any closer communist life nor lasting relations between man and woman, his ideal being an aggregate of free, independent persons, mainly bent on the utmost development of their individuality (b. 8, ch. 6). Finally, he has no misgivings whatsoever as to the increase of mankind beyond their means of subsistence. The whole question of population was to him either too remote a contingency to be considered or of no importance in the face of the omnipotence of reason. The time would surely come when mind would control matter. The reign of reason would not only deal with so trivial a matter as increase of population and means of life, but would make man immortal (b. 8, ch. 7). The main task of all who desire to establish political justice was therefore the cultivation of reason through independent thinking, free and fearless enquiry into all ideas and opinions, and careful education.

In 1797, Godwin published the *Enquirer*, a collection of essays, two of which are relevant to our subject. One is entitled " Riches and Poverty," the other " Avarice and Profusion." In the former he warns against an intemperate use of philosophy, and then proceeds to declare that the real evil of poverty was not bodily privation, but lack of leisure to cultivate the mind. Real wealth was leisure. In the other essay he refutes the idea that capital, by giving employment to the poor, was their benefactor. The growth of manufactures aggravated the misery of the poor by prolonging their working time from eight to ten hours, and by fastening the yoke of slavery upon the working classes. The rich did not pay the poor, since there was no wealth but labour. The only way for the rich to help the poor was to take off their shoulders a part of the burden of labour.

Godwin's communist position was discussed, in 1797, between Thomas Robert Malthus and his father ; the latter was favourable to some of its elements, while the former opposed it. The result of this discussion was the *Essay on the Principle of Population* (1798), the most formidable weapon against communism and social reform in the first half of the nineteenth century. Its main thesis is essentially that of Robert Wallace, whose *Various Prospects* are referred to by Godwin in the following manner : " An author who has speculated widely upon subjects of government, has recommended equal, or, which was rather his idea, common property, as a complete remedy to the usurpation and distress which are at present the most powerful enemies of human kind. . . . But, after having exhibited this picture, not less true than delightful, he finds an argument that demolishes the whole and restores him to indifference and despair, in the excessive population that would ensue." [1] In his argument against social reform Malthus goes farther than that : according to him

[1] William Godwin, *Pol. Justice*, book 8, chap. 7 ; Malthus, *Essay*, Preface and book 3, chap. 2.

there was no need to wait for communism in order to detect the law of population, for it was in full operation to-day.

4.—WORDSWORTH, COLERIDGE, SOUTHEY, PANTI-SOCRACY

Carried away by the moving spectacle of the French Revolution William Wordsworth hoped to see the reorganisation of society on the basis of freedom and justice. He regarded the travails of the time as the forebodings of the moral rebirth of humanity, and the establishment of Utopia not on " some secreted island, but in the very world, which is the world of all of us—the place where, in the end, we find our happiness or not at all." His poetic imagination was all aglow and filled his whole being with an enthusiasm which seemed to render him capable of any sacrifice for the salvation of mankind :—

> " Bliss was it in that dawn to be alive,
> But to be young was very Heaven ! . . .
> I had approached, like other youths, the shield
> Of human nature from the golden side,
> And would have fought even to the death, to attest
> The quality of the metal which I saw . . .
>   I began
> To meditate with ardour on the rule
> And management of nations, what it is
> And ought to be ; and strove to learn how far
> Their power or weakness, wealth or poverty,
> Their happiness or misery, depends
> Upon their laws, and fashion of the State."

And when the acts of terrorism began to shake his belief in the emancipating mission of the Convention, Godwin's book restored his confidence and taught him " to look through all the frailties of the world, and with a resolute mastery . . . build social upon personal liberty." By Godwin's book " a strong shock was given to old opinions ; all men's minds had felt its power, and mine was both let loose and goaded." [1]

Samuel Taylor Coleridge and Robert Southey, young students

[1] William Wordsworth, *Prelude*, book II. *Cf.* Leslie Stephen, *The English Utilitarians*, II., pp. 368-73.

at Cambridge and Oxford, felt the same shock, wrote hymns on
the author of *Political Justice*, and welcomed the dawn of human
liberty and equality. Projecting their revolutionary sentiments
on English history both wrote dramas, of which Southey's *Wat
Tyler* is the more important. Wat Tyler and John Ball are
brought on the scene as natural law communists, and Tyler tells
Piers :—

> " No fancied boundaries of mine and thine
> Restrain our wanderings ! Nature gives enough
> For all ; but Man, with arrogant selfishness,
> Proud of his heaps, hoards up superfluous stores
> Robb'd from his weaker fellows, starves the poor,
> Or gives to pity what he owes to justice ! "

And Piers replies :—

> " So I have heard our good friend John Ball preach."

The peasantry sing the song, " When Adam delved and Eve
span ; " finally, John Ball preaches his sermon on Blackheath.

Coleridge, not satisfied with hymns, odes, and dramas, proposed
to Southey, in 1794, the establishment of a communist colony,
where all-equality should reign. " Pantisocracy ! Oh, I shall
have such a scheme of it ! My head, my heart, are all alive. I
have drawn up my arguments in battle array " (Coleridge,
Letters, 1895, I. p. 81). It is not enough to write about equality
and justice, they must be practised. " The heart should have fed
upon the truth, as insects on a leaf, till it be tinged with the
colour, and show its food in every minutest fibre. In the
book of pantisocracy I hope to have comprised all that is good
in Godwin . . . I think not so highly of him as you do "
(*Ib.* p. 91). Southey, less enthusiastic and more cautious of
communist experiments, for he was the only one among the
prospective pantisocrats who possessed some property, gradually
abandoned the whole scheme, whereupon Coleridge wrote to
him :—

" You are lost to me, because you are lost to Virtue. As this
will probably be the last time I shall have occasion to address
you, I will begin at the beginning and regularly retrace your con-

duct and my own. In the month of June, 1794, I first became acquainted with your person and character. Before I quitted Oxford, we had struck out the leading features of a pantisocracy. While on my journey through Wales you invited me to Bristol with the full hopes of realising it. During my abode at Bristol the plan was matured, and I returned to Cambridge, hot in the anticipation of that happy season when we should remove the *selfish* principle from ourselves, and prevent it in our children, by an abolition of property. . . . But alas ! a short time passed ere your departure from our first principles became too flagrant. . . . Your conversation scorched my throat. Your private resources were to remain your individual property, and everything to be separate except a farm of five or six acres. In short, we were to commence partners in a petty farming trade [in Wales]. This was the mouse of which the mountain Pantisocracy was at last safely delivered. . . . Thus your system of prudentials and your apostasy were not sudden ; these constant nibblings had sloped your descent from virtue. . . . My indolence you assigned as the reason for your quitting pantisocracy. Supposing it is true, it might indeed be a reason for rejecting *me* from the system. But how does this affect pantisocracy, that you should reject *it ?* " (Coleridge, *Letters*, 1895, I. pp. 137–51).

However, the time was to come when this fiery apostle of all-equality would follow the example of Southey. Before the eighteenth century expired the French Revolution was discredited and Godwin was sinking into oblivion. Disillusionment and despair took hold of the spirit and heart of those who had been so full of hope, enthusiasm, and exaltation, and " sick, wearied out with contrarieties, yielded up moral questions in despair" (Wordsworth, *Prelude*, II. 304–5), and returned to the institutions of government, law, and authority. Wordsworth, Coleridge, and Southey became, in the course of time, the spiritual leaders of the new conservatism, imbuing it with a sense of social righteousness and love of the people. They are the fathers of the Tory Democracy and Christian social reform. Of the anti-capitalist spirit Southey possessed the most ; he was an assiduous reader of the socialist literature of his time, and one of the keenest and most one-sided critics of the industrial revolution. Some of his *Letters from England* (1807) might have been written by a communist. Manufactures appeared to him as the source of misery, depravity, and rebellion, threatening England with destruction.[1] Coleridge worked by fits and starts on a philosophy which was diametrically opposed to that of the Radicals. And Wordsworth was, to the end of his life, in sympathy with the social movements of the masses. There is a curious utterance reported of him by Crabb Robinson : " I recollect once hearing Mr. Wordsworth say, half in joke, half in earnest, ' I have no respect for Whigs, but I have a great deal of the Chartist in me.' To be sure he has."[2]

5.—LONDON CORRESPONDING SOCIETY : JOHN THELWALL

The same agitated period saw the beginning of the independent political action of the working classes, the London Corresponding Society (L.C.S.) forming the preface of its history.[3] The programme of the L.C.S. was democracy and social reform. Its founder was Thomas Hardy (1752–1832), a Scotch shoemaker, who had come to London from Stirlingshire in the year 1773. Its intellect was John Thelwall (1764–1834), an orator, poet, and journalist of considerable power. The L.C.S. was formed in March, 1792, and soon attracted the attention of the democratic and revolutionary intellectuals who supplied the working class organisations with speakers and lecturers, among them being Horne Tooke, Thomas Holcroft, John Richter, and John Thelwall. Holcroft and Thelwall were friends of Godwin, and Thelwall lectured before the working men of London on Godwin's " Political Justice." Hardy was not only moved by the ideas of the French Revolution, but by the views which had gathered

[1] Robert Southey, *Letters from England* (1807), I. 306–8 ; II. 139–44, 147-151 ; III. 114–19, 132–4.
[2] H. C. Robinson, *Diary*, ed. 1872, II., p. 290.
[3] Francis Place, Add. MSS. 27808, 27814 (British Museum) ; E. Smith, *English Jacobinism*, 1881 ; *State Trials*, vols. 24, 25 ; Graham Wallas, *Life of Francis Place*, pp. 20–8 ; Charles Cestre, *John Thelwall*, 1906.

round the agitation of Wilkes, "Junius," the American War of Independence, Major Cartwright and the Duke of Richmond. Also Thomas Spence was very active in the interest of the L.C.S., two branches of which used to meet in his lodgings in Holborn. The connection of the L.C.S. with the French Convention, their attempts to hold, in conjunction with the Scottish Reformers, a National Convention at Edinburgh (1793), finally their growing and insurrectionary activity among the industrial population of London and the Midlands, alarmed the Government. Mr. Pitt, informed by spies of the turmoil produced by the L.C.S., took at once measures for their suppression. In May, 1794, Hardy, Horne Tooke, Thelwall, etc., were arrested ; at the same time the Government prevailed upon Parliament to agree to the suspension of the Habeas Corpus Act ; and in October, 1794, the leaders of the L.C.S. were tried at the Old Bailey for high treason. The redoubtable Erskine was chief counsel for the defence, and the prisoners were acquitted. John Thelwall had prepared a speech in his defence, which, however, he had no opportunity of delivering ; he published it, in 1795, under the title "Natural and Constitutional Rights," which is a defence of universal suffrage and the rights of labour. He ascribed the power of property and monopoly to the fact that the richer classes were represented in Parliament. " If, once in every year, the poor man's vote were as important as his employer's, the poor could not be forgotten. But it is property, we are told, that ought to be represented, because by property government is supported. What ? Does property man the navy or fill the ranks of the army ? . . . Let us not deceive ourselves ! Property is nothing but human labour. The most inestimable of all property is the sweat of the poor man's brow ; the property from which all other is derived, and without which grandeur must starve in the midst of supposed abundance. And shall they who possess this inestimable property be told that they had no rights, because they have nothing to defend ? . . . No ! Man and not movables is the object of just legislation. All, therefore, ought to be consulted where all are corcerned, for not less than the whole ought to decide the fate of the whole. And if the few are to be the ultimate organ of that decision . . . then only the few are free, the rest are helots, bondsmen, slaves. The few, are, in fact, the owners of the life and liberties and possessions of the many " (pp. 42–3). Thelwall was connected by bonds of friendship with Coleridge, at least in the last decade of the eighteenth century. They exchanged many letters, in which Coleridge took great pains to cure Thelwall of his atheism. Both came to despise Godwin, although Thelwall remained to the end of his life a democratic reformer, while Coleridge became one of the formative minds of New Toryism. Thelwall delivered the funeral oration at the grave of Hardy (October, 1832), and was denounced by the Government spy, named Poppay, whom old Cobbett exposed in the first Reform Parliament.

Hardy's last years were, from a financial point of view, not happy. He retired in 1815, at the age of sixty-three, from business, with a competency which he reckoned would last him another ten years. But Providence ordained otherwise. He outlived his resources, and, but for the generosity of Francis Place and Sir Francis Burdett, would have had to spend the evening of his life in the workhouse and die a pauper's death.

The L.C.S. constituted a sort of democratic and social reform seminary for labour leaders. From it issued most of the ideas and men that made themselves conspicuous in popular movements up to the year 1820. Thomas Evans, leader of the Spenceans in the fateful years 1816–18, Colonel Despard (executed for high treason in 1805), John Gales Jones, later a supporter of Owen, Francis Place, and many others received their education, or impulses, from the L.C.S. The United Irishmen, when preparing for the insurrection, entered into communication with its leaders.

By the Corresponding Act, 1799, which prohibited all communication between political societies, the L.C.S. was suppressed, but it had already done its work ; the movement had spread to Lancashire and Yorkshire.

6.—CHARLES HALL

The sources of information concerning the life of Charles Hall are but few and scanty. Even the years of his birth and death are uncertain. It is only known that he published his book, *Effects of Civilisation*, in 1805, in the preface of which he relates that he practised as physician in the West of England. In the last years of his life he made the acquaintance of John Minter Morgan, a Christian Owenite, who left a few notes about him. " Hall's book," says Morgan, " contains an able analytical examination of the errors of the existing system. The author was in very reduced circumstances ; his work was published without funds to make it known. . . . Dr. Hall reached the age of eighty years, but he died in the Rules of the Fleet Prison, where I frequently saw him ; occasionally, when he could obtain a day-rule, he dined at my chambers ; his conversation was particularly animated and intelligent ; although learned in the classics, he was more distinguished for attainments in natural philosophy. He had friends who would have released him from prison, but he was confined through a lawsuit, as he considered, unjustly ; and rather than permit the money to be paid, he had resolved to remain incarcerated for life."[1] In the collection of Francis Place, there are two letters written by Hall to Thomas Spence. In one of the letters, dated Tavistock, August 25, 1807, he writes that he was nearly seventy years of age, a widower, and father of eight sons and two daughters ; his intention was to leave the country for London and get rooms at Furnival Inn.[2] From the reminiscences of Morgan and the letter to Spence it may be inferred that Hall was born about 1740, and died about 1820.

Hall's book [3] is evidently based on personal observations of the effects of the Industrial Revolution in particular, and private

---

[1] J. M. Morgan, *Hampden in the Nineteenth Century*, 1834. I., pp. 20–1.

[2] Place, Add. MSS. 27808 (British Museum).

[3] Only the second edition, published by J. M. Morgan in 1850, is extant, and here quoted or referred to.

property in general, but it also shows distinct traces of wide reading in economic and socialist literature, particularly Adam Smith, David Hume, Thomas Paine, and Godwin. The author is a determined opponent of manufacture, trade, and commerce, and regards agriculture as the most useful and beneficial occupation. He elaborates the doctrine of the antagonistic interests between the capitalist and working class, a doctrine found in embryo in Adam Smith's *Wealth of Nations* (book I, ch. 8), but developed to a revolutionary stage by Hall, who was the first socialist to make a statistical attempt at demonstrating the enormous injustice of profit, which he regards as a wholly illegitimate deduction from the produce of labour and the natural reward of labour.

Hall's position in the history of socialism is an intermediary one between natural law or ethical socialism and proletarian or revolutionary socialism. It is the first interpretation of the voice of rising Labour.

Following, evidently, Thomas Paine, Hall defines civilisation as that state of society in which, on the one hand, science, knowledge, trade, and manufacture flourish, while, on the other hand, the large majority of the population is poor, or sinking into poverty, and therefore excluded from enjoying its advantages. It is a state opposed to natural and simple life, where there is neither riches nor misery. The division of society into rich and poor is, for the social investigator, the most striking mark of civilisation. The life of the poor is short, hard, and deprived of all bodily and mental care. No government thinks it worth while to examine into their conditions, though they form the large majority of the population. It was mainly the establishment of manufactures that brought about this state of things, and is now aggravating it by withdrawing the mass of the population from agriculture, and thus starving the land of the necessary labour. The results are scarcity of agricultural produce and continual rise of the cost of living, which reduce the purchasing power of the wages and further depress the condition of the poor (pp. 25-37).

The motor power of these changes is wealth or capital. Economists have hitherto looked upon it from one side only ; they have but seen its workings and effects on production, and have neglected to investigate it with regard to its effects on the structure and welfare of society. In this rôle it reveals itself as a tremendous political power. Wealth is pre-eminently power ; in it resides the real sovereignty of the nation. It has the absolute command of the labour of those who are propertyless. This power of the rich is as strong and effective as that of the most despotic monarch, and probably more so. To condemn so many to the mines, to confine such numbers to such nauseous, irksome, unwholesome, destructive employments in factories and work-shops, is more than equal to any kingly power on earth (pp. 39–40). The possessors of wealth govern the distribution of the whole produce of labour and the lion's share falls to them. The so-called contract of labour is a sham, since the poor have only the choice between starvation or slavery (pp. 58–9). The interests of Capital and Labour, of the non-producers and the producers, are absolutely opposed to each other. The acquisition of the one is the spoliation of the other. What the possessor has the non-possessor is deprived of. " The situation of the rich and the poor, like the algebraic terms plus and minus, are in direct opposition to, and destructive of each other " (pp. 53–4). If every one had an allotment of land from which he could live and on which he could fall back in times of need, the accumulation of the few could have no such injurious effect on the masses, for there being no destitute the rich would be unable to force anybody to work for them at their discretion. Wealth, without labour to fertilise it, represents a harmless heap of goods, giving no power to its possessor. It is, then, the poverty of the many that results in the despotism of the capitalists. Altogether, manu-facturers are the cause and symptom of the poverty of the masses, they render them more ignorant and barbarous and weaken the nation.

How is wealth produced and distributed ? Trade and com-merce consist in buying and selling articles already produced by the poor, and gaining a profit on them. These goods are all the products of the hands of the workmen, from whom they are bought for less than their full value, else a profit could not be realised. The tradesman shares or takes part of the fruits of the labour of the poor. The means enabling tradesmen to share in the product of labour is their capital, from which they furnish materials and immediate subsistence to the artificers to work on. This loan of capital to the workman is supposed to give the capitalists the right to direct the distribution of the produce (p. 56–7). How the distribution is accomplished, the following data may help us approximately to ascertain. The rent of all lands in England about twenty years before was supposed by Adam Smith and others to have been twenty millions ; since that time the amount of rent had considerably increased ; the rapid rise of rent in the last thirty years was a well-known fact. Smith also supposed that the rental represented one-third of the value of the produce. Dr. Grey, in his late treatise on the income-tax, estimated the value of agricultural produce to amount to £112,000,000. The amount of exported manufacture according to Mr. Pitt's statement was the previous year (1804) about £50,000,000 ; the home consumption was supposed to be treble the foreign. The total produce of labour in agriculture and manufactures was therefore £312,000,000. The labouring population forms eight-tenths of the whole ; supposing their families to consist of five persons each, in a nation consisting of ten millions there will be 1,600,000 working men's families ; the average annual income of such a family is £25. This multiplied by the number of families give a total wage bill of £40,000,000.

Result : Eight-tenths of the population—or the large majority who produce all the wealth—receive one-eighth of it, while two-tenths who produce nothing receive seven-eighths of the produced wealth.

Or, a working man labours seven days for the capitalist, and one day in eight for himself, wife, and children (pp. 94–6).

> " Sic vos non vobis mellificatis, apes ;
> Sic vos non vobis fertis aratra, boves."[1]

The sum total of civilisation is to enable a few of mankind to

---

[1] You make the honey, but not for yourselves, bees ;
You make the land fruitful, but not for yourselves, oxen.

K

attain all possible enjoyments both of mind and body that they are capable of, but at the expense of the bulk of mankind, by which a great proportion of them are destroyed, and the remainder stunted in body and mind. All this is brought about in a regular, orderly, silent manner, under specious forms, with the appearance of law, order, and liberty, and even charity.

Wealth which is so injurious to national life is also the principal cause of one of the most fateful international calamities—viz. war, the objects of which are to increase trade and territory or to stifle internal revolutionary movements provoked by the infinite lust of the rich for power. The education given by the rich to the children of the poor is calculated to impart to them a warlike spirit ; the books they read are little else than a glorification of bloodshed ; the most destructive battles are called brilliant and glorious, but the horrid spectacle presented by the " field of glory," the day or the night after the battle—the mangled carcases, the groans of the dying, the ghastly aspect of the hospitals full of wounded and dying, are not mentioned. How overwhelming then must be the power of wealth that it is able even to extinguish the light of reason and morality, to suppress the feelings of the human heart, and cause man to slaughter his fellow-man !

This state of things was not brought about by the express design or contrivance of any set of men, but was the result of forces working unconsciously. The division of the land into large dominions, and the inequality consequent upon that division, gave to the rich an absolute power over the non-possessors, whom they use for the purpose of increasing the stock of wealth. Private property in land led to manufactures, trade, and commerce, by which the poor are made poorer still, and the small possessors are deprived of the little they possess and thrown into poverty.

The division of the land being thus the original cause of the evil, the reform of society must evidently start by removing the cause. The land, therefore, should be nationalised and settled with small farmers. The land to be restored to the nation, and the nation to the land. Agriculture should be the main occupa-

tion of all. Of the sciences and arts only those should be preserved and promoted that are necessary for the prosperity of
agricultural pursuits.

The significance of Hall's book is, however, not to be sought in
its reform schemes, which are evidently nothing else but an
elaboration of the sentimental reaction against industrial progress.
Its place in the history of socialist thought is assured to it by its
critical part, in which the rising opposition of the working classes
against the factory system found so keen an expression. It is
the edge-like sharpness and mathematical precision of the nascent
class antagonism which makes it into a herald of the approaching
revolutionary period. At first the book remained unheeded.
It was published in the year of Trafalgar and in the midst
of internal inaction. The youth of the nation, the strong
and adventurous, were either in the army and navy or
profitably employed in the factories, mines, and commercial houses ; glory and prosperity kept them quiet. The course
of the French Revolution and the repressive measures of Mr. Pitt
either damped the ardour of the intellectuals or brought them
back to a more conservative frame of mind. Hall's book fell
flat or was regarded as a paradox by the few papers which thought
it worth while mentioning or reviewing it.[1] These reviews had
only the effect of calling the attention of Thomas Spence to
Hall as a fellow-labourer. He sent him his Newcastle Lecture
and other pamphlets and asked for his opinion. Hall at first
replied with a few polite commonplaces, but after having been
urged again and again to speak freely, Hall told Spence that his
scheme was worth little, since it left capital and wage labour
untouched. The capitalist system was so complicated and
injurious an arrangement that it could not be mended, but must
be completely abolished.[2]
Hall's book is also mentioned by George Mudie, an Owenite

[1] *Monthly Review*, 1806, Vol. 51 ; *Monthly Magazine*, May, 1807.
[2] Place, Add. MSS. 27808. Reply of Hall to Spence, June 7,
1807 ; Letters of Spence to Hall, June 28, Aug. 13, 1807 ; Reply of
Hall, Aug. 25, 1807.

and journalist, in the *Economist* (1820–1, No. 4), who points out that Hall had not taken sufficient account of the evil of competition, and that the remedy was not a return to simpler conditions, but co-operation.

On the whole it would appear that in socialist and reform circles the book was read.

III

STORM AND STRESS

I.—REBELLIONS OF LABOUR

ONCE a communist, always a communist. This applies, as far as social criticism is concerned, to Robert Southey. His *Letters from England*, published two years after Hall's book, contain as destructive and one-sided a criticism of the new industrial era as the *Effects of Civilisation*. Southey only saw the poverty of the masses and he argued that, " if religion were out of the question, it would have been better for them (the lower classes) to have been born among savages than in a civilised country, where they are in fact the victims of civilisation " (*Letters*, I., pp. 306–8). This is curiously reminiscent of Hall. The wealth which the new era brought in its train was " not equally and healthfully distributed through the whole system ; it sprouts into wens and tumours, and collects in aneurisms which starve and palsy the extremities " (*Ib.*, II., p. 147). It needed the pen of a Dante to describe the horrors of the Manchester factories (*Ib.*, II., pp. 139–44). The result of that system would be a violent revolution. " The introduction of machinery in an old manufacturing country always produces distress by throwing workmen out of employ, and is seldom effected without riots and executions. . . . A manufacturing population is always ripe for rioting. They have no local attachments ; the persons to whom they look up for support they regard more with envy than with respect, as men who grow rich by their labour ; they know enough what is passing in the political world to think themselves politicians. . . . Governments who found their prosperity upon manufactures sleep upon gunpowder. . . . If the manufacturing system continues to be extended, increasing as it necessarily does the number, the misery, and the

133

depravity of the poor, I believe that a revolution must come, and in the most fearful shape. And the tendency of the present system is to lessen the middle classes and to increase the lower ones " (*Ib.*, II., p. 157, III., pp. 132–3).

Three years later the *Edinburgh Review* diagnosed the condition of the nation in no less gloomy colours. " The great body of the nation appears to us to be divided into two violent and most pernicious factions : the courtiers who are almost for arbitrary power ; and the democrats who are almost for revolution and republicanism. . . . If the two opposite parties are once permitted to shock together in open conflict, there is an end to the freedom and almost to the existence of the nation. In the present crisis, we have no hesitation in saying, it is to the popular side that the friends of the constitution must turn themselves. If the Whig leaders do not first conciliate and then restrain the people ; if they do not save them from their leaders they are already choosing in their own body . . . the Constitution itself, the Monarchy, and the Whig aristocracy will, in no long time, be swept away. . . . The nation is on fire at the four corners. . . . That the number of democrats is fast increasing with a visible and dangerous rapidity, any man may satisfy himself by the common and obvious means of information. It is a fact which he may read legibly in the prodigious sale, and still more prodigious circulation of Cobbett's *Register*, and several other weekly papers of the same description ; he may learn it in every street of the manufacturing and populous towns in the heart of the country. . . . The storm is most evidently brewing over our heads at this moment, and if it cannot be dispersed before it bursts upon them, we do not know where is our chance of being saved from destruction." [1]

And the storm burst. First in the form of Luddism. The infuriated workmen destroyed machinery. In March, 1812, Parliament passed a law for the protection of machinery, punishing Luddite actions with death, and in the second week of January, 1813, eighteen workmen died on the gallows at York.[2] Lord

[1] *Edinburgh Review*, 1810.
[2] Henry Brougham, *Life and Times*, II., pp. 76–7.

Byron, who had opposed that law in the House of Lords, evidently regarded this movement as one for freedom, and composed, in December 1816, the following song of the Luddites :—

> " As the Liberty lads o'er the sea
> Bought their freedom, and cheaply, with blood,
> So we boys, we
> Will die fighting, or live free,
> And down with all Kings but King Ludd !
>
> " When the web that we weave is complete
> And the shuttle exchanged for the sword,
> We will fling the winding sheet
> O'er the despot at our feet,
> And dye it deep in the gore he has pour'd.
>
> " Though black as his heart its hue,
> Since his veins are corrupted to mud,
> Yet this is the dew,
> Which the tree shall renew
> Of liberty, planted by Ludd ! "

Quite different from the attitude of the rebellious aristocrat was that of the fighting democrat, William Cobbett. Though in his cheap weekly edition of the *Register*, begun in the autumn, 1816, he represented Labour as the creator of all wealth and the foundation of the State (*Political Register*, November 2, 1816), he soon appealed to the Luddites to desist from destroying machinery, and to join, instead, the movement for Parliamentary reform. Not machinery, but oligarchic rule, the debased state of currency, the heavy load of taxation consequent upon the enormous expenditure for war, pensions and sinecures, borough-mongering and Jewish Stock Exchange jobbery, were at the bottom of the misery of the working classes. These evils could only be removed by a popularly elected Parliament (*Ib.*, November 30, 1816). Indeed, soon after Waterloo, Radicals began to revive the democratic traditions of the years from 1760 to 1794, and to undertake the political education of the working classes. The City of London became again one of the foci of Liberal thought, and on December 9, 1816, the Common Council told the Prince Regent that the

Government was corrupt and wasteful, and that the late war was unjust and senseless. Following Cobbett's cheap *Register*, a Radical and popular press, mostly weeklies, appeared, such as Wooler's *Black Dwarf*, John Wade's *Gorgon*, Carlile's *Republican*. An alliance between the middle and working classes was being formed ; Cobbett, Hunt, Major Cartwright, Sir Francis Burdett, took the lead, and the working men, abandoning sporadic revolts, which only led to executions and to the suspension of the Habeas Corpus Act, joined the Hampden Clubs, the first of which was formed at Westminster in 1812. This club was, however, exclusively for rich reformers, while the Hampden Clubs formed after the war bore a popular character, and demanded not only Universal Suffrage and the abolition of the Corn Laws, but also the abrogation of the Combination Acts.

While Cobbett and Hunt were beginning to dominate the popular platforms, a writer of vastly superior intellectual and literary powers was meditating upon the problems of the time— Samuel Taylor Coleridge composed his *Lay Sermons*. He retraced " the progress of things from 1792 to 1813, when the tide was at its height . . . and the ebb from its first turn to the dead low-water mark of the last quarter," *i.e.*, end of 1816, and then generalised the events under the following heads : " Fluctuations in the wages of labour, alternate privation and excess, consequent improvidence, and, over all, discontent and a system of factious confederacy—these form the history of the mechanics and lower ranks of our cities and towns. In the country a peasantry sinking into pauperism, step by step, with the rise of the farmer's profits and indulgences." The trading and huckstering spirit predominated everywhere, and to excess within its own sphere. How should this state of things be remedied ? First, as to agriculture : This " requires principles essentially different from those of trade." A gentleman ought not to regard his estate as a merchant his cargo, or a shopkeeper his stock. The marketable produce of the land ought to be made a subordinate consideration to the living and moral growth that was to remain on the land—a healthful, callous-handed, but high-hearted tenantry, twice the number of the present landless, parish-paid labourers.

" Our manufacturers must consent to regulations ; our gentry must concern themselves in the education as well as in the instruction of their natural clients and dependents ; must regard their estates as secured indeed from all human interferences by every principle of law and policy, but yet as offices of trust, with duties to be performed, in the sight of God and their country. Let us become a better people, and the reform of all public griev-ances . . . will follow of itself. . . . Let us palliate where we cannot cure, comfort where we cannot relieve ; and for the rest rely upon the promise of the King of Kings by the mouth of His Prophet, ' Blessed are ye that sow beside all waters.' " [1]

This was the first voice of Christian Socialism.

2.—STRIKES AND DEMONSTRATIONS

Andrew Ure, in his *Philosophy of Manufactures*, goes to the root of strike movements when he declares that the concen-tration of industry brought them in its train. " The textile manufactures consist of two distinct departments ; one carried on by multitudes of small, independent machines belonging to the workmen ; another carried on by concentrated systems of machinery, the property of the masters. The workmen of the first class being scattered over a wide tract of country, and being mutual competitors for work and wages, can seldom conspire with one another, and never with effect against their employers. . . . The operatives of the other class are necessarily associated in large bodies, and have no capital sunk in machinery and work-shops. When they choose to strike they can readily join in the blow, and by stopping they merely suffer a loss of wages for the time, while they occasion to their master loss of interest on his capital, his rent, his taxes, as well as injury to the delicate moving parts of metallic mechanism by inaction in our humid climate." [2]

As soon as the textile industry reached a sufficient degree of concentration the struggle between Capital and Labour began,

[1] S. T. Coleridge, *Lay Sermons* (in *Constitution of Church and State*), 1830, pp. 414–30.
[2] A. Ure, *Philosophy of Manufactures*, Bohn's Library edition, 1861, p. 281.

and that was at the commencement of the nineteenth century.[1]
Both parties soon formed separate and mutually hostile organisations, and by 1810 the North of England was in the throes of
large strike movements, the cotton spinners and miners leading.
Sporadic turn-outs occurred in the following years, which
culminated in the great Lancashire strike of 1818, the textile
workers fighting not only for higher wages, but for factory legislation, and particularly for the regulation of female and child
labour. From Lancashire the movement spread to Scotland,
where the weavers, taught by their English brethren, formed
trade organisations and entered with zest into the struggle.

These agitations, occurring at a time of political crisis, drew
the trade unionists into the vortex of radical reform. Hunt and
Cobbett fraternised with the trade union leaders ; the organised
workmen formed the bulk of their audiences or readers, and even
the female workers formed Female Reform Associations, at whose
meetings not only the thoughts and vigorous utterances of Cobbett
were repeated, but also the particular demands of Labour found
expression. On July 5, 1818, the Female Reform Association of
Blackburn held a mass meeting of working people of both sexes,
in which a woman was the chief speaker. The meeting carried
the following characteristic resolution :—

" By means of the improvement of machinery, the means of
producing most articles of agriculture and manufacture have
been increased in an astonishing degree ; it necessarily
follows that the industrious labourer ought to have a far greater
quantity of produce than he had previous to those improvements ;
instead of which, by means of taxation and restrictive laws he is
reduced to wretchedness. Borough-mongering and tyranny
must be exterminated. If this is not done, thousands of our

---

[1] " It is well known that the seeds from whence these troubles
have sprung up, first began to vegetate amongst the weavers of
Lancashire, in the latter end of 1799 and the beginning of 1800,
changing the aspect of the manufacturing districts from that of
wealth, peace, and godliness to that of complaint against masters,
murmurs against ministry, and a general cry for peace ! "—i.e.,
against the war with France (W. Radcliffe, *Origin of the New System
of Manufacture*, 1827, p. 73).

countrymen must starve in the midst of plenty. No man can have a right to enjoy another man's labour without his consent. And we do contemplate with horror the many placemen and pensioners, whilst at the same time we live in poverty, slavery, and misery. We protest against those unjust and unnatural regulations—the Corn Laws and the Combination Acts. We demand Universal Suffrage, annual Parliaments, and the ballot."[1]

A week later the men of Birmingham assembled in public meeting, and, as protest against borough-mongering and the restricted franchise, " elected " Major Cartwright and Sir Charles Wolseley to Parliament. The culminating point of these demonstrations was Peterloo (August 16, 1819), which led to the Six Acts, and put a stop to the public agitation in England. In Scotland, however, the agitation went on at an accelerating pace. English Radicals from the South and trade union leaders from Lancashire and Yorkshire won the ear of the Scottish working men and tradespeople, particularly of Paisley, Glasgow, and Carlisle, and formed unions in most of the manufacturing districts. " The devil seems to have come among us unchained," wrote Sir Walter Scott at that time to one of his correspondents, " and bellowing for his prey. In Glasgow, Volunteers drill by day and Radicals by night, and nothing but positive military force keeps the people under." The workmen had formed societies, and were led by the cleverest and most impertinent fellows, " bell-wethers in every sort of mischief." [2] In March, 1820, considerable unrest and alarm began to prevail in Scotland, and on April 2 the alarm grew into extreme anxiety by a proclamation, posted on the walls of many houses in the commercial and manufacturing centres, calling upon the people to close their factories and workshops, and to desist from work until Universal Suffrage was granted. " Equality of rights (but not of property) " was the cry. The proclamation, which the authorities considered as " highly seditious and treasonable," was signed by " The Committee for Organisation of a Provisional Government." Many workmen obeyed the appeal and struck work. At Paisley, Glas-

[1] *Black Dwarf*, July 14, 1818.
[2] Sir Walter Scott, *Familiar Letters*, II., p. 78.

gow, Carlisle, and in the colliery district the strike was all but general. Small bands of people took up arms, but only at Bonny-muir did some of them come in contact with a military detach-ment. After a short skirmish the insurgents suffered defeat ; many of them were wounded, and nineteen made prisoners. Numerous arrests in other parts of the country soon put an end to the rising. In July and August the prisoners were brought to trial for high treason, and many of them found guilty, but only three, among them being Andrew Hardie, a forebear of Mr. James Keir Hardie, suffered the extreme penalty.

3.—THE SPENCEANS

In 1812 Thomas Spence formed an association of his adherents and friends, who became known later as Spencean Philanthropists. This association consisted of four groups of ten persons each, all of them skilful propagandists and agitators, who by their organising activities created the impression that they were controlling the whole working class democratic movement in the metropolis. The most prominent members were : Thomas Evans, a traces-maker, who after the death of Spence became the literary mouthpiece of the Spencean doctrines ; Thomas Preston, a leather worker ; John Hooper, a labourer ; Dr. James Watson, physician ; and Arthur Thistlewood, later of Cato Street fame. Evans had been a member of the London Corresponding Society and its secretary in 1798 when the whole Executive were arrested and kept in prison, without any trial, for nearly three years. In 1816 he published a pamphlet entitled *Christian Policy*, which went through a second edition in the same year. It is devoted to a demonstration of the necessity of a reform or rather " revolution of property " by giving back the land to the people as the only means of removing the distress caused by the war. The people in possession of the land would become con-sumers of industrial commodities, and extended consumption would promote production. Instead of a revolution in the land system the ruling classes were treating the poor with Malthus's theory that they had no claim whatsoever to the smallest portion of food, " and, in fact, had no business to be where they are."

Also, the whole foreign policy was wrong. The Napoleonic Wars had only served the interests of Russia, which had become overwhelmingly powerful by swallowing Poland—the granary of Europe. The right policy would have been an alliance between England and France with the purpose of checking Russia.

The same author published, probably in 1817, another pamphlet entitled *Christian Policy in full practice among the people of Harmony, a town in the State of Pennsylvania . . . to which are subjoined a concise view of the Spencean system of Agrarian Fellowship, and some observations on the manifest similarity between the principles of the system and the truly practical and Christian establishment of the Harmonites.* It contains a description of the communist colony of the Rappists, which Robert Owen bought up seven years later.

While Evans was spreading the socialistic doctrines of his master, the other Christian philanthropists were busily engaged in organising popular demonstrations for political and social reform. They were the organisers of the Spa Fields meetings (November–December, 1816), which led to rioting and to the high treason trial against Dr. Watson and his son, Preston, Hooper, and Thistlewood. Their acquittal was due to the advocacy of Sir Charles Wetherell, who in a severe cross-examination exposed the chief witness for the Crown as a spy. In March, 1817, Parliament carried a Bill for the suppression of clubs and associations known as Spenceans or Spencean Philanthropists, for they were aiming at the confiscation and division of the lands as well as at the repudiation of the national debt. Parliament at the same time renewed the Corresponding Act, 1799, which prohibited all communication between political societies. Of the Spenceans only Thistlewood remained active. For a defamation of Lord Sidmouth he was sent to prison for twelve months. After his release he was active more than ever for reform, but his past experience and the events on the St. Peter's Fields in Manchester (Peterloo) caused him to abandon all peaceful methods, and with the help of Government spies he organised the Cato Street conspiracy, for which he and four of his fellow-conspirators paid with their lives on the gallows at Newgate, on May 1, 1820.

Peterloo, Bonnymuir, and Cato Street closed one of the most agitated and terrible and at the same time mentally most active and prolific decades in British history. The chaotic fires of popular rebellions and aspirations, in passing through the preternatural imagination of Percy Bysshe Shelley, flamed up in fury and splendour in " Queen Mab," " Poems of the Time," and " Prometheus Unbound." The baffling problems of the Economic Revolution and financial distresses excited the logical and concentrated thought of David Ricardo. The new conditions of the working classes found in Robert Owen a reformer of exceptional energy and constancy. All men of understanding were searching for knowledge of social affairs, the modes of distribution of the national income, the cause and cure of the nation.

IV

THE ECONOMISTS

I.—PATRICK COLQUHOUN

THE first writer who attempted to satisfy the desire of the educated classes for information concerning the new economic conditions of the country was Patrick Colquhoun. As a trained jurist, municipal administrator, director of commercial enterprises, and London magistrate, he possessed the requisite knowledge and opportunity for such a work. The circle of his friends and acquaintances included Adam Smith, Robert Owen, and probably also David Ricardo. As a loyal supporter of the Government and staunch adherent of the existing order he had access to contemporary State documents. In possession of these advantages he wrote his *Treatise of the Wealth, Power, and Resources of the British Empire*, published in 1814, in which he gave a statistical account of the population, agriculture, manufactures, commerce, and distribution of the national income among the various classes of the United Kingdom and the British Colonies in 1812. A second edition appeared in 1815, so great was the curiosity of the nation with regard to its economic position.

But even apart from this legitimate curiosity the thought of the nation became increasingly economic. The industrial revolution appeared to reveal the new truth that the basis of society was economic rather than philosophical or spiritual. The idealists lamented the new turn which mental speculations were taking. "Absorbed in the contemplation of material objects," lamented Isaac D'Israeli, "and rejecting whatever does not enter into their own restricted notions of utility, these old arithmetical seers, with nothing but millions in their imaginations, . . . value the intellectual toils of library and studio by the law of supply and demand. In their commercial, agricultural,

143

and manufacturing view of human nature . . . they confine
the moral and physical existence of man in tables of population.
Planning and levelling society down to their carpentry of human
nature, they would yoke and harness the loftier spirits to one
common and vulgar destination. Man is considered only as he
wheels on the wharf, or as he spins in the factory. But man as
a recluse being of meditation, or impelled to action by more
generous passions, has been struck out of the system of our
Political Economists."

Colquhoun's treatise was the book of revelation after which
the nation thirsted. It gave statistical tables and glowing descriptions of the new wealth of the country. But also the critical
socialist found in it what he wanted. In fact, the book may be
regarded as one of the most important bases of economic and
socialist researches and criticisms during the Ricardian and
Owenite period. This applies particularly to its tables on the
distribution of the national income.[1] The socialist interpretations of Colquhoun's distribution tables played in working class
agitation of those times a rôle similar to that of Mr. Chiozza
Money's *Riches and Poverty* in our time.

Colquhoun was fully acquainted with the revolutionary
movements. As London magistrate since 1792 he studied the
doings and proclamations of the Corresponding Society and the
revolutionary intellectuals. He appears to have had a hand in
the composition of the secret reports with which the Government
justified, in Parliament, the measures they proposed for checking
those movements. He also knew his Adam Smith and told his
readers that labour was the source of wealth. " Millions of
individuals," he declares, " pass through life without being aware
that the food, clothing, and the other conveniences and comforts
which they enjoy, proceed entirely from the labour of the people
employed in agriculture, mines and minerals, in manufactures
and handicrafts, in trade, commerce, navigation, and fisheries.
It is by the labour of the people . . . that all ranks of the

---

[1] *Life of Robert Owen*, 1857, I., pp. 150, 125–7 ; J. Gray, *Lecture
on Human Happiness*, 1825 ; *Midland Representative*, June 25, 1831 ;
Bray, *Labour's Wrongs*, 1839, p. 85.

community in every condition of life annually subsist ; and it is by the produce of this labour alone that nations become powerful in proportion to the extent of the surplus which can be spared for the exigencies of the State." The people who produced all these things were poor, and it was quite true that " every State is supported by the poverty of the community composing the body politic. Without a large proportion of poverty there could be no riches, since riches are the offspring of labour, while labour can result only from a state of poverty. Poverty is that state and condition of society where the individual has no surplus labour in store, or, in other words, no property or means of subsistence but what is derived from the constant exercise of industry. Poverty is therefore a most necessary and indispensable ingredient in society, without which nations and communities could not exist in a state of civilisation. It is the lot of man. It is the source of wealth, since without poverty there could be no labour, no riches, no refinement, no comfort, and no benefit to those who may be possessed of wealth, inasmuch as without a large proportion of poverty, surplus labour could never be rendered productive in procuring either the conveniences or luxuries of life." [1]

What is the amount of wealth produced annually, and how is it distributed ? The question of distribution began at that time to interest the bulk of the nation. This curiosity arose from two sources—first, from the manufacturing and commercial class, who felt that, for all their efforts and risks, the largest part of the national income fell to the landed interests ; it was the beginning of the struggle for the abolition of the Corn Laws ; secondly, from social critics who, as we have seen from Hall, were quite sure that Labour was the producer of all wealth and received very little, but wanted accurate data to base their arguments upon ; it was the beginning of economic socialism or the agitation for the abolition of Capitalism.

Colquhoun appeared to satisfy this quest for facts and figures of distribution by giving approximately correct, at any rate.

[1] Patrick Colquhoun, *Resources of the British Empire*, 1814, p. 110 ; the same, *Treatise on Indigence*, 1806, pp. 7–9.

L

authoritative replies drawn from official records and papers. The new wealth produced, in 1812, in the United Kingdom, he found to have amounted to over 430 millions sterling. The number of the population was then 17,096,803. The distribution of the national income was as follows :—

The higher and lower nobility (numbering with their families 416,000 persons) received fifty-eight millions sterling, or from 200*l.* to 400*l.* each member, including women and children ; the yeomanry (1,400,000 persons, including women and children) received forty millions, or from 20*l.* to 50*l.* each ; farmers (1,540,000 persons, including their families) received over thirty-three millions, or 22*l.* each member ; merchants (194,000 persons, including their families) received twenty-seven millions, or from 112*l.* to 260*l.* each member ; shopkeepers (700,000 persons, including their families) received twenty-eight millions, or 40*l.* each member ; manufacturers (264,000 persons, including their families) received thirty-five millions, or 134*l.* each member ; agricultural labourers, including miners (3,154,142 persons, including families) received 33,400,000*l.* or 11*l.* each ; industrial workers, mechanics, artisans (4,343,389 persons, including their families) received over forty-nine millions, or 11*l.* each member. The remainder was distributed among royalty, the services, professional classes, clergy, small tradespeople, commercial assistants, finally among the paupers, who numbered 1,647,900 persons, and received either allowances or full relief.

The stress laid by Colquhoun on labour producing all the wealth could not but painfully emphasise the small reward that fell to the share of Labour. The contrast was striking. Likewise, the profits of the manufacturers compared unfavourably with the rent of the landowners, all the more so as Colquhoun sometimes regarded the work of the manufacturers and, generally, the manufacturing capital as productive labour (*Resources*, p. 109). The indefiniteness of the concept of Productive Labour, as we shall see later, is one of the weakest points of classical Political Economy and has been a fruitful source of error. Still, the general impression which Colquhoun's treatise left on the mind of its readers was that labour formed the source of wealth.

Reasoning from this premise there appeared to be no justification for the mode of distribution. Where lay the error ?

This problem was taken up by Ricardo and by Owen. Ricardo asked, what were the principles that ought to govern the distribution, and why were they ineffective ? How did it come that such a large part of the national income was absorbed by Rent ? And Owen asked, why did Labour receive so small a share, and why was the nation, as a whole, in the face of the enormous productive forces created by invention and science, still so poor that poverty fell to the lot of the great majority ?

Ricardo believed he had discovered the source of mischief in the Corn Laws and Poor Laws ; Owen in the new machinery being exploited exclusively in the interest of the capitalists, and, generally, in the ignorance of the rationalist truth that man did not make his own character, but that it was made for him by the past and present conditions.

Other reformers, like Thomas Attwood and John Gray, believed the medium of exchange (gold) and the whole process of circulation of commodities were at the root of all social misery. They were, therefore, currency reformers, or proposed a different form of exchange.

The Radicals, as we know, thought the cause of discontent and social unrest was the oligarchic form of government.

All those streams of opinion intertwined or crossed and formed, in their courses, large movements which filled British history from 1815 to about 1850.

2.—DAVID RICARDO

Among the theorists of Political Economy there has been none more inductive, and less abstract in method, than Ricardo. The misconception regarding his method arose, first, from his assumption that the problems which preoccupied him were known to everybody, and that, therefore, his main business was to supply the commentary and solution ; secondly, from the erroneous view prevailing until recently, that a great writer was enunciating eternal truths, instead of merely attempting to interpret a minute segment of the passing waves of human history.

But, taking Ricardo as he really was—viz. the economist of the latter phase of the Economic Revolution and the transition from the Napoleonic Wars to peace, there is no difficulty in judging his work.

Ricardo's problem was distribution. It engrossed his attention to such a degree that he regarded it as " the principal problem of Political Economy,"—a view in which Adam Smith would not have concurred, for, in his time, it was production which formed the principal economic problem ; and Thomas Mun, in his turn, would surely have opposed the opinion of Smith, and maintained that the balance of trade was the principal problem of Economics. Time and place control economic theory, and the England of the first half of the nineteenth century desired to know how the wealth produced by the new industrial system was divided. Ricardo, being a rationalist, lacked the historical sense and assumed that there was a natural law which regulated distribution and would, if not deflected by class or government legislation, equitably divide the produce of labour into rent, profit, and wages (*Principles of Political Economy and Taxation*, third edition, Preface, and conclusion of chapter 4). Ricardo, in speaking of natural law, has nothing to do with the state of nature. He, like Adam Smith, held the system of private property as far superior to any other system. In his eyes, property was sacred,[1] and he, like Smith and the Physiocrats, assumed the commercial system to be governed by inherent laws, acting through the nature of man. So, too, had Edmund Burke, the great opponent of the state of nature, assumed that commerce was governed by inherent laws, " which are the laws of nature, and, consequently, the laws of God." [2] There was, further, in the mind of Ricardo, not a shadow of doubt that Capital was the creator of civilisation, progress, and all that was good in society. He never regarded Labour as a separate and independent factor. Labour was the instrument of Capital. Only on one point there appeared to him a divergence of interest between Capital and Labour,—viz. in point of machinery (*Principles*, chapter 31),—

[1] Hansard's *Parliamentary Debates*, 1820, Vol. II., p. 122.
[2] E. Burke, *Thoughts on Scarcity*. 1795, p. 157.

and at this view he arrived comparatively late (about 1819), through the propaganda of Owen and the Owenites. On the other hand, he always believed that there was an irreconcilable opposition of interests between Capital and the landed aristocracy who lived on ground rent.

Although Ricardo was profoundly convinced that Capital was the creative and driving power of society, and that Labour was merely the appendage and instrument of Capital, he nevertheless made labour the foundation of his theories, without defining, in an unambiguous manner, the concept of labour. We shall deal, in the following chapter, with the erroneous inferences caused by that ambiguity; meanwhile, let us consider the law which, according to Ricardo, governed economic life.

It is the law of exchange-value.

Given utility, the exchange-value of a commodity arises from labour, and is measured by the quantity of labour necessary to produce the commodity. Political Economy deals, as a matter of course, with commodities that can be increased at any time and in any country, by human industry. The quantity of labour which measures value, is that which is necessary under the most unfavourable circumstances of production. It is, to use a modern economic term, marginal labour, or final utility labour, that measures value or forms the standard of value (*Ib.* I. 2, II.). Exchange-value and natural price are identical.

Value and riches are not identical. Riches or wealth consist of utilities, of an abundance of useful things, while value depends on the difficulty or facility of production. A person may possess for a period of, say, ten years, the same quantity of useful things, or the same quantity of wealth, yet its value may have increased or diminished according to the changes that have taken place during that period in the quantity of labour necessary for production. If, in the meantime, new machinery had been brought into operation which displaced a certain quantity of human labour, the exchange value of those goods will have decreased ; or, conversely, if, in the meantime, a larger quantity of labour will have to be employed in order to produce the same amount

of wealth as ten years ago, its exchange-value will have increased
(*Ib.* ch. 20.).

It is thus marginal human labour that forms the standard of
exchange-value. It measures the volume of wealth of a person or
country. Machinery, or natural agents used as motor power, may
increase the volume of wealth or useful things, but add nothing
to exchange-value ; they rather decrease it, since they displace
or save human labour.

In order to produce commodities three things are necessary—
land, labour, and capital.

The most important factor is capital, or accumulated labour.
It is the motor power of social life. It consists of tools, implements, machinery, buildings, raw materials, food, and clothing,
used for purposes of manufacture, agriculture, trade, and commerce. It is divided into two portions—fixed and circulating.
Fixed capital consists of machinery, buildings, raw materials ;
circulating capital is that which is spent on wages. Capital used
in such a manner yields a profit or a surplus over the prime cost.
Prime cost, plus profit, is the cost of production. The movement of capital, particularly circulating capital, determines the
increase or decrease of population ; for, the larger the circulating
capital, the greater the opportunity for steady work and good
wages, and, therefore, the possibility of bringing up large families, and *vice versa* ; growth of population results in a greater
demand for agricultural produce, consequently, in an extension
of agriculture and rise of rent (*Ib.*, ch. 2 and 5).[1]

Rent is a surplus profit on the cultivation of land, paid by the
cultivator to the owner. It presupposes private property in
land, and arises from three causes—(1) Land is limited in quantity ; (2) it varies in quality and advantages ; (3) with the
progress of population inferior soils are taken into cultivation.
Suppose there are, in a new country, three qualities of land—
Nos. 1, 2, 3. Land of the first class is abundant relatively to the
population. It is, therefore, taken first into cultivation, and it
yields a hundred quarters of corn. With the growth of the population, however, the cultivated area proves inadequate, and

[1] See also *Essay on the Influence of Low Prices of Corn*, 1815.

therefore, the farmers have recourse to soil No. 2, which yields but ninety quarters of corn. As soon as this is accomplished there is a surplus profit on No. 1, amounting to ten quarters. With the further increase of capital and population the soil No. 3 must be cultivated, which yields but eighty quarters. In this case the rent of soil No. 1 will be twenty quarters, and that of No. 2 will be ten quarters. And in the same proportion as we descend the scale of land qualities and reach marginal land which just covers the cost of production and thus produces no surplus profit, the rent of the superior qualities rises.

It is, as we have seen, marginal land that determines rent, and marginal labour that determines exchange-value. And as the inferior qualities of agricultural land require a greater quantity of labour to reproduce the cost and yield a profit, the exchange-value of agricultural produce must rise.

Had Ricardo thought out his theory of marginal labour to its last consequences, he would have come to the conclusion that the profits of all better equipped manufacturing establishments also partook of the nature of rent. For, if labour under the most unfavourable circumstances forms the standard of exchange value, all establishments which work under more and more favourable circumstances must yield surplus profits or rents. But he has not gone beyond stating the theory of marginal labour.

Having dealt with value and rent, we must consider Ricardo's theory of wages. Wages are not the price paid to the workman for the produce of his labour, but they represent a certain amount of food, clothing, shelter, and conveniences of life according to the habits and customs and the degree of civilisation of the country or district in which the workman lives, in order to enable him to exist and perpetuate his race without increase or diminution Or, in other words, wages are intended to restore to the labourer the physiological wear and tear caused by his exertions in field, factory, mine, office, and shop. In progressive countries the money wages have a tendency to rise, since the price of agricultural produce, according to the law of value, must rise, and the bulk of wages consists of agricultural produce. The only

factor which depresses wages is machinery, for through its introduction a part of the capital which would have been allotted to
the circulating portion (for wages) is added to the fixed portion.
But the introduction of machinery is only profitable when
money wages rise, and this rise is the effect of the extension of
agriculture to inferior soils, or the rise of agricultural prices.

On the whole, in a progressive country, rent and money wages
have a tendency to rise.

How does this rise act on the reward of Capital ?

The value of the produced commodities, after deducting the
cost of the fixed capital, is divided into profit and wages. And
as wages have the tendency to rise, profit must have the tendency
to fall. For, if one whole consists of two portions, one portion
must decrease when the other increases. Wages and profit stand
in an inverse ratio to each other. Experience shows also that
the rise of agricultural prices is more prompt and rapid than that
of wages. The workman is therefore less benefited than the
landowner.

Before we sum up Ricardo's theories, in so far as they
are relevant to our subject, it must be pointed out that we
have been dealing with pure theory, leaving out of account such
factors as supply and demand, and fluctuations in the market
which lead to deviations from the theoretical laws and which
cause the natural price to become the market price. Ricardo
has not neglected those disturbing factors, but he always assumes
that the natural price forms the centre of gravitation round
which the market price fluctuates. The exchange-values or
natural prices are, in John Stuart Mill's simile, the sea level,
while the market prices are the ripples and waves.[1]

Ricardo's theories may be summed up as follows : The centre
of his system is the law of exchange-value. Labour, under the
most unfavourable circumstances, is the foundation of value ;
the quantity of such labour, or marginal labour, is the standard
of value or the natural price. This price is represented in the
cost of production (fixed capital used, wages paid, profit). Higher
or lower wages do not appreciably affect the price, but they do

[1] J. S. Mill, *Principles of Pol. Econ.*, book 3, ch. 3, § 1.

considerably affect the volume of profit. Wages rise or fall according to the movement of agricultural prices, and if wages rise
profit sinks, and *vice versa*. With the development of capitalist
activities, the population increases, agriculture extends to
inferior soils, rent rises, corn prices go up, wages go up, but profit
sinks. The more Capital risks and undertakes, the less its relative income, the greater the income of the landowning class,
which does nothing for the growth of civilisation. Moreover,
manufactured commodities are losing in value, since the improvement in machinery lessens the quantity of labour, and,
therefore, decreases their value, while the corn prices rise, since
inferior soils are taken into cultivation which, as a matter of
course, require larger quantities of labour. The result of the
progress of civilisation is prosperity of the landowning classes
and severer struggle of the capitalist classes. And yet it is Capital
which creates civilisation ! Were this result the natural outcome
of economic life nobody would have any right to complain.
But it is not the natural effect. It is produced artificially by
class legislation,—viz. the Corn Laws. By closing the English
markets to foreign corn English agriculture is forced to have
recourse to inferior soils, and thus to larger expenditure of labour
quantities, which, by the law of value, raise the natural price.
Diminished supply, limited competition, marginal labour and
marginal lands combine to produce that effect. The interests
of the landowning classes are thus opposed to the interests of the
whole community.

This is the Ricardian interpretation of the Economic Revolution and the social turmoil produced by it. The middle classes
found in it a clear and logical exposition of their own feelings ;
they knew now their real enemy ; and they gained some insight
into the movement of population, prices, profits, rents, and wages.
The agitation for Parliamentary reform and the abolition of the
Corn Laws appeared theoretically established and justified.
Ricardo's treatise, while it undoubtedly contributed to the
aggravation of the warfare between the people and the Tory
aristocracy, softened the antagonism between Capital and Labour.
The manufacturers learned the cause of strikes and the reason

of the desire of Labour for coalition, and Labour discovered that oligarchic legislation, and not capitalism, was at the root of their distress. And that was essentially what Cobbett taught them. For the next fifteen years the capitalists and the mass of the working classes marched hand in hand in the struggle for Radical reform. And it was the sympathy of the middle classes which enabled the working classes to arrange demonstrations, to get rid of the Combination Laws, and to appear on the scene as a political factor. Without that sympathy such an event, for instance, as Peterloo would have passed comparatively unnoticed, or as little noticed as the Luddite hangings in January, 1813. Liberalism stood godfather to Labour politics. Most of the leaders of the organised workmen were cognisant of that fact.

But at the same time the socialists appeared and began to make use of the Ricardian theory of value as a weapon against the middle classes and to teach Labour that not the Tory landowner but the Liberal capitalist was their real enemy. Ricardo made labour the corner-stone of his system and yet he permitted the capitalist to appropriate accumulated labour and to decide the fate of the working classes. Ricardo looked upon social life from the point of view of Capital, the socialist looked upon life from the point of view of Labour. Ricardo asserted that the capitalist was everything and the landowner nothing, and yet the latter received the lion's share of the national income. Rent swallowed up profits and wages :—

> " See these inglorious Cincinnati swarm,
> Farmers of war, dictators of the farm ;
> *Their* ploughshare was the sword in hireling hands,
> *Their* fields manured by gore of other lands ;
> Safe in their barns, these Sabine tillers sent
> Their brethren out to battle—why ? for rent !
> Year after year they voted cent. per cent.,
> Blood, sweat, and tear-wrung millions—why ? for rent !
> They roar'd, they dined, they drank, they swore they meant
> To die for England—why then live ?—for rent ! "
>
> (Byron, *The Age of Bronze*, xiv.)

While Byron was voicing the sentiments of rising Liberalism, the socialists asserted that the capitalists and the landowners were nothing, the working men everything, and yet the latter, even under the most favourable circumstances, received but food, clothing, and shelter as a compensation for the produce of their labour or for the national wealth they created : Society rests on injustice, on the robbing of Labour, and ought to be either radically mended or ended :

> " Men of England, wherefore plough
> For the lords who lay ye low ?
> Wherefore weave with toil and care
> The rich robes your tyrants wear ?
>   *   *   *   *
> " Wherefore, Bees of England, forge
> Many a weapon, chain, and scourge,
> That these stingless drones may spoil
> The forced produce of your toil ?
>   *   *   *   *
> " The seed ye sow, another reaps ;
> The wealth ye find, another keeps ;
> The robes ye weave, another wears ;
> The arms ye forge, another bears."

Shelley created the song of rising socialism. Ricardo, Byron, and Shelley were ushering in a period of social warfare, in which England was transformed from an Oligarchy into a Democracy. Manufacturing and trading capital found its theorist in Ricardo ; Liberalism its bard in Byron ; Communism and social justice found in Shelley, a poet,—visionary, passionate, and transcending reality.

3.—CURRENCY AND SOCIAL REFORM

The period of the Economic Revolution and Napoleonic Wars gave rise to prolonged and intricate controversies on currency which also influenced the social agitators for many years and played no small part in the Owenite and Chartist literature. Up to the foundation of the Bank of England the media of exchange were gold, silver, and bills of exchange. With the establishment of the Bank the nation soon realised that paper, even when only partly covered by gold and silver, could be made into money.   This was a new experience which, at first, met with difficulties, but finally won the day.   Since 1774, gold began gradually to be regarded as the only proper and legal basis of money, and in 1816 Parliament declared it to be the only legal tender—England accepted monometallism.   It was this period (1774–1816) which bristled with difficulties, theoretical and practical, about money.   The expansion of agriculture (rapid enclosing of lands), manufacture, and commerce, on the one hand, and the enormous expenditure and loans for war purposes on the other, led to the Bank Restriction (1797) which made paper the legal tender.   The country was suffering from a lack of gold and silver, the Bank suspended specie payment and issued one-pound-notes, and many private business men issued token money for the purpose of paying wages to their workmen.   Although the price of gold gradually rose and paper money suffered depreciation, many currency reformers could not rid themselves of the new and astonishing experience that paper could be made into money even if totally deprived of its metallic basis.

As far as our subject of social reform is concerned there were two kinds of currency writers.   Some of them argued that the proper basis of money was the productive power of the nation. Money being the medium of exchange of goods and labour there ought to be as much money in the country as to facilitate the exchanges.   No good standing business man ought to be hampered by lack of the circulating medium in his transactions. The banks which were licensed to issue notes should issue and lend him as much paper money as he needed.   Other reformers were of opinion that money was merely a receipt for goods produced, which receipt enabled the producer to exchange them for goods of equal value.

The former writers on currency were numerous and had their representatives in Parliament, who, in the first decade of the nineteenth century, spoke in favour of their theories.   One of their most active pupils was Thomas Attwood (1783–1856), the son of a Birmingham banker, who in the years from 1816 to 1819 issued several pamphlets on currency reform, and in the years from 1829 to 1839 was prominently associated with, and often the leader of, all popular movements in Birmingham and the Midlands. In 1816, the year of the final victory of gold over silver and the year of the beginning distress, he published a pamphlet entitled *The Remedy, or Thoughts on the present Distress;* one year later he issued *A Letter to Mr. Vansittart on the Creation of Money,* and in 1819 a pamphlet *Observations on Currency, Population, and Pauperism,* in form of a letter to Mr. Arthur Young ; the latter pamphlet being intended to show that the resumption of specie payment by the Bank of England in conformity with the so-called Peel's Act (1819), *i.e.,* on the basis of gold, was injurious also to the landed interests.[1] Attwood's theory may be outlined as follows :—

All riches come from labour in agriculture, manufacture, and trade. All labour comes from the population. With the increase of the population the needs multiply, and also the resources and exertions of society to satisfy those needs. Increase of the population means therefore increase of production and wealth. This progress has no limits. But the employment of labour and the production of wealth are only rendered possible through the agency of the circulating medium. The invention of money has done more for the progress of society than any other. It facilitated division of labour and thus led to all the other inventions and improvements of which Adam Smith speaks. Hence it follows that if the population increases the quantity of the circulating medium must be increased, else it becomes unequal to its increased duties, and the population becomes redundant, which really means a shortage of the circulating medium. Labour and employment cannot be brought together, goods remain unexchanged, with the result that stagnation and misery overtake society. It is therefore evident that the well-being of the society depends on the facility with which capital is exchanged for industry, and consumption for production. The medium which facilitates this process of circulation is money, which not only must exist in an adequate quantity, but must be elastic enough to expand with the expansion of population,

[1] A summary of these currency theories and an elaboration of their arguments are given in *Gemini Letters,* 1844.

labour, and wealth.   Has the Government, whose chief business
is supposed to be the promotion of the welfare of society, given
us such an expansive currency ?   No !   Instead of an elastic
circulating medium it took great pains to establish a restricted
and restricting currency.   Were gold a home commodity easily
procurable there would be nothing to object to it ; such a commodity would be capable of satisfying the needs of an expanding
productive population.   Gold is, however, the product of oversea
countries ; it is not easily procurable ; moreover, it is subject to
fluctuations which are beyond our control.   We are thus suffering
from the contradiction of an expanding society and a restricted
medium of exchange.   Population, trade, and commerce are
being strangulated.   Hence the distress.

Attwood belongs to the usual type of revolutionary thinkers,
who are possessed with one idea which they use for the interpretation of past and present history.   They bend, stretch, and
break the facts until they are made to prove that that idea under-
lies or controls the whole course of human history.   Attwood
argued that it was the paper currency following upon the Bank
Restriction which enabled England to carry the Napoleonic Wars
to a successful issue.   In his eyes this period was prosperous,
trade and commerce flourished, and the working classes were
peaceful.   But as soon as the Government, giving way to the
financiers, jobbers, and Jews, began to prepare measures for the
resumption of specie payments, business slackened and distress
set in.   After 1819 it was Peel's Act to which he ascribed every
evil, and when, in the course of the trade cycle, distress gradually
disappeared and the country enjoyed years of prosperity, Attwood
was quite sure that they were preceded by a large issue of paper
notes.   On the whole, he refused to believe that England could
ever prosper as long as Peel's Act remained in force.   The remedy
for this deplorable state of things was of course a return to the
period of the Bank Restriction and creation of paper money on
the basis of the productive power of the nation.   To make gold
the basis of the circulating medium, he argued, was tantamount
to making the social pyramid stand on its apex.

To the objection that England was not suffering from a shortage of money, but of markets, Attwood replied with the question, What were markets ? Markets were created by our needs, and most of the needs of the productive classes or the great majority of the nation remained unsatisfied. The home market should be first supplied. The productive classes were the creators of wealth and would form a most profitable home market if the opportunity were given to them to employ their skill at remunerative wages. The capitalists were comparatively few in number and their whole work consisted in accumulating property. The labouring classes, on the other hand, formed the great majority of the population and would consume most of the goods if capital could be readily converted into industry. And this would be the case if the currency were based on reasonable principles. The cry of the nation should therefore be, Break the strangulating gold chains from our body politic ! Let the circulation move freely and easily ! Without such measures all other reforms must prove futile. Parliamentary reform, abolition of the Corn Laws, reduction of taxes, emigration, sexual restraint, etc., etc. would avail nought as long as the circulation was fettered.

The establishment of gold as legal tender had also caused much harm to the farmers, debtors, and taxpayers. For, in consequence of the gold basis of money, the prices fell considerably, while the contracts, national debt, and private debts, made during the war period, when prices ruled high, remained, and no corresponding abatement was arranged.[1]

The influence of the currency controversies on Owen and John Gray will be dealt with in a subsequent chapter.

[1] For a refutation of the paper money theorists see J. S. Mill, *Principles of Political Economy*, book 3, chap. 13, § 4.

V

ROBERT OWEN

I.—PERSONALITY AND INFLUENCE

THE central figure of British Socialism in the first half of the nineteenth century was distinguished neither by original philosophic speculations nor outstanding literary achievements, but by strength of character and untiring reform activities. He witnessed and took part in the rise and development of the industrial revolution, the social agitations, the struggles of the working classes for economic and political power. His influence on the movements of this period was considerable, and is still being felt. His strong and simple intellect, perfect bodily health and even temper, always under the control of reason, resulted in an unbroken, energetic, and straight-aiming volition, in a self-confidence and rapidity of resolution which destined him for the leadership of men. These qualities, mostly the result of heredity and natural gifts, were ascribed by Owen to his having early gained the conviction that the character of man was formed for him by the circumstances into which he was born, and in which he lived. As soon as Owen had attained to that truth, which was with him one of his few leading principles, his " mind became simple in the arrangement of ideas," and " in consequence, gradually became calm and serene, and anger and ill-will died within " him.[1] But he has failed to explain why so many of his brother rationalists, who were imbued with the same opinions, never attained to that simplicity of reasoning, serenity of mind, capacity for leadership, and social reform activities, which made him so conspicuous a personality.

That was one side of Owen's character.

Beneath his armour of dispassionate logic burned a

[1] *Life of Robert Owen* (Autobiography), 1857, I., p. 30.

heart with the glow of compassion for the labouring poor, and an imagination fed by social visions. He united in his personality the shrewdness and keen eye of the business man with the emotionalism and ecstasies of the prophet. As long as the management of textile workers and the business of cotton spinning in Manchester and New Lanark were uppermost in his mind, his emotions and imaginings were controlled by his strong and cool reason. He then marched from success to success ; the apprentice in a drapery shop at Stamford became, at the age of twenty years, manager of one of the largest factories in Manchester, then factory owner, finally partner of one of the greatest manufacturing establishments in Scotland and rationalist educator of his numerous employees. Wealth and fame were his. Without any conscious effort on his part, he exacted cheerful obedience from his subordinates, and even men of incomparably superior education and higher station of life than Owen's willingly paid their tribute of respect to his understanding and sterling worth. Princes, dukes, and lords admired his educational and philanthropic work, and New Lanark became, for a time, particularly from 1815 to 1820, the Mecca of reformers. The son of a Welsh saddler and ironmonger, with a scanty education at a village school, became one of the best public speakers and writers of lucid and vigorous English.[1] As soon, however, as he had left the sphere of trade, commerce, and philanthropy, and dedicated himself to the mission of a saviour of mankind, his shrewd realism, exactness of statement, and wonderful executive capacity came to an end. Of his long life from 1771 to 1858, the years from 1817 onwards increasingly exemplified to the second phase of his career, which was strewn with failures, material losses, disappointments. His outlook on society became blurred, his social criticism marred by exaggeration, his inferences degenerated into prophecies, and his charming and disarming *naïveté* had much of the credulity of a child.

Still, his infinite charity and love of humanity cover a multitude of shortcomings ; and his insight into some of the meanings of the new inventions, the services rendered to infant education,

[1] Robert Southey, *Sir Thomas More, or Colloquies*, 1829, I., p. 144.

M

factory legislation, and the co-operative efforts of the working classes have secured for him one of the foremost places in the history of socialism.

Owen was the first British socialist who did not turn to the past for inspiration, but attempted to put the productive forces, unlocked by modern science, into the service of collective production and distribution, first on behalf of the unemployed, and afterwards of society as a whole. He was immensely impressed by the facilities for wealth production which the new machinery afforded. It seemed to him that inanimate machinery, tended by a comparatively small number of manual labourers, would soon be capable of supplying the needs of mankind. What was, then, to become of the working classes ? Yet, for all his propaganda among the labouring population he was no democrat. He was always with them, but never of them. He could be their self-sacrificing father and teacher, their authoritative adviser and leader, but never the *primus inter pares*. He was perfectly free from all demagogy. In telling the working classes that labour was the source of wealth, he never failed to qualify it by adding that only " well-directed " or " properly-directed " labour was the fountain of riches and standard of value. Moreover, it was only modern machinery which caused the sources of wealth to flow abundantly.[1] He, at first, used to speak of them as " lower orders " ; then, with the rise of co-operation, trade unionism, mechanics' institutes, and Chartism, he called them " productive classes." From him they learned socialism, but it was essentially co-operative socialism and not militant socialism. He was strongly opposed to strikes, trades-unionist policy, and class warfare. His struggle was not primarily against usurpation and wickedness, but against error and ignorance, of which both the possessing classes and the labouring poor were the victims.

Which was that cardinal and fateful error ?

[1] *On the Proposed Arrangements of Mr. Owen,* 1819 (Three Letters to Mr. Ricardo).

2.—LEADING PRINCIPLES

Bentham's formula is Owen's premise. The object of all human exertions is happiness. Yet, happy individuals are rare exceptions, and happy nations do not exist at all. This state of things cannot have been caused by a perversion of the human will, since volition is not the prime mover of human actions. Like all rationalists, Owen is of opinion that reason, the prime materials of which are impressions, governs man. Reason, badly or falsely trained, creates evil. Hence the cause of the failure of man to achieve his object must be sought in some error of judgment. It consists, according to Owen, in the current and generally accepted belief that man makes his own character, while the truth is that man's character is made for him by the circumstances into which he is born and in which he lives and works. Inferior conditions produce inferior men ; good circumstances create good characters. Evil conditions are those that favour ignorance, selfishness, misery, illness, fear, untruthfulness, hypocrisy, superstition, enmity, and war. These conditions prevail to-day, and their fruit is unhappiness,

The first business of the reformer is, manifestly, to spread the truth concerning the formation of character in order to gain universal consent for such a change of circumstances that would create good characters. These views he elaborated in his four *Essays on the Formation of Character*, written in the years 1813–15.[1]

The creation of good circumstances depends, next, on an abundance of wealth. Without such an abundance the lot of the many must be poverty, and poverty is one of the evil circumstances, for it causes ignorance, bad health and cowardice. These ideas are dealt with in Owen's pamphlets, *Observations on the Effect of the Manufacturing System*, *Report on the Poor*, *Memorial to the Allied Powers*, and *Report to the County of Lanark*, written in 1815–20.[2]

Rationalist psychology and social economics are Owen's main fields of research. The spreading of the principles of both

[1] Reprinted in *Life of Owen*, I., pp. 257–332.   [2] *Ib.*, IA.

are alike important. For as long as the old conception of character-building prevails the infinite multiplication of wealth will only be exploited by the few to the detriment of the many, while as long as the material resources are scanty the opposition of the possessing and ruling minority to any reform will be overwhelming, and poverty will remain the lot of the majority.

The great importance of our times is that both requisites for universal happiness are at hand. The new truth concerning the formation of character is being revealed, and wealth is being produced at an unprecedented rate. The time for human emancipation has arrived. Owen, as the new character-builder, on the one hand, and the inventors of the industrial machinery, on the other, are creating that great crisis or turning-point in human history. He has shown what could be done by education and benevolent care for the working people, and under modern industrial conditions, with the machinery created by science, wealth can be made as plentiful as water. The rich will therefore sacrifice nothing by consenting to a change of conditions by social arrangements in favour of all. And the poor need no more envy and hate the rich, since the opportunity will soon be given to them to produce as much wealth as they liked.

Owen exclaimed : " Any general character, from the best to the worst, from the most ignorant to the most enlightened, may be given to any community, even to the world at large, by the application of proper means ; which means are, to a great extent, at the command and under the control of those who have influence in the affairs of men." Given the proper circumstances, it is best to begin with the formation of the character of the infants, for these being " passive and wonderfully contrived compounds . . . can be trained to acquire any language, sentiments, belief, or any habits and manners, not contrary to human nature " (*First Essay on the Formation of Character*). Side by side with training must go the opportunity for " honest and useful employments to those so trained," by which means " some of the circumstances which tend to generate, continue, or increase, early bad habits " will be withdrawn. This truth, combined with the evident fact that the world is now being saturated with wealth, render the emancipation of mankind possible. And it is high time to prepare the way for it, for, " those who have duly reflected on the nature and extent of the mental movements of the world for the last half century, must be conscious that great changes are in progress ; that man is about to advance another important step toward that degree of intelligence which his natural powers seem capable of attaining. Observe the transactions of the passing hours ; see the whole mass of mind in full motion ; behold it momentarily increasing in vigour, and preparing, ere long, to burst its confinement " (*Third Essay on the Formation of Character*).

Owen was evidently a careful observer of the growing ferment and agitation among the working classes, and the knowledge gathered therefrom accelerated his reform activity. He gradually entered upon his missionary career of emancipating mankind from misery. It must have been a moment of ecstasy when the full import of his mission flashed upon his mind. The elements had been slowly gathering, and in 1817 they coalesced. The shrewd cotton spinner of New Lanark was reborn as a socialist. Private initiative, he saw, would give to the labouring poor neither education nor employment, " for the children of commerce have been trained to direct all their faculties to buy cheap and sell dear ; and, consequently, those who are the most expert and successful in this wise and noble art, are, in the commercial world, deemed to possess foresight and superior acquirements ; while such as attempt to improve the moral habits and increase the comforts of those whom they employ, are termed wild enthusiasts " (*Third Essay*). Owen, therefore, asked the Government to carry out the task of national education and national employment in order to create those circumstances which were favourable to the formation of good characters. It was in 1817 that he began to see the evil and good circumstances, in the shape of an antithesis of capitalism and socialism or competition and co-operation.

3.—FACTORY LEGISLATION.

Prior to 1817, Owen's definition of bad circumstances did not go beyond sweating, ignorance, and enmity. It did not imply any radical change of the system of property, but amelioration through private initiative and legislative action. In 1813 or 1814, Owen exhorted his fellow-manufacturers and superintendents to devote more attention to the welfare of the operatives. " Experience has also shown you," he told them, " the difference of the results between mechanism, which is clean, well-arranged, and always in a high state of repair ; and that which is allowed to be dirty, in disorder, without the means of preventing unnecessary friction, and which, therefore, becomes and works out of repair. In the first case the whole economy and management are good ; every operation proceeds with ease, order, and success. In the last, the reverse must follow, and a scene be presented of counteraction, confusion, and dissatisfaction among all the agents and instruments interested or occupied in the general process, which cannot fail to create great loss. If, then, due care as to the state of your inanimate machines can produce such beneficial results, what may not be expected if you devote equal attention to your vital machines, which are far more wonderfully constructed ? . . . Will you not afford some of your attention to consider whether a portion of your time and capital would not be more advantageously applied to improve your living machines ? " [1]

In the years 1815–18 Owen devoted a great deal of his time and money to the propaganda of Factory Legislation and relief of the unemployed. His success was by no means equal to his efforts, but his insight into the effects of the Industrial Revolution widened and deepened from the necessity imposed upon him of proving the truth of his propositions and the practicability of his demands. He had started as a rationalist educator and psychologist, he now became a social economist. In order to interest his fellow-employers in his plans, he, in 1815, convened a meeting in Glasgow of the Scotch manufacturers, with a view to consider

[1] *Life of Owen*, I., pp. 260–1.

the advisability and policy of asking the Government to remit the heavy duty on the importation of cotton, and, further, to consider measures for the improvement of the condition of the young children and others employed in the various textile manufactures. Owen spoke on the objects of the meeting, but while the audience was enthusiastically in favour of the remission of the cotton duties, not one person rose to second his motion for the protection of the textile workers. The preparations he had made for the address to this meeting and the experience he had gained from the attitude of the audience enabled and impelled him to write his first economic pamphlet, *Observations on the Effect of the Manufacturing System* (1815). Having shown the growing preponderance of trade and manufacture over agriculture, he proceeds to describe the cause of those changes. " The change has been owing chiefly to the mechanical inventions which introduced the cotton trade into this country." The foreign trade extended, and the wealth, industry, population, and influence of the British Empire increased so rapidly that by their aid the nation was able to carry on the war against France for twenty-five years. But " these results have been accompanied with evils of such a magnitude as to raise a doubt whether the latter do not preponderate over the former. Hitherto, legislators have appeared to regard manufactures from the point of view of wealth. The other mighty consequences which proceed from extended manufactures when left to their natural progress have never yet engaged the attention of any legislature. The general diffusion of manufactures throughout a country generates a new character in its inhabitants ; and as this character is formed upon a principle quite unfavourable to individual or general happiness, it will produce the most lamentable results, unless the tendency be counteracted by legislative interference and direction."

Owen then proceeds to draw a dark picture of the deterioration of the character of the commercial and working classes, through the lust of gain and exploitation, and urges upon the Government to limit the regular hours of labour in mills of machinery to twelve per day, including one and half for meals ; to prohibit the employ-

ment of children under ten years, or for longer than six hours
daily, until they reach the age of twelve years ; after a time to
be named, children shall not be admitted into any factory until
they can read and write and understand the first four rules of
arithmetic.   For the success of this legislative measure he worked
for three years, until it was embodied, in form of a compromise
with the opposing interests, in the Factory Act, 1819.

Owen always believed that he had been the main driving power
of that Act.   On the other hand, Alexander Ure, whose knowledge of the history of the factory system was considerable,
ascribed that law to the " strikes and turmoils " of the Lancashire
cotton spinners in the years 1817 and 1818.[1]

Owen's pamphlet contains also a curious prophecy.   He
thought it was highly probable " that the export trade of this
country has attained its utmost height, and that by the competition of other States possessing equal or greater advantages
it will soon gradually diminish.   The direct effect of the Corn
Bill lately passed will be to hasten this decline and prematurely
to destroy that trade.   It is deeply to be regretted that the Bill
passed, and I am convinced that a repeal will be ere long absolutely necessary in order to prevent the misery of the people."

This was written in 1815, and during the whole of the nineteenth century the export trade was increasing and is still
increasing.   Of the unfulfilled prophecies concerning the down-
fall of capitalism there is no end.

4.—UNEMPLOYMENT AND SOCIALISM

The distress which set in towards the end of 1816 was the first
crisis caused, not by scarcity, but by over-production.   The supply
was outstripping demand.   The number of unemployed increased
at an alarming rate, public opinion became agitated, meetings
were convened and committees appointed to investigate the
cause of the distress and find a remedy for it.   The demands of
the poor for parish relief increased to such an extent that the
House of Commons appointed a Committee on Poor Laws.
Robert Owen, having found it impossible to explain his views

[1] Ure, *Philosophy of Manufactures*, Bohn's Library, p. 288.

upon the matter to a committee appointed by a meeting of the leading men of London, wrote a report for the Parliamentary Committee on Poor Laws, March, 1817.[1] A year later he further elaborated his reforms on behalf of the working classes in a Memorial to the Allied Powers assembled in Congress at Aix-la-Chapelle,[2] and in 1819 he caused one of his literary friends, probably George Mudie (editor of the *Economist*, 1821–2), to write a number of open letters to Mr. Ricardo on the same subject.[3] The gist of these pamphlets is that machinery facilitated production to such a degree that the world was becoming saturated with wealth. As long as manual labour was the main source of wealth demand and supply balanced. Production and population were to each other as 1 to 1. In the years 1792 to 1817 the proportion changed enormously. Production and population were now as 12 to 1. As machinery worked cheaper than manual labour, the latter was being depreciated or displaced. The total wage bill of the country diminished ; the working classes lost, therefore, much of the fund from which they satisfied their needs, the home market contracted, and the produced commodities remained unsold in the barns and warehouses. When the invention of the steam engine and other machines was made, either the greatest blessing or the greatest curse was bestowed upon society. At present, the latter prevailed, and a considerable portion of the British population was doomed to pauperism. It was in vain for manual labour to contend, under the present conditions, with the sinews of mechanism. On the other hand, if it were possible to make consumption keep pace with production, labour and capital would be beneficially employed, and distress would be unknown. But this could not be the case as long as private gain, and not social welfare, ruled economic life. As things stood now, production would more and more outstrip consumption, for the export trade must gradually decrease, and the home market contract, and, therefore, unemployment and insecurity of existence increase, until the working classes, finding their remuneration either gone or reduced below the means of

---

[1] *Life of Owen*, IA., pp. 53–63.   [2] *Ib.*, pp. 212–22.
[3] *Mr. Owen's Proposed Arrangements*, 1819.

subsistence, would be goaded into fury and despair, and suddenly overwhelm our noble and beneficent institutions and lay them in ruins. " We resemble individuals standing on the narrow causeway of a surrounding abyss." And all that happened because the human mind, after countless ages of struggle with poverty and ignorance, finally succeeded in unlocking the sources of wealth ; in multiplying the productive forces ; in rendering the production of goods easy. It was abundance that brought upon us misery ! Large masses of producers were being thrown upon the Poor Laws because they had produced too much wealth ! How paradoxical it all looked ! What was the remedy ? Some said Poor Law Reform ; others advised emigration. But all remedies of that kind would do no good, for they did not touch the problem. The real cure lay in arrangements that would enlarge consumption and make it tally with production. Such arrangements were conditioned upon combined labour and expenditure, or communism.

However, the remedy could only be applied gradually. First of all, the problem of unemployment must be dealt with. " Under the existing laws the unemployed working classes are maintained by, and consume a part of, the property and produce of the wealthy and industrious, while their power of body and mind remain unproductive. They frequently acquire the bad habits which ignorance and idleness never fail to produce ; most of the poor have received bad habits from their parents ; and as long as this present treatment continues those bad and vicious habits will be transmitted to their children, and through them to succeeding generations." The care of the unemployed must therefore include education, and circumstances must be created for them in which duty and interest would coincide. The bodily and mental power of the poor should be used for their own benefit as well as for that of society as a whole. All those advantages could be realised by establishing Villages of Unity and Co-operation, consisting each of 500 to 1,500 persons and 1000 to 1,500 acres of land for agricultural and manufacturing purposes, with blocks of houses erected in such a manner as to enclose large squares. The establishment of such a co-operative village would require a capital outlay of £96,000. This sum, divided by 1,200 (the number of persons), gave £80 per head, or, at 5 per cent. interest, the sum of £4 per annum. With so small an expenditure, an unemployed workman could be made to maintain himself and family, educate his children, and even repay the capital charge. In the squares of the Co-operative Villages would be erected public buildings so as to divide the squares into parallelograms or quadrangles.

Owen's unemployed reform remained on paper, and became known jocularly as Owen's Parallelograms. He was opposed practically by the whole nation. Even the working men of London voted against his string of resolutions on Unemployment, which he had laid before two public meetings, in August, 1817, in the City of London Tavern. The London artisans sided at that time with the advocates of Parliamentary reform as against social reform of a coercive or patriarchal nature. An Owenite complained that the " lower orders are quite assured that a radical reform of the House of Commons must prove the grand panacea for all our woes." [1] Owen ascribes his defeat to machinations of the Churches and the Political Economists. Owen always regarded these two London meetings as the turning-point in his life.[2] Speaking on August 21, 1817, in the City of London Tavern, he denounced all religions of the world as now taught as gross errors. It was they that prevented mankind " from knowing what happiness really is." And the Political Economists, "including Malthus, Mill, Ricardo, Colonel Torrens, Hume, and Place . . . were all well-intentioned, clever, acute men, close reasoners, and great talkers upon a false principle. . . . I was most desirous to convince them that national education and employment could alone create a permanent, rational, intelligent, wealthy, and superior population, and that these results could be attained only by a scientific arrangement of the people, united in properly-constructed villages of unity and co-operation. While they, on the contrary, strongly desired to convert me to their views of instructing the people without find-

[1] *Mr. Owen's Proposed Arrangements*, 1819, p. 4.
[2] *Life of Owen*, IA., p. 161.

ing them national united employment, and of a thorough
system of individual competition. The one may be called the
system of universal attraction ; the other, that of universal
repulsion." [1]

Owen was now fast drifting into socialism. On September 6,
1817, he wrote a letter to the press on " Relief of the Poor and
Emancipation of Mankind." Soon after he published a brief
sketch, written by Mr. Warder, a Philadelphian Quaker, dealing
with the communistic arrangements of the Shakers, in order to
show that " even with an inferior communistic life, wealth could
be easily created for all " ; he also republished John Beller's
Colledge of Industry, to which Francis Place had called his attention.[2] Owen was now clear in his mind that the first step of social
reform was to create a superior physical and mental character
for all ; the second step was to produce abundance of wealth
for all ; the third step would be to unite the two first by basing
society on its true principle, *i.e.*, " by placing all within such
arrangements of surroundings as will well-form the character,
create the wealth, and cordially unite all in one interest and
feeling over the world." [3]

Undeterred by the failure of his plan to form villages of co-
operation for the unemployed, he laboured assiduously in London
for his ideas, and, in 1819, a committee consisting of the Duke of
Kent, Sir Robert Peel, David Ricardo, and W. Tooke, was formed
in order to raise subscriptions for an experimental establishment of a " Parallelogram," but no adequate amount of subscriptions came in, and the committee dissolved in November,
1819. Robert Southey, evidently grieved at the failure of Owen's
committee, comments upon it, saying that if Owen " had not
alarmed the better part of the nation by proclaiming, upon the
most momentous of all subjects [religion], opinions which are
alike fatal to individual happiness and the general good," he
might have, ere this, seen the firstfruits of his labours. " For the
connection between moral truth and political wisdom is close
and indissoluble ; and he who shows himself erroneous upon one

[1] *Life of Owen*, I., p. 129.   [2] *Ib.*, IA., pp. 119–60.
                     [3] *Ib.*, I., p. 243.

important point, must look to have his opinions properly dis-trusted upon others." [1]

5.—SOCIAL RECONSTRUCTION AND CURRENCY REFORM

The enormous efforts made by Owen in the years 1815–19 produced no tangible result. Apart from the Factory Act, 1819, the honours of which he must undoubtedly share with the Lancashire cotton operatives, nothing was achieved in the way of the relief of the unemployed or communist experiment. In 1819, he issued an *Address to the Workmen*, offering them his whole-hearted assistance in their striving for emancipation from misery and ignorance, but under the condition that they should first accept and imbue themselves with his doctrine of the formation of human character in order to renounce all violence and hatred against the possessing and ruling classes. As long as they showed themselves impervious to that truth, there was no hope of saving them from the depths of misery and darkness ; the new light which he had to reveal might then prove too strong, and cause more mischief than good. Owen was evidently of opinion that it would do no good to society to reveal to the workmen the mysteries of wealth-making and the principle of communism before they had made a successful attempt to re-moralise their character, to extinguish their violent class-warfare against the rich. He therefore explained to them his psychological theory, and told them that (*a*) Rich and Poor, the governors and the governed, had in reality the same interests ; (*b*) The upper classes had no more the desire to degrade the workmen or to keep them in subjection ; (*c*) The labouring masses possessed now the means for emancipating themselves and their posterity from economic misery, but that the knowledge of those means must be withheld from them until they fully comprehended that rich and poor were alike the creatures of circumstances, and that, therefore, all personal enmity was senseless ; (*d*) The past ages belonged to the history of human irrationality, and that now the dawn of reason was beginning.[2]

[1] Robert Southey, *Sir Thomas More, or Colloquies*, 1829, I., pp. 130–2.
[2] *Ib.*, Ia., pp. 224–31.

The working classes, however, were at that time fully occupied with the agitation for Parliamentary Reform, and Owen's exhortations remained unheeded. He then returned to Scotland, where he twice stood as a Parliamentary candidate, and was defeated. In 1820, the County of Lanark applied to him for a remedy against lack of employment and falling wages. Owen wrote his *Report to the County of Lanark* (1820), in which he gave a full exposition of his communist teachings as well as of currency reform.

This document deals also with one of his minor proposals—the discarding of plough cultivation for spade cultivation, but for the understanding of Owenism it is of no importance, it being accidental and logically unconnected with communism, although it played, later, some part in the Owenite movement.

As far as the communist teachings are concerned, there is nothing new in the Report ; they present a good and clear summary of Owen's economic views, which he had treated in his pamphlets in the years 1815–19. They are only bolder and more complete as coming from a courageous thinker who had passed the Rubicon, and who, moreover, had come to the conclusion that agriculture and manufacture on commercial lines were " on the eve of bankruptcy." [1] On the other hand, the views on currency and value, which this Report contains, are a substantial addition to Owenism. They exercised a considerable influence on the later movement, and led to practical experiments. Prior to 1820, Owen believed that the sources of evil were the error of character-building and mal-distribution of wealth ; he now began to disseminate the view that the form of exchange and the circulating medium were also at the root of social misery. His premise was the same as Attwood's, but the opinion of John Bellers on money appears also to have influenced him. In his *Colledge of Industry* (1696) Bellers declares that the " colledge fellowship " or communistic establishment " will make labour, and not money, the standard to value all necessaries by." Money had its mischiefs, and was called by

[1] *Report to the County of Lanark*, in *Life of Owen*, IA., p. 270.

the Saviour the Mammon of Unrighteousness ; although land and labour were the true riches, yet they could not be made productive if money was lacking. In reality, " money in the body politic is what a crutch is to the natural body, crippled ; but when the body is sound the crutch is but troublesome. So when the particular interest is made a public interest, in such a colledge money will be of little use." [1]

Owen, stimulated by Attwood, Bellers, and the public discussions on money which were caused by the introduction of monometalism (1816) and resumption of specie payment (1819), treated also currency and standard of value reform in his *Report*. He argues that the distress for which the County of Lanark was looking for a remedy showed that, under present arrrangements, no remedy was procurable. The wealth of the country had grown too rapidly and no measures had been taken for directing the overflow into proper channels. Society was suffering from an excess of production and weakened by maldistribution, caused partly by the mode of property, and partly by bad circulation. Effective measures must, therefore be taken for a re-arrangement of the system of property and the standard of value or the circulating medium. In taking such measures the following principles must be borne in mind : (a) " Manual labour, properly directed, is the source of all wealth and national prosperity ; (b) When properly directed, labour is of far more value to the community than the expense necessary to maintain the labourer in considerable comfort ; (c) Manual labour, properly directed, may be made to continue of this value in all parts of the world under any supposable increase of its population for many centuries to come ; (d) Wealth will grow faster than population." There need be no fear of change. With reasonable measures, such a change would literally " let prosperity loose on the country." One of the measures was a change in the standard of value. It was quite true that, in the civilised parts of the world, gold and silver had long been used for this purpose, but they had changed the intrinsic values of all things into artificial values, promoted fraudulent commerce and specula-

[1] Reprint in *Life of Owen*, IA, pp. 164 *et seq.*

tion, and, in consequence, materially retarded the general improvement of society. It was fortunate, however, that the Bank Restriction (1797) had taught Englishmen that gold and silver could no longer represent the increased wealth. Paper became legal tender, but this measure at the same time placed the community at the mercy of a trading company, which was ignorant of the mighty machine it wielded. Gold was restored to its ancient dignity, but, being inadequate for the circulation of the increased wealth, it aggravated the crisis, poverty, discontent, and danger. The restoration of the metallic currency was like forcing a grown-up person to put on the swaddling-cloth of its infancy. It cramped the body politic. Hence the unparalleled depression of agriculture, commerce, and manufacture, and the total annihilation of the value of labour. The remedy was a change in the standard of value. " The natural standard of value is, in principle, human labour, or the combined manual and mental powers of man called into action." A certain quantity of such labour should form the unit of value, and the labourer who performed it should get a paper note certifying the number of units of value he had produced, with which note he would be able to obtain the necessary goods containing an equal number of units of value.

It might be objected that human labour was unequal, and therefore could not form the measure of value. Against this it was only necessary to point out that horse power was also unequal, and yet served as the measure of mechanical power. Surely, average human power could be found out, and, as it formed the essence of all wealth, its value in every article of produce might be ascertained and the relation of its exchange-value to other values fixed accordingly ; the whole to be permanent for a given period, until progress of science had brought further facilities for wealth production and made a revaluation necessary. Human labour would thus acquire again its natural or intrinsic value, which would increase as science advanced ; and this was, in fact, the only useful object of science. The demand for human labour would no longer be subject to caprice, nor would the support of human life be made a perpetually varying article of commerce, and the working classes made the slaves of an artificial system of wages, more cruel in its effects than any slavery ever practised by society. This change in the standard of value would immediately open the most advantageous home markets, until the wants of all were supplied, nor, while the standard continued, could any evil arise in future from the want of markets. For, if the labourer was rewarded according to a natural standard of value, he would receive a fair proportion of the product of labour. Consumption would keep pace with production.

There is much confusion of thought in these reasonings. Owen believed money and standard of value to be identical, whereas money but expresses the standard of value. He regarded gold and silver as artificial values, and did not see that they could only serve as measures of value because they are real values in themselves. Owen applied his reform also to conditions of private property. If, then, a labourer is to be remunerated according to the standard of labour value—*i.e.*, if a labourer received for six hours' work a certain quantity of goods embodying six hours' work, he would really receive also the additional value produced by machinery, management, organisation, or the profit of capital. Where should, then, the new capital come from ? Or the cost of maintenance, of science, and of administration ?

It seems, however, that Owen did not mean that the labourer should receive the full product of labour, but a fair wage, or a fixed proportion of the product, for after much discussion he finally arrives at the conclusion that a fair proportion of the product would be for the labourer sixpence an hour. The truth appears to be that Owen was caught in the whirlpool of the currency controversies in the years 1816–19, without having been able to extricate himself. A discordant and fissiparous character was hereby imparted to his social economic reasonings, which made itself felt in the course of development of the Owenite movement. Some Owenites became merely currency reformers, and busied themselves with remedies for the improvement of exchanges and the circulating medium. From the Owenites it

N

passed to the Chartists, and from the latter to the International Working Men's Association (1864–73).

There are thus in Owen's social system two currents of thought : (*a*) Social misery arises from the error concerning the formation of character, the excess of production over effective demand, and consequent mal-distribution ; (*b*) Social misery springs from or is considerably aggravated by artificial currency, deficient circulation. Against the former evils he recommends communism ; against the latter, labour notes as the circulating medium, and he leaves private property untouched. Owen undoubtedly preferred communism, but some of his followers regarded circulation and currency as the main point.

Although Owen and Attwood started from the same premise, and had the same views regarding the history of currency in the years 1790–1819, they differed considerably as regards the remedial measures. Attwood and his school desired a paper currency in order to enable manufacturers and merchants to get loans and to facilitate production. Owen, on the other hand, desired labour notes in order to enable the community to fix a fair rate of wages and to render the exchanges equitable.

The *Report to the County of Lanark* was held by Owen to be one of his best publications ; it gave, as he thought, " a full view of society in its whole extent, including every department of real life necessary for the happiness of our race. It was the first time that the outlines of a science of society were given to the world ; . . . and it was after the circulation of this report that the imaginative Fourier imagined his notions for forming a practical community society, mixing old and new principles and practices, which never can continue long to work together." [1]

In 1821, Owen wrote a treatise, *Social System*, published in 1826–7, in the *New Harmony Gazette*.[2] His way of thinking is completely communist, without any admixture of private property institutions. He was then already determined to retire from business and form a community in order to act by example. He directs his critical shafts against the political

[1] *Life of Owen*, I., pp. 238, 234.
[2] *New Harmony Gazette*, February 14, 1827 (note).

economists. They had totally misunderstood their subject. They had, in all cases, supposed that the sole object of society was the accumulation of riches and that men would necessarily obtain all they required in proportion as their wealth increased. They had always reasoned as though man were an inanimate machine, without the capacity of suffering, understanding, or enjoying. They had led the nation from error to error, until it had become evident that production was easier than distribution. At this moment the main sufferings of mankind arose from the excess of wealth and the excess of ignorance ; the political economists were powerless to alleviate the lot of the greatest number of the population ; their praise of individualism, competition and foreign trade had resulted in the degradation of the many by mal-distribution. The main problem was, therefore, not production, but proper distribution.

The real object of political economy or a science of society should be happiness for all. This object could only be attained to by a system of mutual aid and co-operation, or communities with equality of labour and equality of distribution. The achievements of science would then be accessible to all, and therefore cease to be a curse for the many. Every new mechanical invention would lead not to the displacement of the labourer, but to the abridgment of labour time. It would not aggravate the opposition of interests, but strengthen the community and harmony of interests, since under a system of equality of labour every member would have the interest of abridging and facilitating the process of production. Ignorance could not exist in such a society, since it was in the interest of all to educate and train every member and make him an efficient producer. Abundance of wealth joined to equal distribution would put an end to all economic crises. Equality of distribution would under such conditions appear quite natural. " With means thus ample to procure wealth with ease and pleasure to all, none will be so unwise as to desire to have the trouble and care of individual property. To divide riches among individuals in unequal proportions or to hoard it for individual purposes, will be perceived as useless and injurious as it would be to divide air or light into unequal quantities for different individuals, or that they should hoard them."[1]

In the years 1812–21, Owen was at the zenith of his mental powers. His activities in the following forty years, or from 1821 to his death in 1858, were either reiterations and propaganda of his views, at which he had arrived in the second decade of the nineteenth century, or attempts to put them into practice.

The leading representatives of the country of Lanark having refused to put the *Report* into operation, Owen made an effort to form a community at Motherwell, but failed to interest a sufficient number of wealthy people to subscribe the necessary capital. For all his authority and persuasive powers, he did not succeed, at that time, either in getting in touch with the leaders of the working classes, or in bringing his communist views to the test of experience. Baffled in his ardent desire for immediate and tangible results, interfered with even in his educational experiments in New Lanark, he failed to notice that he was making proselytes among intellectuals, stimulating several critics, and creating an Owenite school of thought destined to leave a deep impress on the movement of the working classes and their socialist leaders. His first adherents were Scotsmen, Irishmen, and Welshmen—George Mudie, Abram Combe, Archibald James Hamilton, William Thompson, John Gray, J. M. Morgan, who subsequently became the pioneers of Owenism, spreading its doctrines among the working classes and forming communities.

However, the disappointments and defeats which Owen had suffered since 1815 induced him to retire from business, and to leave Great Britain for America, where he thought to find free men, brought up in the spirit of the Declaration of Independence, and to form there a community. In 1824 he carried out his plan. He bought the Rappist community "Harmony," in the State of Indiana, for £30,000, and converted it into a New Harmony after his own model. His attention to that community had been drawn by reports of travellers, which were

[1] *The Book of the New Moral World*, 1836, Introduction, xxi.

reproduced by Evans, the Spencean, in his *Christian Policy* (1818), and by the anonymous writer of *Mr. Owen's Proposed Arrangements* (1819), at the end of the third letter to Ricardo. The Rappists, simple religious peasants from Germany, had bought, in 1814, about 30,000 acres of land, then a mere desert, and converted it, within a few years, into a flourishing communist settlement. Thither Owen repaired, and about 900 people, a motley of idealists, adventurers, and craftsmen, joined him. Only very few of them were capable of sustained effort or animated by the true pioneering spirit. After three years of much disharmony and constitution-making, the communist experiment ended in dismal failure. Owen lost his money, and finally returned to England, where, in the years 1832–44, he displayed great activity among the working classes. This period of his eventful life belongs, however, to the history of Chartism.

OWENITE AND RICARDIAN INFLUENCES

I.—SOCIALISM BASED ON CO-OPERATION

IN the years 1820 to 1830 the doctrines of Owen, supported by anti-capitalist deductions from Ricardo's theory of value, entered the wide field of working-class agitation, and coalesced into a system of socialism. The industrial, commercial, and political life of the nation favoured the dissemination and growth of the new views. The reign of George IV. marks the rise of Liberalism and the birth of the modern Labour Movement, political and socialistic. This decade saw the repeal of the Navigation Act, of the Combination Laws, of the Corporation and Test Acts ; it witnessed the destruction of the last remnants of the yeomanry, and the bulk of the handloom weavers ; in it occurred a short, but phenomenal spell of manufacturing and commercial prosperity (1824–5), accompanied by the biggest and hardest-fought strikes which the country had until then experienced ; after which one of the severest commercial crises overtook the nation, and the temper of agrarian and industrial labour became restive and rebellious. " King Ludd " reappeared in the manufacturing centres, and " Captain Swing " devastated the counties by fire. Capitalism appeared to be on its trial. Thinking people began to read Adam Smith again, to pore over Ricardo, with a critical eye, and even Owen, the visionary, found favour with some intellectuals. An era of economic criticism and co-operative experiment was ushered in, which laid the foundation of modern socialism, in the midst of a gloomy atmosphere and full of forebodings of the impending bankruptcy of capitalism. Socialism, at its birth, imbibed the dogma that industrialism meant short spells of prosperity, followed by chronic crises, pauperisation of the masses, and the sudden advent of the social revolution.

Two sets of social reformers and critics made then their appeals to the nation, and, particularly, to the working classes, whom they were beginning to designate producers or industrious classes. They were making their appeals to the workers, not as wage-slaves, but as producers of the wealth of the nation. One set consisted of individualists, who, whilst unsparing in their criticism of the capitalists, whom they regarded as non-producers, were not favourable to socialism, and practically demanded a return to the pre-capitalist era, but completely freed from the fetters of mercantilism ; they demanded, in short, a society of free, independent, small producers, agricultural and manufacturing, governed by natural laws of exchange—without any Government interference. The other set of reformers, though in agreement with the former as to the injurious effects of capitalism and State regulations, recommended socialism as the remedy for the wrongs of Labour and the ills of the nation at large. With the former we shall deal in a subsequent chapter. Our first business is the exposition of the doctrines of co-operative socialism.

This movement as it issued from purely Owenite sources, though supplemented by deductions from the Ricardian theory of value, was pacific, constructive, educational, and non-political. Class warfare, passionate appeals to the feelings of Labour, demands for legal enactments, and government reforms were regarded not only as utterly futile, but directly detrimental to the cause of the people ; even trade union activities, strikes, and coercion, were often condemned, and they were but tolerated in so far as they could lead to co-operative-socialist unions. The Owenites believed that all social evils and wrongs had their origin in error, in the neglect of natural rights, but not in ill-will and class antagonisms. Society was suffering because the nation allowed itself to be actuated by erroneous conceptions. The most mischievous effect of error regarding society was competition. Hence the proper methods of removing evil and wrong were the spreading of truth and the formation of co-operative communities, or other co-operative forms of economic life. The main representatives of these views were George

Mudie, Abram Combe, William Thompson, John Minter Morgan, and John Francis Bray, writers of ability and men of action. The most distinguished among them was William Thompson. The views they were spreading and practising may be called Orthodox Owenism. After the failure of Owen to enlist the sympathies of the ruling classes for his plan, he and his faithful adherents mainly appealed for the sympathies of the working classes, or rather of the more intelligent and better situated elements of Labour, and as these were generally organising themselves for fighting purposes into trade unions, the orthodox Owenites made great efforts to persuade them to convert these unions into co-operative-socialist societies, and to invest their funds in production on socialist lines, instead of wasting their money on bitter and futile strikes.

Organised labour never accepted complete Owenism. As a rule, they added to certain parts of it political action or trade union action. One of their most gifted leaders, William Lovett, relates that he and his friends, after having read and admired the writings of Robert Owen, Peter (probably a mistake for William) Thompson, Morgan, Gray, and others, " resolved to be instrumental to the extent of their means and their abilities in spreading a knowledge of these works throughout the country. They intended, however, to avoid the course taken by Robert Owen. He had all along, though in his mild manner, condemned the radical reformers, believing as he did, that reform was to be effected solely on this plan ; the radical reformers of the working classes believing that his plan could only be carried out when the reforms they sought had been accomplished. . . . They resolved to take up such parts of his (Owen's) system as they believed would be appreciated by the working classes, and be the means of uniting them for specific purposes, taking care that these purposes should not interfere more than was possible with opinions in the proceedings to be adopted in matters on which great differences of opinion prevailed."[1] In short, the leading spirits of the working classes took up only certain parts of Owen's teachings, at the same time adhering to the Radical

[1] *Lovett's Memorandum* in Place, Add. MSS. 27791, III.

movement for Parliamentary reform. They believed that only through political power would the labouring masses be able to bring about the co-operative commonwealth, while the orthodox Owenites emphasised the priority of economics, arguing that forms of government and legislatures were the superstructure and economics the basis of society; the main business of socialists consisted therefore in changing the forms of wealth production, for as soon as this was accomplished the superstructure would adjust itself to the new basis.

Finally, parallel with these two main streams of Owenism ran a third which concentrated its activity on the process of exchange and the function of currency. Its foremost representative was John Gray, who attempted to combine individualisation of production with a socialisation of the exchange of commodities through national storehouses and labour notes.

Common to all Owenites was the criticism and disapproval of the capitalist or competitive system, as well as the sentiment that the United Kingdom was on the eve of adopting the new views. A boundless optimism pervaded the whole Owenite school, and it filled its adherents with the unshakable belief that the conversion of the nation to socialism was at hand, or but a question of a few years. Commercial crises, plethora of wealth, and widespread misery, dissatisfaction and general ferment, proved that society was out of joint. " And when these things begin to come to pass, then look up, and lift up your heads ; for your redemption draweth nigh."

2.—RISE OF THE TERM " SOCIALIST "

The centre of co-operative socialist thought was the London Co-operative Society, founded in the autumn, 1824, for the purpose of " formation of a community on the principles of mutual co-operation," and to restore " the whole produce of labour to the labourer." The founders declared that happiness was the true object of human exertions, and that it could not be attained to without a knowledge of the principles of society ; the inventions and discoveries that led to the production of an abundance of wealth could not produce happiness unless corresponding progress was made in moral and political science. Only through such knowledge could man come to see that competition and private accumulations or excessive inequality could never produce happiness ; society must, therefore, be built up on a system of mutual co-operation, community of property, equal labour, and equal enjoyment. Accordingly, the members of the London Co-operative Society resolved to " renounce all the evils of trafficking or mere commerce, likewise profit, which implies living on the labour of others ; all our exchanges being proposed to be for fair equivalents, representing equal labour, and destined for immediate or gradual consumption, and not for accumulation to command the labour of others."

The best periodical publication of orthodox Owenism was *The Co-operative Magazine* (1826–30), which contains a great amount of instructive matter. It was the central organ of co-operative thought and experiment of the time. It expressed the views, arrived at by serious and long discussions, of the London Co-operative Society. This Society and its organ were the common meeting-place of the adherents of communist co-operation. Here are some of the subjects of their debates :—

" May not the greater part of the moral and physical evils which afflict mankind be traced to individual competition in the production and distribution of wealth ? "

" Is the labourer entitled to the whole produce of his labour ? Why is, in the present state of society, the lot of the producing classes poverty and wretchedness ? "

" What are the objections to a state of voluntary equality of wealth and community of property ? And can they be satisfactorily answered ? "

" Is the position of Mr. Owen correct, that man is not properly the subject of praise or blame, reward and punishment ? "

" Would the arts and sciences flourish under the co-operative system ? "

" Is there any principle in human nature which presents an insurmountable obstacle to the co-operative system ? "

" Can the working classes permanently improve their condition by combinations to raise the rate of wages, or by benefit societies and similar means now adopted by them ? "

" Is the right of property derived from nature, or from social compact ? "

" Are the present distresses of the country attributable to redundant population ? "[1]

In these debates the term " Socialist " must have been coined. It is found for the first time in *The Co-operative Magazine* of November, 1827—in the same year in which Robert Owen published, in *The New Harmony Gazette*, a series of articles under the heading " Social System." The adjective " social " in juxtaposition to self-love is of course much older ; its origin may be traced back to Alexander Pope's well-known verses in the *Essay on Man* :—

> " So two consistent motions act the soul ;
> And one regards itself, and one the whole.
> Thus God and Nature linked the general frame,
> And bade self-love and social be the same."

With Owen and his adherents, however, self-love and social were not only not the same, but in direct opposition to each other. Self-love found its expression in individual competition, while social meant communist co-opération. In a footnote to a communication of the Brighton co-operators, the editor of *The Co-operative Magazine* observes that the value of a commodity consisted both of present and past labour (capital or stock), and the main question was " whether it is more beneficial that this capital should be individual or common." Those who argued that it should be in the hands of individual employers were the modern political economists of the type of James Mill and Malthus, while those who thought it should be common were " the Communionists and Socialists "[2] They based their demands on moral grounds, on the doctrines of Robert Owen,

---

[1] *Co-operative Magazine*, 1826, 1827 ; John Gray, *Lecture on Human Happiness*, 1825, Appendix ; William Thompson, *Labour Rewarded*, 1827, p. 106.

[2] *Co-operative Magazine*, 1827, p. 509 (footnote). *Cf. Archiv. für die Geschichte des Sozialismus*, 1912, 2 und 3 Heft, pp. 372, *seq.*

and on the theory of labour value, from which they deduced the injustice of the existing order.[1]

3.—SOCIALIST DEDUCTIONS FROM RICARDO : A CRITICISM

It is hardly possible for an Englishman of to-day to form an adequate idea of the charm which Ricardo's *Principles* exercised on his ancestors of nearly a century ago. Only a German is still able to feel it, for he lives nearer the industrial revolution and all the social ferment that it produces, and he has to study also Karl Marx—the last great disciple of Ricardo who developed the labour value theory to its final consequences. Most of the controversies of German and Eastern European scholarship concerning Marx's *Capital* were, in their essence, fought out in the years between 1820 and 1830 in England round Ricardo. Englishmen, at that time, still liked a good logical tussle, and found pleasure in economic theories.

Adam Smith and David Ricardo, in assuming that labour was " the original purchase money that was paid for all things," and that in the " early and rude state of society which precedes both the accumulation of stock and the appropriation of land," [2] exchange-value was known, committed the error of transferring concepts of advanced commercial societies to an age and social state in which economy was self-sufficing and exchange a rare exception. Any Christian missionary or traveller in non-civilised lands could expose that error by relating his experience with members of tribal societies. When a " savage " gives handfuls of gold nuggets for a necklace of glass beads, or a bag of diamonds for a cart and a span of oxen, he merely follows desire or utility, without any reference to the quantity of labour embodied in the goods exchanged. The meaning of worth or intrinsic value is utility, or the virtue of a thing, a quality which resides in it and renders it desirable. Aristotle regarded the utility of a thing as the foundation of value. He held barter or exchanging things for use as proper and natural, while trading or

[1] See *supra*, pp. 175–177.

[2] Adam Smith, *Wealth of Nations*, book 1, ch. 5 ; Ricardo, *Principles*, ch. 1, sec. 1.

buying things for the purpose of selling them at a higher price than they cost was improper or unnatural. Aristotle thought that a trader was buying up utilities in order to extort a profit from the people who need them.[1] In regarding trade as unnatural he implicitly showed that he had no idea of exchange-value, which really means exchanging equal quantities of labour to the mutual benefit of both buyer and seller.

Shakespeare's view of value is similar to that of Aristotle. In *Troilus and Cressida* (act 2, scene 2), Hector and Troilus are discussing the meaning of it.

> *Hect.* Brother, she is not worth what she doth cost
> The holding.
> *Tro.* What is aught but as 'tis valued ?
> *Hect.* But value dwells not in particular will ;
> It holds his estimate and dignity
> As well wherein 'tis precious of itself.

John Locke also held " intrinsick value " to mean utility.[2]

The concept of exchange-value arose only with the ascendancy of the commercial classes, who had to defend and justify their property against mediaeval views. Labour, as the title to property and the foundation and measure of exchange-value, is a theory in opposition to feudal conceptions of property. Ethically, the theory of exchange-value justifies commerce against Canon Law and against Aristotle by demonstrating that trading meant an exchange of equal quantities of labour and was, therefore, equitable and just and good.

This theory, having its origin in a comparatively advanced trading and manufacturing society, where capital and labour were largely united in the same hands, means capitalist labour, *i.e.*, labour exercised by the craftsmanship and skill as well as organising, managing, and superintending capacities of the capitalist. It is an English theory, and it arose in the seventeenth century, and no English economist ever thought of propertyless labour as the foundation and measure of value. From Sir William Petty to Ricardo the great English leaders of political

---

[1] Aristotle, *Politics*, I. 8 (Jowett's translation).
[2] John Locke, *Of Civil Government*, II. 5.

economy were so clear in their minds about the meaning given here of labour-value that they neglected to emphasise it. Hence the confusion that arose when that theory was taken up either by their less discriminating followers or by the socialists. Only a careful analysis of the history of that concept will reveal its original meaning.

The author of the exchange-value theory is Sir William Petty, the son of a clothier, the observer of many arts and crafts, and a realistic intellect of the highest order. His economic reasonings do not form a separate treatise, but are interwoven with enquiries concerning public affairs. His *Treatise on Taxes* and *Political Arithmetic* contain his most original thoughts. The latter book was written in refutation of one of those periodic panics occasioned by cries and lamentations about the decay of England and the overwhelming and increasing power of foreign nations. Living in the seventeenth century, when middle-class economics, trade and commerce were growing, when the whole life of the nation was being commercialised, Petty asked himself, What was money, and what did it measure ? And he replied :—

" Our silver and gold we call by several names, and in England by pounds, shillings, and pence. But that which I would say upon this matter is that all things ought to be valued by two natural denominations, which is land and labour ; that is, we ought to say, a ship or garment is worth such a measure of land with such another measure of labour, . . . for Labour is the father and active principle of wealth as Lands are the mother."[1] But what labour ? Is it only labour in factory, mine, and field, done by propertyless hands ? Petty's reply was :—

" Suppose a man could, with his own hands, plant a certain scope of land with corn, that is, could dig, plough, harrow, weed, reap, carry home, thresh, and winnow ; and had withal seed wherewith to sow the same. I say that this man after having subtracted his seed out of the proceed of his harvest, and also what himself has both eaten and given to others in exchange for clothes and other natural necessaries, the remainder of corn is a

[1] Sir William Petty, *Economic Writings*, Hull's edition, 1899, pp. 68, 44–5

natural and true rent of the land for that year. . . . But a further, though collateral, question may be, How much English money this corn or rent is worth ? I answer, so much as the money which another individual can save within the same time over and above his expense, if he employed himself wholly to produce and make it, viz. let another man travel into a country where is silver, there dig it, refine it, bring it to the same place where the other man planted his corn ; coin it, etc., the same person working all the while for his silver, gathering also food for his necessary livelihood and procuring himself covering, etc., I say, the silver of the one must be esteemed of equal value with the corn of the other ; the one, perhaps twenty ounces, and the other twenty bushels. From whence it follows that the price of a bushel of this corn to be an ounce of silver."[1] Trade and commerce thus consist in exchanges of equal quantities of labour. Or " if a man can bring to London an ounce of silver out of the earth in Peru in the same time that he can produce a bushel of corn, then one is the natural price of the other. Now, if by reason of new and more easy mines a man can get two ounces of silver as easily as formerly he did one, then corn will be as cheap at ten shillings as it was before at five shillings, *caeteris paribus*. . . . Natural dearness and cheapness depends upon the few or more hands requisite to the necessaries of life."[2]

It is clear that Petty, in formulating his exchange-value theory, had in mind a man with capital who works and manages his business. All this work, comprising outlay of capital, planning, managing, production of commodities, transport, and exchange, constitutes the value of a thing. Such labour is the foundation, and the quantity of such labour is the measure of value.

And now, what was the opinion of Petty with regard to wage labour employed under the management of the capitalist, at any part of the process of production, transport, and exchange ? Petty said, " It is observed by clothiers and others who employ great numbers of poor people that when corn is extremely plentiful the labour of the poor is extremely dear, and scarcely to be had at all, so licentious are they who labour only to eat or rather

[1] *Ib.*, p. 43.   [2] *Ib.*, p. 51.

to drink. Wherefore, when so many acres sown with corn
. . . shall produce perhaps double to what is expected or
necessary, it seems not unreasonable that this common blessing
of God should be applied to the common good of all people . . .
much rather than the same should be abased by the vile and
brutish part of mankind to the prejudice of the commonwealth."[1]

Wage labour was, evidently, regarded by Petty as something
inferior or a necessary evil, and by no means as a creator of value.

Exceedingly instructive, in this respect, is the view of Gregory
King. In his treatise on the various classes of society, in 1686,
he drew up a table of the national income and expenditure,[2] in
which he stated that there were at that time, in England and
Wales, 511,586 families who increased the national wealth by
2,447,000*l* annually, and 849,000 families who decreased the
national wealth by 622,000*l* annually, among the latter being
the families of wage-labourers—*i.e.*, the masses of propertyless
working men, who thus not only created nothing, but actually
decreased the national income. King was no economist, but
merely gave expression to the opinions that prevailed in the
seventeenth century. Labour, as the foundation of value, was
the labour of the capitalists or of handicraftsmen and artisans,
who worked in their own workshops and with their own tools,
and generally managed their business of buying, producing, and
selling ; and the same applies to the yeomen, farmers, and other
land-possessing peasantry.

John Locke, in speaking of labour as making things valuable,
does not discriminate between capitalist labour and wage labour,
but his whole point of view was that of the proprietors of land
and workshops, since his arguments were intended to establish
the truth of his proposition that labour was the only legitimate
title to property, for " 'tis labour which puts the greatest part
of the value upon land, without which it would scarcely be
worth anything. . . . I think it will be a very modest computa-
tion to say that of the product of the earth useful to the life of

[1] Sir William Petty, Economic Writings, Hull's edition, 1899,
pp. 274–5.
[2] Gregory King, *Natural and Political Observations*, 1694, p. 3.

man, nine-tenths are the effects of labour . . . in most cases, ninety-nine hundredths are wholly to be put on the account of labour," and by this creation of value labour became the real title to property. Middle-class property was, therefore, justified. This was the inference which Locke drew from his labour theory. For the labouring poor he only asked parish relief. The labourer's share being but rarely more than a bare subsistence, he must, in times of unemployment, come to the parish. Also, when the prices of commodities rise the labourer's wages " must rise with the price of things to make him live, or else, not being able to maintain himself and family by his labour, he comes to the parish." [1]

In the eighteenth century, many popular writers, not being trained economists, failed to discriminate between capitalist and wage labour, and merely wrote of labour being the source of wealth.

Adam Smith, by his great and well deserved authority, spread the confusion, although he was fully aware of the meaning of the labour concept. In treating of wages he speaks of wage labour as the creator of that fund which supplies the nation with the necessaries and conveniences of life. " It is but equity," he says, " that they, *i.e.*, the wage labourers who feed, clothe, and lodge the whole body of the people, should have such a share of the produce of their own labour as to be themselves tolerably fed, clothed, and lodged " (*Wealth of Nations*, book 1, ch. 8, section 4). In treating of the different employment of capital, he holds, as a matter of course, that " the persons whose capitals are employed in any of those four ways *i.e.*, in procuring the raw materials, in manufacturing those raw materials, in transporting raw and manufactured materials, in distributing those goods, are themselves productive labourers ; their labour, when properly directed, fixes and realizes itself in the commodity upon which it is bestowed, and generally adds to its price the value at least of their own maintenance and consumption. The profits of the farmer, of the manufacturer, of the merchant and retailer, are all drawn from the price of the goods which the

[1] John Locke, *Works*, 1812, Vol. 5, pp. 57, 71. *seq.*

o

two first produce, and the two last buy and sell. . . . No equal
capital puts into motion a greater quantity of productive labour
than that of the farmer. Not only his labouring servants, but
his labouring cattle are productive labourers. . . . The labourers
and labouring cattle," etc. (*Ib.*, book 2, chap. 5). In this chapter
we have a transformation of the scene and actors. As the main
agents in the creation of wealth and value, appear the capitalists,
while wage labourers are put on the same level as cattle. The
further we proceed in our reading of Adam Smith, the clearer
grows the conviction that he meant that capitalist labour constituted the source of wealth and value. In dealing with the rise
of civil government, Smith unhesitatingly states his opinion
that the owners of property acquired it " by the labour of many
years, or, perhaps, of many successive generations," while the
labouring poor are described as swayed by the passions of " hatred
of labour and love of ease and enjoyment," and driven by these
passions " to invade property " (*Ib.*, book 5, chap. 1, part 2).
It is but necessary to collate these passages in order to perceive,
at a glance, the inconsistencies and confusions in which Adam
Smith was entangled.

The same remarks apply to Colquhoun. On page 109 of
his *Treatise*, the manufacturers, proprietors and farmers, are
accounted as productive labourers, while on page 110 he sings
the song of poverty as the creator of the wealth of nations.

David Ricardo is free from these inconsistencies and confusions, but fails to think out his theories to their final consequences. He regarded labour, as directed and managed by the
capitalist, as the foundation and measure of exchange-value.
But which labour ? The labour of wage-earners and cattle, *i.e.*,
living labour, or circulating capital, to the exclusion of fixed
capital. Ricardo assumed that capital employed in manufacture, agriculture, etc., was composed of two portions—viz.
fixed and circulating ; the fixed capital or machinery and raw
materials do not create any new value, but only add to the produced or handled commodity as much value as they lost by their
being used up, or written off, in the process of production and
distribution. On the other hand, circulating capital was the

real source of exchange-value, and from it flowed the new values. Not machinery, but living labour augments the values or the annual fund which supplies the nation with all it needs. This theory is, however, quite incapable of explaining the problem of the distribution of profit. Suppose two capitalists start cloth manufacturing with equal capitals. But one possesses more expensive machinery, or a higher portion of fixed capital, and, therefore, has less to spend on living labour, since his circulating capital is smaller. The other capitalist, following the theory of Ricardo, cares more for circulating capital, and makes it as large as possible. Were Ricardo right, the latter manufacturer would create a larger amount of new values and earn higher profits than the former. Experience, however, shows that equal capitals employed in the same industry, or in the whole field of industry, yield, or tend to yield, equal earnings. In the market all differences in the composition of capital, all differences between the amounts of fixed and circulating capital, disappear, while the total amount of the employed capital determines profit and price. It is no use replying that supply and demand or competition equalise price and profit, for Ricardo knew all that, and regarded it as a disturbing, but not an invalidating factor of his theory. Moreover, were Ricardo's theory in consonance with the realities of economic life, the enormous and astonishing increase of wealth, as measured by exchange-values, since the Economic Revolution, would be inexplicable. Ricardo himself admitted that the introduction of machinery displaced living labour, *i.e.*, diminished circulating capital, and yet the national income grew by leaps and bounds. China and India employ relatively and absolutely more living labour than either Great Britain or the United States of America ; none the less the former countries are suffering from lack of capital, while the latter countries are constantly on the look-out for new markets and investments in order to place their surplus capitals. Or take the development of England since the end of the seventeenth century. According to King, England and Wales, with a population of five millions, had then a national income of about forty-three millions sterling. In 1913, England and Wales, with a population of thirty-seven millions, had a national income of about fourteen hundred millions sterling. The population and the manual labour increased sevenfold, the national income thirty-three times. What had happened in the meantime to account for this growth of wealth and value ? The advent of applied science, new discoveries, and higher organisation. It is altogether an absurd belief that an illiterate boy and female worker tending a machine should create new values, while steam, electricity, chemistry, the embodiments of genius, and the highest exertions of countless ages of collective human thought and endeavour, should be barren of economic values.

The surplus earnings over the prime cost, or the new wealth produced annually, can therefore not be the result of living labour (circulating capital) only, but of the accumulated labour (fixed capital) as well. A factory, a modern farm, a commercial establishment, embody the labour of centuries of invention, discovery, organisation, management, transport, production, and distribution. Indeed, the periods of technological inventions, scientific and geographical discoveries, and introduction of new forms of economic organisation constitute epochs in the history of wealth and value. And these are mainly the work of mental qualities of a high order. The active agent, then, in the production of wealth is mind, and as it was mainly under the system of private property that the human mind brought about those inventions, discoveries, and organisations, the new wealth which they have been yielding takes therefore the form of property and capital. And by the expenditure and new creations of capital the exchange values of the commodities are measured. Exchange-value has just as much to do with wealth as the yard or the pound has to do with the length or weight of things. It is merely a measure, and its expression, under the present system, is money. In order to preclude error it is necessary to add that just as the yard can only measure dimensions because it has itself certain dimensions, or just as the pound measures weight because it has itself gravity, so money measures value because it is itself valuable or based on valuable things, i.e., on things which embody a certain quantity of capital.

We have seen the confusions into which such writers as Smith and Ricardo have fallen with regard to the concept of productive labour. Errors of great minds are generally but a degree less instructive than their truths. There is reason in such errors. Smith and Ricardo erred, because they had not seen and could not have seen the developed form of capitalist production. They were still thinking of domestic industries, farmers, small traders, and independent craftsmen, rather than of wage-labour divorced from the mental functions and tools of labour, which is the main characteristic of the factory system and large agriculture. This can be clearly perceived from the reasonings of the social critics of the time of the Economic Revolution. All of them saw in the capitalist, who was then re-organising the economic basis of society, a mere speculator and cunning moneymonger, and in the labourer the real producer. It is remarkable that by " manufacturer " the writers of those times mean a " workman employed in manufacture." Manufacturer, as meaning the owner of the factory and employer of labour, is of later origin. " Trade or traffic," says Charles Hall, " consists in buying and selling articles produced by the poor, and gaining a profit by them. These articles are all the products of the hands of the labourers, manufacturers, etc., from whom they are obtained for less than their full value ; a profit otherwise could not be made. The tradesman, therefore, shares or takes part of the fruits of the labour of the poor. . . . The means enabling tradesmen to share or take a part of the product of the labour of the poor, is their capital, which puts it into their power to furnish materials to the artificers to work on, and to provide them with immediate subsistence, and on that account is supposed to give the tradesman a just claim to a part of the production of the workman's hands."[1] Substantially the same views are to be found in the whole socialist and anti-capitalist literature since 1820 onwards. Ravenstone, Gray, Hodgskin, William Thompson, and the leaders of Chartism, assumed that the capitalist as such was non-productive and was merely a lender of the means of production to the wage-labourers, from whom he extorted a usurious rate

[1] Charles Hall, *Effects of Civilisation*, edition 1850, pp. 56–7.

of interest on his capital. Moreover, they either misunderstood or corrected Ricardo by assuming that the foundation of value and source of wealth was exclusively the labour in field, factory, and mine, while the labour of transport and distribution was not productive of value. This is not the opinion of Ricardo, for he includes in the definition of labour-value all kinds of labour necessary " to manufacture (the commodities) and bring them to market." He says : " First, there is the labour necessary to cultivate the land on which the raw cotton is grown ; secondly, the labour of conveying the cotton to the country where the stockings are to be manufactured . . . ; thirdly, the labour of the spinner and weaver ; fourthly, a portion of the labour of the engineer, smith, carpenter, who erected the buildings and machinery . . . ; fifthly, the labour of the retail dealer, and of many others. . . . The aggregate sum of these various kinds of labour determines the quantity of other things for which these stockings will be exchanged " (Ricardo, *Principles*, chap. 1, sec. 3).

So much as to value. Another critical conclusion was drawn by the more revolutionary socialists from the Ricardian concept of wages. " Labour, like all other things which may be purchased and sold," says Ricardo, " has its natural and its market price. The natural price of labour is that price which is necessary to enable the labourers to subsist and to perpetuate their race, without either increase or diminution. . . . With a rise in the price of food and necessaries, the natural price of labour will rise ; with the fall in their price, the natural price of labour will fall." From this statement, which is by no means complete, the conclusion was drawn that, under the capitalist system, the wages of labour could never amount to more than a minimum of means of subsistence. No matter how much the workman produced, his real wages would always tend to that minimum. Moreover, by this Ricardian law of wages, the poor must get poorer and the rich richer. If, for instance, the workman produced necessaries enough for two persons, he would get half the produce ; if, by reason of inventions and improvements, he produced enough for ten persons, he would only get one-tenth of the produce of his labour, while his employer would get nine-tenths. Thus, the more goods he could create the smaller the proportion of his reward. It really did not matter to the workman how the country was governed, what the taxes were, or what the political parties did, for the main thing that concerned him was the law of wages, which, being inherent in the capitalist mode of production, could only perish with it. All reforms that did not touch the wage problem were mere tinkering, and therefore not worth the attention of Labour.

This criticism, which bears all the marks of a mechanical conception of social life, must, however, not be laid at the door of Ricardo. He clearly points out that " notwithstanding the tendency of wages to conform to their natural rate, their market rate may, in an improving society, for an indefinite period, be constantly above it " (*Principles*, chap. 5). And even his natural price includes conveniences as well as necessaries of life. But the revolutionary socialists simply refused to believe that capitalist society could be improving, or progressive. Their outlook was statical, and they failed to perceive the dynamic forces that were operating on social life. By their exaggerations and one-sided assertions they hampered rather than promoted the recognition of the rights of Labour and the moral essence of Socialism.

The truth appears to be that most writers on subjects of moral philosophy, social and economic science, and history of nations, form their conceptions not from phenomena which are in the process of shaping themselves, but from phenomena which already belong to the past. The external world moves faster than the operations of the human mind. Objective creation precedes subjective logic. Or, as Hegel says, " the owl of Minerva emerges from its hiding after sunset." [1] To this purely objective and, perhaps, inevitable source of error must be added all those sources of error that have their origin in the passions and prejudices of man. They combine to turn the dominion of history, politics, economics, ethics, and religion into arenas of warring doctrines, contradictory hypotheses, and heated controversies.

[1] G. W. F. Hegel, *Philosophic des Rechts* (Preface).

VII

THE CO-OPERATIVE SOCIALISTS

I.—GEORGE MUDIE AND THE "ECONOMIST"

ROBERT OWEN'S failure to win the confidence and the ear of the London artisans was retrieved by George Mudie, a Scotch journalist and printer, who came to London about 1820. There are but few biographical data of this Owenite pioneer. He studied at Edinburgh, where he made himself obnoxious by his opposition to established ideas, and apparently did not finish his studies. He gradually drifted into journalism, and in 1818 or 1819 was employed at a newspaper in Glasgow. At that time he was already acquainted with Owen's teachings and ideals. By the end of 1820 he was reporter to the *Morning Chronicle*, then the great Liberal daily of the metropolis. It appears from notes left by Francis Place that Mudie owed his position to a recommendation of James Mill, who was an intimate friend of Mr. Black, the editor-in-chief of that paper. Place speaks disparagingly of Mudie, from which it may be inferred that the latter was from the beginning an Owenite agitator among the working men. From January, 1821, to January, 1822, he edited *The Economist*, a weekly paper devoted to the propaganda of Owenism and co-operation. It describes itself as "A periodical paper, explanatory of the New System of Society projected by Robert Owen, and of a plan of association for improving the conditions of the working classes during their continuance of their present employment." Its leading principles were : (1) That poverty was not necessarily the lot of civilised societies, but afflicted them merely from their ignorance of true principles and the influence of other principles based on error ; (2) that while the erroneous principles prevailed, poverty must necessarily increase, and the bulk of human misery grow ; (3) that the knowledge and practice of true principles would assuredly banish poverty, and place mankind above the fear and danger of want ; (4) that the power of producing superabundance of all the goods of life was so great, even in this thickly populated country, that England was capable of sustaining several times the number of the present population in security and comfort ; (5) that the application of the true principle would also disseminate knowledge as certainly as it would diffuse plenty for all ; (6) that knowledge and plenty would build up the physical and intellectual strength of the nation, would in a great measure subdue vice, destroy misery, promote virtue, and lead to happiness—the aim and end of all human effort.

Looking at the productive capacities of nature and man, there was no reason why misery should exist. Even in a very early stage of society each individual had been capable of producing more than several individuals could consume. The first progressive steps in the cultivation of the soil and the making of implements had already raised production, and taught man how to protect himself against poverty. And this was all the more so in the present stage of society in England, where science and mechanism were creating all the facilities for the production of wealth ; one Englishman was now capable of producing more than twenty individuals could consume. None the less, misery and distress were rife in the land, for the productive powers had been misapplied and distribution vitiated.

Some people ascribed this condition to the spread of machinery. It was, however, clear that the natural or the theoretical tendency of mechanical inventions and the progress of science was not to increase the number of the poor, but to increase the number of the rich, and every addition made to the number of the rich must be taken from the ranks of the poor. The natural tendency of mechanical inventions was not to render the poor poorer, but to enrich them and render all mankind rich, by furnishing all with an abundance of goods. The realities appear to belie that theoretical tendency, and to justify the assertion of those who saw in mechanism an enemy of the labouring classes.

Which was the truth ? The truth was that society was based

on erroneous principles, the effects of which were counteracting the natural tendencies, and did not allow them to assert themselves. The fatal error was that " the interest of each individual has been placed, in almost every circumstance and situation, in direct opposition to the interest of other individuals, and to the interest of society." In consequence of this error the productive powers of society were never brought into full and healthful operation, but on the contrary, production, particularly of really useful and necessary articles, was ever kept within the bounds of demand. The possessors of the means of production always had in view, not the interests of society, not the needs of all, but only of those who could pay remunerative prices. Consumption governs production ; not a single wheel was set in motion unless it promised to promote the interests of capital. And as, in present circumstances, the circle of consumption was narrow, the productive forces could not expand to their full capacity. The result was poverty. Quite apart from the wretched condition of the labouring classes, it must be asserted that even the possessing classes were not nearly as rich as the facilities for the production of riches would warrant. The opposition of interests, the waste that competition brings in its train, were paralysing production, and impeding the progress of knowledge.

The civilised nations did not, in reality, form societies, but aggregates of warring individuals. Everybody cared only for himself ; there existed no bond of union ; the nations were kept together by force and compulsion, press laws, militarism, prisons, and gallows. The constitutions and institutions rested on anti-social principles. The imperfections of government or the misconduct of rulers were not the causes of the multifarious evils from which mankind was suffering, but the consequences of the anti-social principles on which society was based. As long as they prevailed there was no remedy for poverty. No addition to our productive powers and no reduction of the population could avert the calamities that threatened us. If Providence were to bless our plains with double fertility, if foreign nations were to pour a superabundance upon us, they would but accelerate the arrival of our greatest woe. For they would cause unemployment, and, consequently, a shrinkage in the consumption of the masses and a narrowing of the circle of production.

Having recognised the source of evil, it was easy to discover the remedy. It consisted in basing society on a harmony of interests or on co-operation, instead of antagonism and competition. The working classes being the greatest sufferers from that system must follow the advice of Robert Owen and form villages of unity and co-operation. But how could that be accomplished without the aid of capital ? Was not capital the source and power of production ? The belief in the creative powers of capital had been spread by the political economists, but, in reality, capital was neither the true source nor the true power of production. The source of production was the land, and the real power of production beyond the spontaneous gifts of nature was the labour of man, rendered infinitely more productive when combined. Capital, far from being the source or power of production, was the product of labour, or rather of human co-operation. Capital did not precede, but follow, production. Labour might go on without capital, but the latter had no power of multiplying itself without labour.

These views, developed in the first numbers of *The Economist*, Mudie had spread, in 1820, among the London journeymen printers and he succeeded in persuading the most enterprising of them to make an experiment. This happened towards the end of 1820, and it seems that it was this success that encouraged Mudie to issue *The Economist*.

2.—THE CO-OPERATIVE AND ECONOMICAL SOCIETY

The London printers, influenced by Mudie, appointed a committee to investigate a co-operative scheme by which they would be able to continue their usual employment, and save enough money for the purpose of establishing a co-operative society of production. The first stage of the experiment was to be an association of co-operative householding. By clubbing together their household expenses they would be able to buy larger quantities of the means of subsistence for the same money, and enable their wives to perform their domestic duties more skilfully and in less time than now. The householding community would have its own school for the children, its library, its infirmary and medical practitioners, and thus promote co-operative habits and harmonious action. Detailed estimates of the cost of living of 250 families on private and co-operative lines showed that by co-operation they would save nearly £8,000 per annum and thus establish a fund for co-operative production and become their own employers.

Much more interesting than this plan is the Report which the committee issued. The editor of *The Economist* thought it "the most important document that has ever proceeded from a body of workmen." They argued that " if foreign nations will not take our manufactures in exchange for agricultural produce, we trust that agricultural customers will spring up at home, and that we shall ere long find means to divide among ourselves, by a fair exchange of produce, all the goods and provisions that our domestic industry and ingenuity can create, and indeed so to open, renovate, and enlarge the home market as to render it much more valuable to all the interests of the State, to the labourer, the farmer, the manufacturer, the merchant, and the landowner. The country abounds with means and materials of wealth, and possesses unemployed productive powers (in manual and mechanical energy) of vast extent, and capable of almost unlimited increase. By what fatal error, then, is it that in this land of abundance there is so much wretchedness and want ? . . . By what hitherto unaccountable fatality has it been that this country has been kept dependent on foreign nations for a large portion of its food, though its own soil required only increased culture in order to furnish a redundancy, that the agriculturists complain of inadequate remuneration for their industry and capital, while they are surrounded by so many hundreds of thousands of half-starving consumers ? " Similar questions are directed to the manufacturers and scholars. The working men only desired the opportunity of exchanging their articles for those they were in need of. " Let us but be placed together in contiguous dwellings, and with the command of a small portion of the land, for which we will pay the usual rental, and we shall soon show our legislators what we are capable of doing for ourselves, for our children, and for all." ◦ Poverty could only be banished by combined labour and expenditure and by education. Such associations would injure nobody, and, if once in full action, would be stable. As to the objection that the success of co-operation might lead to an excessive increase of population, and, consequently, to a recurrence of poverty, the committee replied that if a taste for comfort could be diffused over the whole community, it would constitute a much more effective check upon excessive population than the misery which resulted from blind improvidence could do. They summed up their social ideal with a verse from Robert Southey :—

" Train up thy children, England,
    In the ways of righteousness and feed them
      With the bread of wholesome doctrine.
    Where hast thou thy mines—but in their industry ?
    Thy bulwarks where—but in their breasts ? Thy might
      But in their arms ? . . ."[1]

These lines of Southey enjoyed great popularity in co-operative circles, but, of course, they put on them their own construction. Training of children they meant in the sense of Owen, and " wholesome doctrine " was that of the " New View of Society."

The London printers established the Economical and Co-operative Society and drafted the following Constitution :—

" The ultimate object of this society is to establish a village of Unity and Mutual Co-operation, combining agriculture, manufacture, and trade upon the plan projected by Mr. Owen, of New Lanark. The immediate object of the Society is to form a fund for the purchase of food, clothing, and other necessaries at wholesale prices ; and (where the members reside near each other) to form arrangements for co-operating in the care of their dwellings, the superintendence, training, and education of their children. The Society also proposes, as early as possible, to provide productive employments for such of its members as may

[1] *The Economist* (1821), No. 3.

be without work and to make provision for the members and their families in sickness and old age.

" The fundamental principle is, in proportion as every member shall endeavour to promote the good of the whole Society, will be the amount of respect and happiness enjoyed by each individual.

" Religious and political opinion are a private matter." [1]

Towards the end of 1821 the Society was in full action, but the majority of its members were " men of fortune and individuals of liberal professions."[2] The last number of *The Economist* (end of January, 1822) was printed by that Society. However, the co-operative experiment proved a failure. Robert Southey, who had followed it with close and sympathetic attention, explained the course of the failure. " The founders proposed to raise £12,000 in shares of £100 each. . . . The capital was not forthcoming. The experiment was commenced with insufficient means, and under circumstances every way inconvenient. Of necessity, therefore, it failed." [3]

3.—ABRAM COMBE'S PARABLE OF THE CISTERN.

The first British Socialist who formed an Owenite community was the Scotsman Abram Combe (1785–1827). He was less original and less comprehensive than Robert Owen, but equal to him in devotion, singleness of purpose, love of humanity, and organising capacity. He possessed, moreover, one great quality which his master lacked—a sense of humour. If the great majority of mankind consisted of men like A. Combe, integral socialism would either be possible or superfluous. In 1820 he visited New Lanark and came at once under the spell of Owen. He was then a well-to-do and prosperous leather manufacturer, and gradually decided to sink his money in an Owenite experiment. How intense his studies of Owenism were may be seen from his *Metaphorical Sketches of the Old and the New System*

---

[1] *The Economist* (1821), No. 1.

[2] *Ib.*, No. 46.

[3] Robert Southey, *Sir Thomas More, or Colloquies*, 1829, I., pp. 134–9.

(1823), in which he attempted to illustrate, by flashes of genuine humour and good-natured satire, the difference between capitalism, as he saw it, and the ideal of communism. The essence of his views is contained in the following parable or " metaphorical sketch," which applies particularly to the British people of the period of the Economic Revolution.

The wealth of this great people was contained in the Cistern of their national resources. This Cistern was supplied from three streams—agriculture, mining, rivers, and seas. These streams were purified and made fit for consumption at special stations by human labour, before they reached the Cistern; and when they were all put together they contained all that was necessary and desirable for the supply of human wants, and it was called Wealth. At the stopcock of the Cistern stood a guardian by the name of Competition, whose duty it was to see that each individual should only draw out in proportion to what he put in, lest the Cistern should become empty, to the injury of the whole people ; it was also his duty to see that, if any particular stream was deficient, encouragement should be given to those who supply it.

Those who conducted the streams received a metal order on the Cistern, which they might draw or retain at pleasure. The labourers who attended the streams received an order for about an eighth part of what they put in ; with this remuneration they were quite satisfied. The other parts went to the proprietors of the streams, to those who directed the labourers, to the merchants who exchanged the produce of the native streams for that of of foreign streams, and to those who managed the affairs of the nation. Owing to the difficulty of furnishing the supplies there was no lack of employment for the labourers, since the demand was equal or even greater than the supply. Things went on in this manner for a long time, till the progress of knowledge pointed out a way by which one stream could be made to flow into the cistern with a tenth part of the labour formerly required ; or, in other words, a discovery was made, by means of which each labourer could furnish ten times the quantity that he did formerly. The individuals whose business it was to furnish the supplies through this stream were compensated by orders on the Cistern, in some degree corresponding to the quantity they sent in. The high remuneration they received stimulated their minds to greater exertions. Those who furnished the supplies from the other streams were also put on the alert by the success of their neighbours.

The streams were augmented from all sides, and the Cistern would have been over full had not this wise people employed force to settle a dispute with a neighbouring nation, and made for this purpose large demands on the Cistern. The wise men of the people drained extraordinary quantities of wealth from the Cistern, but they were unable to see how it had come about that the streams flowed so abundantly. The supplies came into the Cistern so fast, and the demands upon it were so great that metal orders could not be found in sufficient quantity to let the supplies out, and without producing such an order it was believed the stopcock would not open. Moreover, ignorant as most of the people were, they firmly believed that the metal orders were the sources of wealth, and they looked upon the contents of the Cistern as of comparatively little importance. But when these orders were exhausted, a crisis broke out. The wise men of the nation fancied ruin to be inevitable, and, necessity being the mother of invention, they introduced paper orders. To their great astonishment they found that a piece of paper let out the supplies just as well as the piece of metal had done.

For upwards of twenty years did these wise men carry on a destructive war at enormous cost. What industry and ingenuity created, waste and extravagance destroyed ; the one pouring supplies into the national Cistern, the other drawing them off at a great rate. But industry and ingenuity obtained so much aid from art and science that the Cistern was kept brimful. Finally, the war came to an end ; waste and extravagance ceased ; the paper orders were withdrawn, and metal ones again resorted to. The sudden shrinkage of the demands on the Cistern, consequent upon the conclusion of the war and the reintroduction of the metal orders, nearly proved fatal to those who attended the streams. As the Cistern was overflowing and the streams were gorged, guardian Competition dismissed the labourers, who, being deprived of metal orders, could not open the stopcock and draw what they wanted. The labourers then applied to him again, saying that it would not in the least hurt him if he allowed them to pour their stream into the Cistern so that they might be able to draw instantly from there what they wanted, for by doing so the cistern would, in the end, not be fuller than it was at that moment. In this way they could go on working their stream and satisfy their needs, while injuring nobody. Competition, hearing this argument, got into a passion and asked them if they were such fools as to suppose that they would be able to draw from the cistern without metal orders ? And as to giving them any of these, it was what he could not and would not do ; for, he declared, he had already more wealth on his hands than he knew what to do with. So he turned them away, showing no mercy to the poor producers who were starving. Disaffection grew apace, and the country was in a turmoil.

A crisis overtook the nation, and its wise men were at a loss to account for it. Mr. Commonsense, seeing all parties at a standstill, gave the people a hint that a remedy for the distress, occasioned by an excess of supply of all they wanted, might easily be found. He said, " The Cistern contains all that your minds desire, why then do you hesitate to give orders to the producers corresponding to the quantity they send in ? You are in distress because waste and extravagance have ceased to dissipate the contents of your Cistern ; but why not divide the surplus among those who supply the whole, since no one need feel want while the Cistern can be so easily kept up ? You say, guardian Competition would not allow it. Well, why not dismiss him ? You say, further, there were not sufficient metal orders to go round,—why not use paper orders which for over twenty years had served the purpose well and kept the circulation between the streams, the Cistern, and the people in some order ! "

However, the people, not having been accustomed to listen to Commonsense, did not understand what he meant. They rather believed those who told them that Commonsense was a visionary and Utopian who imagined impracticable things.

P

They advised the people to listen to the teachings of the political economists. The latter, being called upon to come forward and explain to the people the cause and remedy of the distress, said that the sources of production were woefully scanty, and what they had been yielding was destroyed by the long and ruinous war ; and even the wealth which would be produced in the next future was, by anticipation, wasted, since the national debt had grown to enormous proportions. There was, then, no other remedy for the producers but strict sexual restraint and emigration. And those who remained in the country should strain every nerve to reform the Government in order to render it impossible for them to fall again into extravagance.

Mr. Commonsense, hearing this interpretation of the crisis, could no longer contain himself, and put the question to the political economists, " Why not give the producers orders on the Cistern equal to what they put in, instead of an eighth part only ? " Whereupon the political economists cut him short by saying, they did not wish to " enter into a controversy on such a subject." [1]

This was Combe's interpretation of the effects of the Economic Revolution, the Napoleonic Wars, the Bank Restriction, and the crisis which overtook the nation in the years 1816-20. As soon as he had grasped the doctrines of his master he began to think of co-operative experiments, and he found a fellow-labourer in Archibald James Hamilton (1793-1834), an ex-officer, who had served under the Duke of Wellington in the Peninsular War and at Waterloo. Hamilton was the son of General John Hamilton, of Dalzell and Orbiston. He met Robert Owen at dinner in Dalzell House, discussed with him the new views of society and, finally, adopted socialism. He fully identified himself with the aspirations of the labouring classes and attempted to educate them in the theory and practice of co-operation. In 1821 he made the acquaintance of Abram Combe, and both decided to establish a co-operative store at Edinburgh. They formed a society which from the beginning enjoyed much popularity It grew in numbers and prosperity, about five

<hr>

[1] Abram Combe, *Metaphorical Sketches*, 1823, pp. 40–51, 184.

hundred families joined it, but within a year it collapsed owing to the dishonesty of a storekeeper. Undismayed by this failure, Combe immediately thereafter formed a community in his tanyard. He encouraged his workmen to live in common and to share in the profits of the factory. This experiment also failed; dissensions among the working men rendered community life impossible. In 1825 Combe made the largest and last socialist experiment of his life. He bought Orbiston (near Motherwell), which belonged to the Hamiltons of Dalzell, and formed a community. Warned by his previous failures he proceeded warily and arranged for a gradual transition from private property to communism. This displeased the communists and they began to look at Combe with suspicion. Also the London Co-operative Society, the theorists of nascent Socialism, became impatient with the slow progress of Orbiston ; only John Gray, of whom more presently, warned against the adoption of complete communism, but his voice was unheeded. While all these murmurings and complaints of the onlookers and beneficiaries went on, Combe quietly devoted all his time and energies and sacrificed, to the irreparable injury of his own family, all he possessed—a sum of over £20,000 —to the building up of the first British communist establishment. Enmity from opponents, who gave to Orbiston the name of Babylon, zealous criticism from friends, and the labour and anxiety which the scheme entailed, impaired the health of this truly noble socialist pioneer, and after an illness, which lasted exactly twelve months, he passed away in August, 1827. Combe died a ruined man, leaving his family destitute. Orbiston then went from bad to worse. Deprived of its master-mind and guiding and helping hand, it was doomed to rapid extinction. At the end of 1827 it was bankrupt.[1]

4.—JOHN GRAY

The idea underlying Combe's Parable of the Cistern forms the subject of the elaborate economic treatises of John Gray (1799–

[1] Register for Orbiston, 1825-7 ; John Gray, *Social System*, 1851, Appendix ; Alex. Cullen, *Adventures in Socialism*, 1910.

1850 ?). He was of Scottish origin, but spent his boyhood in Derbyshire, his school days at Repton, and his youth in London. He left Repton at the age of fourteen years, when he was sent as an apprentice to a wholesale merchant in Cheapside. Being a thoughtful youth, he observed the doings in the metropolis in the agitated years, 1816 to 1820 ; he was probably a careful reader of the newspapers of the day, followed the discussions on the crisis, on currency, on over-production, and " came to the conclusion that the commercial system was at variance with the whole system of nature, and that God could never have intended His creatures to be mere stumbling-blocks to each other," as he saw them at every step he trod.   The final result of his observations and meditations was as follows : " I saw clearly that goods of every description are made either because they are ordered or because there is every prospect of their being so ; and continual reflection satisfied me that this state of things ought to be reversed—that production, instead of being the effect of demand, ought to be the cause of it."[1]   The main conclusion of Gray is, as we see, the same as Mudie's.

After an abortive attempt to put his ideas in a readable form on paper he read Owen, and in 1825 published the first instalment of his system, under the title, *Lecture on Human Happiness*, which was intended to be the first of a series of lectures dealing with the evils of the existing order of society, and the development of means by which they might be permanently removed.   This pamphlet, though Owenite in spirit, betrays also influences of other socialist, social reform, and economic writers.   Its author knew Ricardo, Colquhoun, and probably also Attwood.   The leading ideas are : Society is a natural phenomenon, since nature has implanted in man the desire to associate himself with his fellow-man ; it has likewise implanted in man the desire for happiness.   If this is so, how comes it that society is afflicted with so many evils, so much misery and wretchedness ?   The answer is, the principle on which the association of man with man is founded has been misapplied.   The principle which satisfies the natural desire of man to live in society is barter.

[1] John Gray, *Social System*, 1851, p. 340.

" Barter, and barter alone, is the basis of society, all other
institutions are built wholly and solely upon it." The right
application of this principle is giving and taking equal quantities
of labour. Were this fundamental principle acted upon, society
would have attained to happiness. But it is not acted upon.
Under the existing conditions the labourers are robbed of four-
fifths of their produce, which are distributed among the non-
producers who give no equivalent to society. The whole principle
of exchange is falsified, the basis of society vitiated.

And here we come to the main critical consideration of Gray,
which exercised considerable influence on the subsequent socialist
agitation. The Ricardian concept of labour as the foundation
and measure of value was taken by Gray to mean exclusively
wage-labour in field, factory, and mine. Only these labourers
produced the wealth of the nation. All the other members of
society were either useful, if they rendered services, or useless,
if they rendered no services. Employers, merchants, traders,
physicians, artists, scientists, were non-productive, though
some of them useful, while the remainder were both non-productive and useless. But the useful as well as the useless lived
on the wealth produced by wage-labour in field, factory, and
mine. Gray took Colquhoun's table of production and distribution, and re-classifying it under the heads of Producers and
Non-Producers, he arrived at the following conclusion : In
1812, the population of the United Kingdom numbered 17,096,803
persons, and the new wealth produced amounted to £430,521,372.
This wealth was produced by 7,897,531 labouring persons, who
on the principle of equal exchanges ought to have received £54
each, but had actually received £11 only, or one-fifth of the
produce of their labour. Or, in other words, about eight million
producers received £90,500,000, and nine million non-producers
received £340,000,000. " The rich man, who, in point of fact,
pays nothing, receives everything, while the poor man, who,
in point of fact, pays everything, receives nothing. We put it
to the candour of every honest man whether such a state of
society as this ought to be preserved ! Whether it is not at
variance with every principle of honesty ! " (Lecture, pp. 15–20).

Gray leaves no doubt whatsoever as to his meaning. He believes he has shown " that from human labour every description of wealth proceeds ; the productive classes do now support, not only themselves, but every unproductive member of society. Only these are productive members of society who apply their own hands either to the cultivation of the earth itself, or preparing its materials for the uses of life ; that every individual not so employed is a direct tax upon those who are so employed ; that the whole merchant class are either directors of production or distribution of wealth who are paid by those who create it ; only a sufficient number of all such persons are useful. We have shown that the wealth annually produced is taken from its producers, chiefly in form of rent, interest, and profit. Profit being obtained by buying labour cheap and selling it dear " (*Lecture*, p. 69).

The non-producers and useless will, of course, reply that they live upon their property. But Gray rejoins : " This we positively deny, and, on the contrary, affirm that they live upon the property of others." The foundation of all property is labour or accumulated labour. Property not acquired by labour is injustice. The landed proprietor has no right to the land, for the earth is the habitation and natural inheritance of all mankind. And the capitalist, who lives on the interest of money, lives likewise on injustice. " By what principle can a man lend £10 and receive £12 for them ? " (*Ib.*, pp. 34–5). All just exchanges can only be based on equal quantities of labour, while between the possessing and labouring classes no just exchanges can take place.   From these unjust relations spring the irrational luxurious and unnatural living of the rich, and the misery and wretchedness of the poor. " And yet people think Owen a visionary whose plan is to abol sh the circumstances which now limit production, and to give the producers the wealth they produce. It has nothing to do with turning men into angels, but it is simply the employment of mankind upon the principle of co-operation " (*Ib.*, p. 56).

The evils which flow from the misapplication of the principle of exchange are aggravated by competition. It is competition which puts an unnatural limit upon production. In order to show the restraining influence of competition on the production of wealth, let us assume that society determines to call into action the whole industry of the country, and put all the marvellous mechanical inventions and contrivances at its disposal. Under these circumstances the production of wealth would only be limited either by the amount of productive powers extant or by the full satisfaction of the wants of everybody ; and as the productive forces and the wants of society are great, the volume of wealth will be large. The limits thus imposed upon production would be natural. Under the present system neither the power to produce nor the capacity to consume limits wealth. It is competition that does it. At present, production is limited by effective or profitable demand. This demand depends on the amount of wealth which all the classes of society have for purposes of consumption. And the distribution of this amount of wealth among the various classes is regulated by competition. It is competition that fixes the quantity of wealth obtained, in the form of wages, by the productive classes ; the competition among the workmen for an opportunity to labour presses down the rate of wages. The competition among manufacturers and other employers lowers the rate of profit. The same applies to rent. Thus the consumable income of every individual and consequently of the whole country, except those who have fixed incomes, is lowered.. And this national income forming the effective demand, this demand is lowered ; and limited demand means limited production, for, in the present state of society, not a single commodity is produced unless it promises a profit. No matter, therefore, how great the wants of the people are, no matter how enormous the facilities for wealth production are, nothing will be done to remedy these defects, so long as labour is brought into competition with labour, capital with capital, instead of being brought to act in conjunction with each other.

Gray concludes : " In a further Lecture we shall endeavour to explain another set of arrangements on the basis of a national capital, by the introduction of which the only limits to our wealth would be the exhaustion of our productive powers, and the satisfaction of our wants. The plans to which we allude are altogether different from those proposed by Mr. Owen, and we willingly admit that they are altogether inferior to them ; but we entertain a hope that they will be useful in proving to the world that unity of interest is in every way consistent with individuality and distinctions of property, and at a period like the present, when, we hesitate not to say, society is on the eve of relinquishing for ever the commercial principles on which it has hitherto acted, we think that too many modifications of the same fundamental principle cannot be laid before the public, from out of which something advantageous may perhaps be selected."

No further Lecture appeared. Gray invested some money in Combe's Orbiston venture and, of course, lost it, though it must be said that he warned his friends against the adoption of complete communism. Gray removed to Edinburgh, where, in company with his brother, he published a newspaper, at the same time meditating upon his reform plan. In 1831, he published his *Social System*, which shows him to have been, in his way, a lucid thinker and vigorous writer. He abandoned socialism as far as production was concerned, and based his system solely on a plan of equitable exchange. Also his opposition to the existing order of things lost much of its acerbity, and his book is quite free from the bitter invective and moral ardour which characterise his *Lecture*. The exposition of his reform plan is summarised as follows :—

As it is by labour that all things valuable to mankind are produced, so it is by exchange that individuals are enabled to get a variety of things which their own labour could never have commanded without it. Without exchange man could have never emerged from a state of rudest ignorance and barbarism. The present application of the principle of exchange is faulty. It forms the hiding-place of that giant mischief which bestrides the civilised world, rewarding industry with starvation, exertion with disappointment, and the best efforts of the rulers to do good with perplexity and failure. It is this system of exchange which has produced a confusion of ideas on social matters, which find expression in the various demands for parliamentary reform, universal suffrage, annual parliaments, vote by ballot, free trade, repudiation of the national debt, reduction of taxation, repeal of the union, etc., etc. Even if all these demands are granted, nothing will be altered for the better as long as the present form of exchange is left unreformed.

The medium of exchange is money ; its use is the same as that of scales, weights, and measures ; it is to measure and apportion exchanges, to facilitate the giving and obtaining of equivalents. Money, therefore, ought to be as cheap, as accessible and easily attainable by those who have anything to exchange, as a pair of scales or a pound weight, or a yard. If this proposition is true, gold is totally unfit for this purpose : it does not fulfil these conditions ; moreover, it is itself subject to fluctuations of value. It is no exaggeration to say that ninety-nine out of every hundred marketable articles are easier of production and attainment than gold. For this reason money, when based on gold, renders exchange difficult, and thus checks demand, which, in its turn, checks production. Bank notes are exposed to the same objections as gold, for they are uniformly issued upon securities, which, in the aggregate, contain more value than the money advanced upon them. Therefore the nation suffers constantly from a deficiency of money ; the medium of exchange falls always short of the amount of goods waiting for exchange, though the object of money is to enable any man, at any time, to exchange any article of any value for an equal value of any commodity he desires to have in its stead.

Which kind of money would answer this purpose ? Money should be merely a receipt, an evidence that its bearer has contributed a certain value to the national stock of wealth. The use of the receipt should be to enable the bearer to re-obtain the value that was given for it, whenever he pleases, and in whatever shape he may require. But money should not be intrinsically valuable. For the purpose of carrying out such a reform a National Bank should be established, possessing the sole power of manufacturing paper money, and of issuing it to the accredited agents. Another, and the only other, business of the Bank should consist in keeping the national books, and separate accounts with all the agents. All goods should be transmitted from their respective manufactories and workshops to the national ware-houses, where their direct cost or price of material and labour expended is to be ascertained, and a certain percentage or profit, fixed by the Chamber of Commerce, added, to pay the various expenses of rent, interest, depreciation of stock, incidents, and taxes. This would form the retail price of goods. All the warehouses to be under the supervision of agents who give receipts of the goods delivered with the money received for this purpose from the Bank. Thus the amount of money would always be in exact proportion to the goods. The producers would get the exact amount of money value for their goods, and be able to get in exchange from the warehouses any goods they may need.

The accomplishment of this reform will render exchange smooth and equitable. It will then be as easy to sell as to buy. Under this system, the more one will produce the more will he get. The national warehouses will, in the aggregate, form one large reservoir, into which a constant stream of wealth, arising in different places and partaking of different qualities, will drain ; and from that reservoir every producer will draw accord-ing to the labour values he sends in.[1]

Gray evidently presupposed a simple society of small producers, and he never attempted to show that his plan could apply also to a complicated society, with large manufacturing, commercial, and agricultural establishments, working not only for the national but international markets.

5.—WILLIAM THOMPSON

The ethical philosophy of Jeremy Bentham, the labour economics of David Ricardo, and the social views of Robert Owen, were united into a system of socialism by William Thomp-son (d. 1833). As a prosperous landed proprietor of Cork, with an

[1] John Gray, *Social System*, 1831, particularly chap. 5 ; *An Efficient Remedy*, 1842 ; *Lectures on Money*, 1848.

inquiring intellect and philanthropic disposition, he at first turned to the Utilitarian school for enlightenment. He adored Bentham as the Francis Bacon of moral philosophy, and adopted his doctrines and, unfortunately, also his style. His faith in these doctrines was, for a time, strong enough to make him regard Owenism merely as " an improved pauper management," totally unsuitable for society as a whole. This was about the year 1818. Gradually, however, he came to a different conclusion. " Patient study of the subject of distribution led me to mutual co-operation."[1] The year 1822 marked the turning-point of his life, and he sat down to think out how and why he left Bentham for Owen. His excogitations he published, in 1824, in a large volume under the title, *Inquiry into the Principles of the Distribution of Wealth most conducive to Human Happiness*. Its diffuse style and its reiterations—the effects of the author's painful efforts to satisfy his scientific conscience, make the book tedious reading. Still, it is instructive to watch how a Utilitarian becomes a Socialist.

Thompson starts with the concept of Utility, or the pursuit of the greatest possible sum of human happiness. This is the aim of man and the test of the institutions of society. This aim cannot be attained without the physical means of enjoyment or objects of wealth. An abundant production and a just distribution of commodities are therefore the indispensable conditions of happiness. To make the production of wealth abundant, security is necessary, for nobody will undergo the toilsome labour of producing an abundance of goods unless he is sure that he will enjoy them. But abundance of wealth is, by itself, not sufficient to bring about the greatest sum of happiness. For, the British nation is rich in all materials of wealth, in machinery, inventions, intelligence, and industry, and is none the less not happy ; moreover, poverty and misery are really the lot of the majority of the producers. The truth is that to abundant production must be joined a just or equal distribution, *i.e.*, the abundance of wealth must be distributed over the whole population so as to allow every member of the community to satisfy

[1] William Thompson, *Labour Rewarded*, 1827, pp. 98–9.

its needs, instead of leaving the wealth in the hands of the few. By a just distribution only can the total sum of happiness be greatest, for the whole is greater than a part.

But, are security and equality consistent with each other? Will equality of distribution not defeat all efforts to make production abundant? If the industrious and skilful will only receive as much of the wealth as the less industrious, less skilful, or idle and unskilled—or, in other words, if they are deprived of the security of enjoying the fruits of their exertions, they will cease to produce in abundance, and thus render happiness altogether impossible of attainment.

It is the old problem which occupied Bentham and still occupies all those who discuss socialism. It really amounts to the question whether, under socialism, people will work as hard as they do under the system of private property. Bentham, as it is known, replies that security is more important than equality, and wherever they cannot be reconciled with each other equality must be abandoned; the proper policy is to base society on the foundation of private property, and by gradual reform to approach equality.

At this point Thompson turns away from Bentham, and joins the orbit of Owen. He takes from the Utilitarian school utility, or the test of happiness and the anti-governmental creed. All Radicalism was in theory completely libertarian; all government was compulsion and force; but in practice their libertarian view really meant opposition to a Tory government. On the other hand, the co-operative socialists completely adhered to the creed of anti-government. The difference in the respective attitudes to the State or Government has an important bearing on the respective views concerning distribution. Bentham, in adhering to security or private property, needs government laws to regulate distribution in order to secure to the owner of the means of production his rent, interest, and profit. Thompson, in adhering to equality, rejects government laws and looks for those natural laws that govern distribution. His whole *Inquiry* is devoted to a quest after those natural laws. However, at the bottom of this difference of attitude lies the question as to the identity

be free and voluntary as to direction and continuance ; (2) All the products of labour shall be secured to the producers of them ; (3) All exchanges of these products shall be free and voluntary.

These principles carried into effect will result both in security and equality.

Thompson, when working on his *Inquiry*, was not yet quite clear as to the form of society which could best follow up these principles. It is quite conceivable that he had then in view a society consisting of small independent producers, working on individualist lines. But his predilection for Owen's scheme of socialist co-operation was already strongly asserting itself. " Owen of New Lanark has shown how to reconcile equality of distribution with perfect security. Mutual co-operation and equal distribution are the instruments by which he operates " (*Inquiry*, chap. 6, sec. 1). However, at that time he was still hesitating between a free, primitive, democratic society of independent producers, and united labour under a system of voluntary socialism. The latter form soon got the upper hand, and Thompson adopted socialism. In his second book, *Labour Rewarded*, written in 1826 and published in 1827, there is no trace of any hesitation. Here he pleads for a co-operation against any other system of society, particularly against the scheme of free and competing small producers, suggested in Thomas Hodgskin's *Labour Defended* (1825). While the latter is written in an anti-capitalist spirit, full of fight and class warfare, Thompson devises a constructive plan for the emancipation of labour by establishing co-operative societies of production.

With Hodgskin, trades unions are fighting organisations ; he saw them as such in the years 1824-5. With Thompson, trades unions should have for their aim the saving and accumulation of funds with a view to establishing, by a series of successive steps, the co-operative commonwealth. He admits that trades unions, or voluntary associations openly and legally organised by the industrious classes, are likely to be useful ; they can help those who are thrown out of employment ; they will operate as a check on the caprice and selfishness of employers ; they will keep up wages and keep down profits. Moreover, trades unions

Q

will tend to call the intellectual powers of the industrious classes
into full activity, for questions of remuneration are closely
connected with political economy, statistics, nature of legal
institutions, and moral philosophy—subjects which the working
men have hitherto thought to be beyond their ken. Finally,
they will lead them to the discovery that all their methods are
inadequate to secure to them the full produce of their labour,
so that they will be forced to investigate the teachings of the
political economy of co-operation. The trades unions, in raising
the wages and the intellectual and moral level of the working
classes, will have achieved all they can ever achieve. With the
funds saved by them they will then embark on the real work
of redemption, and build up, first, trade manufactories of their
own on the following plan :—

In those trades which require large buildings and machinery,
the funds of the trades unions, comprised in a general union,
should be permanently devoted to the erection of suitable
buildings, and the purchase of the best machinery to give employment to the industrious who might be thrown out of employment
through disagreement with their employers ; the general union
approving of their conduct and entitling them to work at the
trade manufactories, instead of granting them aid from the
Unemployed Funds and supporting them in their enforced idleness. Near the largest seat of every extensive branch of manufacture these buildings and workshops should be erected—a
kind of industrious refuge for the victims of capital. Out of the
products of the labour of those employed in these trade manufactories, nothing should be withheld from the labourers but the
cost of management and depreciation of capital. The unions
should encourage those who are thus employed to become
shareholders of the trade manufactories. Every individual
labourer paying the amount of a share should become a capitalist-
labourer, and would thus enjoy an increased part of the products
of his labour. The same facilities for independence should,
of course, be opened in every department to women as to men ;
no person being permitted to purchase more than one share.
As these trade manufactories would thus come to be possessed

by joint-stock companies of the labourers themselves, other buildings and always improved machinery should be erected with their funds by the unions to keep up a constant refuge for the honest and industrious losing their employments. These establishments of capitalist-labourers would be something approaching to an efficient check on the exactions of mere capitalists. They would prove that capital can be accumulated without the aid of capitalists. But let not the industrious classes think that trade manufactories, even supposing them established in every branch of industry, would secure the labourers from the vicissitudes of the capitalist system. No, for they would still be burdened with payments of rent on the land on which their buildings stand, and profits on the raw materials —cotton, metals, etc.—which they use ; and they would still be exposed in their transactions to all the uncertainties of competition, the rivalries of similar establishments conducted by capitalists, and the fluctuations of trade dependent on the general markets. The workmen engaged in those trade manufactories would then find themselves under the necessity to have recourse to more advanced measures—to buy land, form agricultural associations, and finally form communities of co-operative production for their mutual wants. The progressive advance of Labour is from trades unions through knowledge and moral character to mutual co-operation.[1]

Thompson was at that time already one of the pillars of the London Co-operative Society, and one of the most assiduous contributors of the *Co-operative Magazine*. In 1830, he published a manual for co-operators under the title, *Practical Directions for the Establishment of Communities*, in which he laid down the principles of the political economy of co-operation : " Want or uncertainty of employment for the industrial classes is the master-evil of society as now constituted. What immediately causes want of employment ? Want of sale or market. Goods when produced cannot be sold at all or not at a price that would repay the cost of production ; therefore manufacturers cannot give permanent and remunerative employment. The remedy

[1] *Labour Rewarded*, 1827, pp. 87–93.

evidently is to find an unfailing market for all sorts of useful produce. The system of co-operative industry accomplishes this, not by the vain search after foreign markets throughout the globe which are no sooner found than overstocked or glutted by the restless competition of the starving producers, but by the voluntary union of the industrious classes in such numbers as to afford a market to each other by working together for each other, for the direct and mutual supply by themselves of all the most indispensable wants in the way of food, clothing, dwelling, and furniture."

Thompson took part in all the co-operative meetings and congresses. He was also one of the most thorough-going advocates of equality of rights for women, and wrote with this view a pamphlet entitled, *An Appeal of one-half of the Human Race* (1825). In fact, the whole co-operative-socialist movement identified itself with this demand. Thompson desired his property to be devoted to co-operative purposes, but his will was contested by his relatives in an action which outlasted the whole period of experimental socialism.[1]

6.—JOHN MINTER MORGAN

" In acute analytical investigation, in just and comprehensive views of society, and in bold uncompromising exposition of error, the *Distribution of Wealth* by Mr. William Thompson is perhaps unrivalled ; it is the most able work upon Political Economy that has appeared since the *Wealth of Nations*." This enthusiastic eulogy was passed by John Minter Morgan (1782–1854), a Christian Owenite, in his *Revolt of the Bees* (p. 81), which appeared in 1826. Morgan belongs to the popularisers of Owenism, and was eminently fitted for his task in virtue of his poetic style, singleness of purpose, and complete lack of originality. He was one of the earliest adherents of Owen, and published in 1819

[1] William Thompson's main teachings are to be found in his *Inquiry*, Preface, chap. 1, sections 6, 9, 11, 14, and Concluding Remarks ; then in *Labour Rewarded*, and *Practical Directions*, Introductory Remarks. *Cf. Poor Man's Guardian*, February 1, 1834.

a booklet entitled *On the Practicability of Owen's Plan.* His most popular work was the *Revolt of the Bees ;* it was much read by working men, and popular writers ; Harriet Martineau, quite a power in those times, knew it,[1] and the *Co-operative Magazine* published lengthy extracts from it. The author looks upon society as a hive of bees which had left its instinctive communal order, the state of nature, and instituted private property and competition, in the train of which came poverty and strife, super-abundance and misery, crime and punishment, lawyers and judges, moral precepts and immoral deeds. They had forgotten that under the primitive system, when each had its moderate portion of honey, there was no repletion, no destitution, and consequently neither theft nor murder. The miseries now occasioned by selfishness, folly, and ambition, to which the new system gave birth, excited the commiseration of the more reflecting bees, and from time to time there would arise individuals who devoted themselves voluntarily to the relief of the distressed. Once it happened that an ingenious bee invented a contrivance by which honey and wax could be made in large quantities with the aid of a few workers only. This scheme was imitated by others to such an extent that the poor working bees lost much of their employment. Then came the political economists, who argued that the misery could only be alleviated by greater accumulations of honey in the hands of the few rich, while one of their cleverest drones declared that the misery was due to the fact that there were too many working bees, and no matter how much honey was accumulated, the increase of the number of bees would always be much greater. This opinion became general, and there appeared to be no other alternative for the unemployed and hungry than to commit suicide. At that juncture a wise bee (Owen) appeared and showed them a way out of all misery, but its advice was regarded as visionary. It therefore flew away to a far-off land. However, since 1824 the poor bees began to shake off the despondency into which they had been thrown by the clever drones and to take to the teachings of the wise bee.

[1] *Poor Man's Guardian,* 1832, p. 383.

No lengthy explanations are needed to show that Morgan intended to give an outline of the state of nature, the introduction of private property, the coming of the inventions, the theory of Malthus, and the doctrines of Owen.

Dropping metaphor Morgan assumes that man had gone through four revolutions, and was now entering on the fifth. In the first stage mankind appeared as a noble savage ; in the second, as a shepherd ; in the third, as an agriculturist ; in the fourth, " science enabled man to produce riches in superabundance, but as yet the right to use them was unknown ; there might have been seen immense wealth in the midst of a starving population, more strife and contention than when less wealth prevailed, and infinitely more discord and crime." In the fifth stage a far greater change was taking place than in any of the preceding. Wealth, which had before lain in masses, was now being beneficially diffused and greatly increased, and with it invaluable riches of mind, knowledge, and virtue were spreading over the land.

7.—THOMAS ROWE EDMONDS

The author with whom we are going to deal cannot be said strictly to belong to the Owenite school of co-operative Socialism, but he is closely related to it by postulating happiness as the object of society; further, by using Ricardian economic concepts; finally, by advocating the social system. He differs from that school only by his appealing to the higher classes, and not to the working men, to introduce socialism, and by his belief in the efficacy of political methods. Edmonds (1803–89) was a Cornishman who graduated at Cambridge and soon after wrote a treatise, entitled *Practical, Moral, and Political Economy most conducive to Individual Happiness and National Power* (1828). For all its dispassionate and sober reasonings it is in its effect as condemnatory of the system of private property as any book which emanated from the Owenite school. Edmonds appears to have been influenced by Paley's *Moral and Political Philosophy*, then by Ricardo's *Principles*, whose views on value and wages he fully accepts, and by the whole socialist and anti-capitalist current of the time. Also Malthus's population theory was not without influence on him, though it was rather disturbing than positive. He argues for socialism in the following manner :—

Every man is in pursuit of happiness, yet he is still very far from having achieved it. The obstacles which stand between him and his object are ignorance, private property, competition, and a relative excess of population. Man, therefore, requires, before all, knowledge—knowledge of the physical and moral world. Useful physical knowledge has for its object the diminution of labour required to provide a given quantity of the necessaries of life, as food, clothing, lodging, and national defence, while mental or moral knowledge has for its object the exploration of the faculties and affections of the mind with the view of their being applied to the improvement of physical and social knowledge, and, consequently, the increase of human happiness (p. 264). But man is prevented from acquiring this knowledge by the love of money. This has become the predominant passion and excludes all really useful mental pursuits. It has even infested the minds of men of cultivated understanding whose opinions rule the opinions of all other men ; and the possessing and ruling classes are not slow in making use of this passion of scholars, and thus array the men of talent against truth (p. 262). Likewise, the Government does not favour freedom of discussion on the subject of social happiness. In consequence, minds of the highest order in England cannot publicly express themselves on subjects most vital to the community. All this is the effect of private property, and the division of society into two classes, masters and labourers.

The labourers work as hard as horses and produce all the necessaries and luxuries of life. The labourers who produce the necessaries are productive labourers, but receive only one-third of the produce of their toil, while two-thirds are taken away from them by the masters (p. 108-9). It is productive labour that supplies the nation with wealth, and it is the quantity of labour that measures the value of all commodities, but labour itself is measured by the necessaries of life. No matter how much a labourer may produce he will only get as much thereof as is necessary to keep him alive. If the arts of a country are so advanced that one labourer can produce necessaries for two men, he gets as wages half of it ; if the arts are so advanced that one labourer produces necessaries for three, as it appears to be the case in England, he will get one-third (p. 100–1) ; and should the arts and sciences advance to such a degree that one labourer could produce for ten, he would but receive one-tenth (pp. 122, 288).

The effect of this division of the produce is in the highest degree deplorable. The labourers, condemned to a life of a beast of burden, follow a principle of action similar to that of a horse, in being always ready to propagate, though they know that the result can only be semi-starvation and pauperism for themselves and their offspring. Pauperism, although apparently it is the effect of over-population, and can only be obviated by sexual restraint of the workmen,[1] is in reality the effect of private property, for there is hardly a country in Europe which could not sustain ten times as many people as they do sustain now (p. 107).

Finally, trade and commerce are at present regulated by competition. There is, therefore, a tendency in all capitals to undersell one another, that is, to diminish the rate of profit, and thus to reduce the revenue of the smaller capitals, while the larger capitals are amply compensated by quicker returns, with the result that, although by lowering the price of the commodities they lower the rate of profit, their total profit is larger than before.

Those are the causes that thwart man in his efforts to attain to happiness.

There are, however, in man and capital, certain tendencies that counteract those causes, and, aided by human endeavour, might lead to happiness. There is the social instinct. " Sociality," or the collecting together of many men for the purpose of united action, is a natural desire and necessity. Nature has so ordered it that the majority of pleasures and improvements depend on

---

[1] Edmonds was so disturbed by the view that over-population was the immediate cause of pauperism that he regarded as " the best cure for pauperism a tax on marriage both of masters and labourers " (*Practical, Moral, and Political Economy*, p. 113).

society. As the number of men forming one society increases the saving of labour increases, happiness increases, and the rapidity of progress made in the physical and moral arts and sciences increases (pp. 238, 268). Then there is the tendency of capital to concentrate or unite together and form one great fund under a single management. Competition soon teaches the merchant and shopkeeper and trader that only by collecting together many small capitals he will be able to reap high profits. By the increase of the size or the amount of single capitals the national wealth or power is increased, because by this increase, and united action, a greater quantity of commodities may be produced by a given quantity of labour. By the decrease of competition in consequence of the decrease of single capitals acting independently of each other, the profits become more regular and secure. When the labour employed in the different arts and crafts has been collected into very large and distinct capitals, all will probably unite and form a single corporation (pp. 128-30).

To these two natural tendencies, viz. sociality of men and association of capital should be added the principle of improved propagation of men and women. " The breed of men, like that of all other animals, is capable of infinite improvement in mind as well as in body. The bodies of the coming generation may be rendered superior in health, strength, activity to the present generation by selecting for the purposes of propagation the individuals of both sexes possessing those qualities, and not allowing the weak and diseased to transmit their diseases and miseries to posterity." The same principle of propagation should be applied to mental qualities. And with the help of training and education the human race could be made fit for the highest tasks.

Finally, there is a law of God and nature " that no man or class of men can increase their happiness by oppressing, or by diminishing the happiness of other men or other classes of men. The law of nature is that the interests of individuals and the interests of the public shall always be inseparably linked together " (p. 261).

If we enlist for our purpose these tendencies and principles we can devise a plan of rendering society happy and powerful. Such a society may be denominated the " Social System " on account of its being based on sociality and equality (p. 281). By way of illustrating the social system the author assumes that about a thousand people, agriculturists, craftsmen, and scientists, decide to settle in some distant isle which contains about 5,000 acres of land. They do not commence by dividing the land into a thousand equal parts and isolate each man on his five acres, but resolve to work together in order to enjoy the benefits of large capital, proper division of labour, mutual defence and assistance. All matters of administration they put into the hands of a small number of elected persons distinguished by the clearest judgment and most firmly rooted principles of justice. These persons form a representative assembly who select from their midst the best and fittest as justices, for no social system can exist if the administration of justice does not command the confidence of all. This secured, the members of the community will direct their attention to the organisation of production. All the men of the same trade will collect together, in one mass, each man's machinery, stock, and labour, in other words, all the capitals of any one trade will be collected into one single capital. At least one half of the community will consist of agriculturists, who, besides their fixed capital (machinery, stock), must possess necessaries (circulating capital) to be consumed by the five hundred men during the process of production. Since all the agriculturists have an equal right to govern their collective capital, the government, or management of this capital must be performed by a small number of their representatives. The management of the capitals of the other trades will be regulated on the same principle. And the governments of all capitals will be subject to the general government.

After providing for equal administration of justice and for the management of collective labour, the community will turn its attention to fostering the gregarious instinct and the increase of sociality by erecting large apartment houses, common dining-rooms, sitting-rooms, lecture halls, theatres, concerts, dancing-halls, libraries, open to the whole population.

The community will then be united by the threefold cord of equal administration of justice, collective labour, and sociality. When these social bonds will have reached a high degree of perfection, injustice will disappear, and with it the necessity of the Courts of Justice. Collective labour and sociality will then be of sufficient strength to keep the community closely together and perpetuate happiness. The only pressure which the assembly of representatives might have to apply would be in matters of propagation. Should over-population threaten, then it would be necessary to prevent the weak in body or mind from multiplying, and to take the quota of children necessary for the existence of the community from the stronger members only.

The benefits to be derived from the social system will be so considerable that the nation which first adopts it will so far exceed in power all other nations that they will fall an easy prey to it and be compelled to adopt the same system. The British nation is the one which, in all probability, will soonest arrive at the social system and which will spread it over the world. England is more powerful than any other nation because its system approaches nearest to the social system. There is equal administration of justice, concentration of capital, division of labour ; only sociality is lacking. The population of English towns is divided and split up into a multitude of different ranks, sets, groups, with no intercourse between them. This lack of sociality is manifest in the pride, self-consciousness, and ferocity of the English. And this is the main cause of the unhappiness so prevalent among them (p. 250). And nowhere are the working classes so degraded as in England, for the upper classes keep them in ignorance. All reform in England must be directed towards fostering sociality.

The social system is the ideal towards which all governments tend, and at which they cannot fail to arrive sooner or later. It is in harmony with nature and the doctrines of Christianity (pp. 270–288). The establishment of the social system should be the work of the thinking and richer classes, for only to them would the bulk of the population pay attention, while any reform undertaken by the working classes would be insecure and finally

fail. Changes proposed by the working classes " even if con-
formable to truth, or conducive to happiness, could not be carrried
by them into effect ; the exceptions to the general truth would
stagger them, they would reject the truth in despair, and things
would return to a worse state than before " (303–4). In other
words, the author is evidently of opinion that working men, by
assuming that a theory must uncompromisingly be carried out,
are bound to fail in their efforts for reform ; they do not see that
a theory can only become workable when it is corrected by, or
enters into a compromise with, practice. This is, indeed, one of
the causes of failure of revolutionary movements.

8.—JOHN FRANCIS BRAY

The synthesis of Owenite teachings and anti-capitalist criticisms
was effected by John Francis Bray in his *Labour's Wrongs and
Labour's Remedy* (1838–9), a book written with great knowledge
and genuine rhetorical fire. He was born June 26, 1809, in
Washington City, U.S.A., as son of John Bray, comedian and
writer, a native of Yorkshire. Father and son returned to
England in 1822 and settled with their relatives at Leeds, where
John Francis attended school and then worked as compositor
at the *Leeds Times*, edited by Samuel Smiles (*Self Help*)[1]. He
was active in the labour movement, read Owen, Gray, and
Hodgskin, and was profoundly grieved at the constant efforts
of the working classes to ameliorate their condition, or to accomplish their emancipation, by trade unionist and political methods,
notwithstanding all the failures and disappointments which
attended their feverish activities in the political and trade
unions. And when he finally witnessed the rising tide of Chartism he summoned up all his energies and his store of philosophic
and economic knowledge for the purpose of demonstrating to the
working classes that the only remedy for their wrongs was
mutual co-operation in production, distribution, and exchange.
His book is the last and most powerful manifesto of Owenism.

[1]Bray returned in 1842 to U.S.A., lived in the state of Michigan
as printer, journalist, and farmer, later on, with his relatives and
grandchildren in and near Boston, and died in 1895. (Compare also
Socialist Review, London, Sept., 1916.)

The doctrines concerning happiness, natural rights, circumstances as builders of character, capitalist production, labour-value, co-operative enterprise, socialisation of exchange, and the priority of economics to politics, are combined and fused into one whole by the concentrated heat of an intensely thinking mind. He argues :

Were we able to take an unprejudiced survey of the human race we should compare it to a group of shipwrecked men thrown upon an almost desert island. There is sufficient room for all to live and move, plenty of materials necessary to support existence, but nothing can be done without labour. It requires labour to gather even the wild fruits from the trees, or the shell-fish from the shore. Without labour we die. Surely, the most rational mode of action for men so circumstanced would be to unite in parties, work and share alike, and render to each other mutual assistance and protection. But men have hitherto done nothing of the kind. They have pursued different tracks, and have moved on alone, each for himself, although they have all been in search of the same object—happiness. The result has been complete failure to achieve it. And it could not be otherwise, since men have neglected the first principles of society, or the rights of nature. We live in an unnatural society. All this restlessness and yearning and dissatisfaction of a great part of humanity is due to that fact. Our whole social fabric is one vast Babel of interests, in which true charity, morality, and brotherly love are absent. The hand of every man is raised against every other man ; the interests of every class are opposed to those of every other class, and all other interests are in opposition and hostility to those of the working class. This unnatural state of things was originally brought about and is now maintained by man's ignorance of the first principles promulgated in the great book of Nature, which may be thus interpreted :

(1) All men are alike in regard to their substance, their creation, and their preservation, the inequalities in men's nature mostly arising from the different circumstances in which men are placed, and from the inequalities produced by the artificial state of things.

(2) The materials requisite for the preservation of life—food, clothing, and shelter—exist everywhere around us, but they are naturally valueless or unobtainable until labour intervenes ; therefore, as the life of man cannot be maintained without a due provision of food, clothing, and shelter, and as these cannot be procured without labour, it follows that every human being ought to labour.

(3) As the nature and wants of all men are alike, the rights of all must be equal ; and as human existence is dependent on the same contingencies, it follows that the great field for all exertions and the raw material of all wealth, the earth, is the common property of all its inhabitants.

Equality of men, equality of rights and duties, common ownership of the soil, are the laws of nature.

Further, it is labour alone that bestows value. Every man has an undoubted right to all his honest labour can procure him ; when he thus appropriates the fruits of his labour he commits no injustice upon any other human being ; but if any individual appropriates the field on which all labour is exercised, he clearly infringes the common equality of rights. And these rights have been destroyed by the appropriation of the land. Or, as the author puts it, " From the very nature of the thing, and the position in which man stands with regard to his fellows, he never did, and never can, individually, possess any exclusive right to one single inch of land. Wherever such an assumed right is set up and acted upon, there will always exist injustice, tyranny, poverty, and inequality of rights, whether the people be under the monarchical or the republican form of government ; for all the wrongs and woes which man has ever committed or endured, may be traced to the assumption of right in the soil by certain individuals and classes to the exclusion of other individuals and classes. Equality of right can never be enjoyed until all individual claims to landed property are subverted, and merged in those of the nation at large " (p. 33–4).

From this prolific source of evil have arisen despotisms, governmental power, domination of class over class, riches and misery—in short, the wrongs of Labour must be traced back to inequality of possessions. No change of forms of government or laws, no struggles for higher wages and a shorter number of working hours can remove those wrongs, for government and laws or conditions of employment are the effects, and not the causes, of the evil. Wherever inequality of possessions prevails, inequality of rights and duties must necessarily exist. Our politicians have always been wont to make laws for rich men as such, and poor men as such, without ever inquiring how it came to pass that some men were rich and some were poor ; or how it happened that one class toiled away, generation after generation, without becoming any richer, and the other class ate, drank, and were merry, generation after generation, without becoming less rich. The politicians have almost always taught the workmen to look for relief to governmental changes and reforms ; but the majority of these advisers have not belonged to the working classes ; and, connected as they are with the rich, and living as they do on rents and profits, they are necessarily hostile to the interests and wishes of labour. The politicians who always descant on the load of taxation, cost of royalty, etc., do not know that taxes form a relatively small fraction of the social burden of Labour. The amount of taxation is now (1838) about fifty millions sterling. On the other hand, the value of the goods produced by the working classes of the United Kingdom is no less than five hundred millions, of which they receive in wages about two hundred millions ; thus the capitalists and landlords deprive them of three-fifths of their labour produce. A right understanding of the tables of production and distribution, as given by Colquhoun and Gray, could teach the working classes more than all the speeches of the politicians and taxation reformers (pp. 76, 85). The insufficiency of political measures to remedy social grievances was long since seen by thousands of the working classes ; they had some sort of conception that the gain of the capitalist was the loss of the producer ; and therefore sought relief by the institution of trade societies and trades unions. But these also had the same ultimate object in view as the political unions—namely, the partial amelioration of the condition of the working class as such.

Likewise, factory legislation can, at best, have no other effect. All these remedies will reduce neither the number of the rich nor the poor ; and therefore they are not capable of curing the evils which this relative position and this division of society inflict upon the workman. The capitalist or employer, by his very position in society as the purchaser and controller of the labour of the working class, has it in his power to suck from them the greater part of the wealth which they produce. Indeed, capital arises from unpaid labour.

" Every accumulation of the capitalist or employers, as a body, is derived from the unsurrendered earnings of the working class, or persons employed ; and wherever one man thus becomes rich, he does so only on condition that many men shall remain poor " (p. 56). All this is done by means of unequal exchanges. The workmen have always given the capitalist the labour of a whole day for the value of only a half day, and even this value had been previously taken from Labour, since the capitalist, being a non-producer, can have nothing to exchange. It is this inequality of exchanges, and not the supposed inequality of bodily and mental powers, that makes the rich richer and the poor poorer (pp. 48-9).

The division of society into two classes, into capitalists and labourers—into those who produce everything and get little, and into those who produce nothing and get the most—is the root of evil. It perpetuates the division of interests, and by bringing individuals into hostile contact in the common scramble for subsistence, destroys those germs of social sympathy which naturally exist in all men, while the germs of self-love are fostered and even forced to a riotously profuse growth and unnatural development. To apply to an evil of this potency the measures advocated by politicians is to equip men with pop-guns for a hunting expedition in a jungle.

However, while reviewing their wrongs and devising remedies, the working class must never lose sight of the fact that their warfare is not against men, but against a system,—not against capitalists as individuals nor against capital itself, but against the present mode of applying capital, against that system which gives to irresponsible individuals the power of grinding masses of labour between masses of capital. There is no remedy for this except a change of system. Without such a change, the cause of the redemption of the working class is a hopeless one !

From the nature of the evil it follows that the remedy can only be found in the establishment of equal exchanges—exchanges of equal quantities of labour. Such an equality, once established, would necessarily lead to universal labour, or to the extinction of the idle classes. The social burden will then be taken off the shoulders of the working classes (p. 110).

This change must be undertaken with a view to a reconciliation of interests, to uniting all into one interest. And this is only possible in a social system based on community of possessions, as devised by Robert Owen. Such a form of society is in every respect the most perfect which is in the power of man to institute, but it cannot be called into existence at one stroke, for it requires a degree of excellence of character and reasoning capacities which but few enjoy to-day. We are all tainted by, and more or less imbued with, the depravity and ill-feeling which the present system generates. The failures which have hitherto attended co-operative experiments have been due either to those causes or to lack of capital. If, then, a changed character be essential to the success of the community system in its most perfect form, and if the present system affords no circumstances and no facilities for effecting the requisite change of character, it is evident that things must necessarily remain as they are, unless one of the two methods are adopted. Either those who commence a new system must possess accumulations of capital sufficient to overcome the drawbacks imposed by the present system until the superior circumstances created by the new system shall have done their work, or else some preparatory step must be discovered—some intermediate resting-place, to which men may go with all their faults and follies, and from which they may move forward, imbued with those qualities without which the system of community and equality cannot exist.

After having dealt with all the familiar objections to com-

R

munism and proved them to have emanated either from prejudice and ignorance or from the failures of rashly undertaken
communist experiments, the author devises, as a preliminary
step to the perfect social system, the formation of communities in
form of joint-stock companies, based on the following principles :
Society is to consist of one class only, labourers, mental and
manual, united together in an indefinite number of communities
or joint-stock companies, in which labour is to be universal and
the remuneration in proportion to the time of labour.   These
communities would hold possession of the land and the productive
capital of the nation ; they would likewise possess a circulating
bank-note or paper medium, amounting to two thousand million
pounds sterling ; they would mutually and universally produce
and distribute wealth, exchanging their labour and their productions on one broad principle of equality. This vast confederation of
labour would have somewhat the character of a modern joint-
stock company, and would bring forth its results by means of
similar appliances.   There would be general and local magazines of
food and necessaries ; this produce would be distributed by means
of large markets or bazaars instead of through innumerable petty
tradesmen ;   and every commodity would be procurable in any
part of the country for its wholesale cost of production, neither
depreciated by abundance—social statistics based on the national
accounts would preclude gluts—nor enhanced by the artifices of
speculators.   The production and transport, and, generally, the
affairs of society at large, would be regulated by national and
local boards of various kinds, the members of which would be
elected by the communities.   A national bank would create the
circulating medium, and issue it to the managers of various companies in proportion to the number of members of each company,
or the character of their occupation.   With this money, all
individuals and companies would purchase commodities and
transact their exchanges, on the present principle of trade ; and,
either by the imposition of a direct tax on persons, or a percentage
on commodities, necessary funds would be forthcoming for the
expenses of administration.   The money issued would always
keep within the limits of actual effective capital existing.   The

money would always be at hand to pay for the labour—the labour would always be ready to exert its power for this universal representative of capital, and thus, while the money would insure the labour, the labour itself would insure the creation of commodities. Production, accumulation, distribution, and consumption would naturally be adjusted to each other, thus precluding confusion, gluts, unemployment, and poverty.

For the rest, no accurate and detailed description of future arrangements can be given by any human being. For, as the knowledge of every man is acquired either through his own experience or the experience of others, he can never accurately foretell and determine how individuals will feel and act, in every instance, when placed in new circumstances. We can only judge from the past and present, and keep in view principles, actions, and incentives to action ; by combining experience with principle, or practice with theory, we can make an approximation to the results sought for. The efforts of the communists are of this character ; although they may not be able to point out every trivial arrangement which might be adopted by a people acting upon such a system, the principles on which it is founded, and the general outline of it, will serve as a standard with which to compare and test existing social arrangements. And it is not the communists or any other individuals who are preparing the change of the social system. " The present crisis is no more than a natural movement attending the course of things—it is but one move of that mighty ocean of events, the billows of which have rolled on from eternity, and will progress in unchecked power for ever . . . it was advancing even when polished Greece and Rome degenerated into semi-barbarism—it was coming on when the French Revolution took place . . . and it is at this moment passing before our eyes and bearing us along, destroying and reinstituting political and social institutions of every character and kind. The present is not a merely local movement, it is not confined to country, colour, or creed—the universe is the sphere in which it acts . . . and whatever may be its immediate prospect, there are to be seen harbingers of brighter and better times. The light of Mind is beaming through the gloomy boundaries of the Age of Might, and ushering in the Age of Right."[1]

[1] Bray's book was regarded by Socialists and Chartists as a standard work (*Northern Star*, May 20, 1843) ; *O'Brien's National Reformer and Manx Weekly Review*, Oct. 24, 1846 ; Karl Marx *Misère de la Philosophie*, 1847.

VIII

ECONOMICS OF ANTI–CAPITALISM

I.—" A LETTER TO LORD JOHN RUSSELL "

The revolutionary ferment consequent upon the rise of the new manufactures and aggravated by the Napoleonic Wars, the distress which had set in at the end of 1816, and the propaganda of Owen, produced a revulsion of feeling and reasoning against the capitalist mode of production and its economic theories, particularly as formulated by Ricardo, whose concise statement of principles and verbal inaccuracies in details offered a favourable front to attack. The writers who led the attack were, as already stated in a preceding chapter, by no means socialists. They only saw in capitalism a destructive or subversive force dangerous to the welfare of the working-classes in particular, and to the nation in general. The comprehensive and sweeping character of their criticism is out of all proportion to their indefinite and halting proposals for reforms. Their leading idea is, capital is really preserved labour ; the foundation of value is labour ; and yet, socially, Capital is everything and Labour nothing ! The reverse ought to be the case. No socialist has ever surpassed these writers in the emphasis they laid on the opposition of interests and the irreconcilable antagonism between capital and labour. Most of their thought was communicated to the rising Labour Movement by Thomas Hodgskin, of whom we shall treat later on. One of the first critics of capitalism was an anonymous writer of an open letter to Lord John Russell on *The Source and Remedy of the National Difficulties* (1821).

Our country, he says, is suffering, and the revenue of the nation is rising. Political economists count those nations richest where the greatest revenue can be raised, " as if the power of compelling or inducing men to labour twice as much at the mills of Gaza for the enjoyment of the Philistines were a proof of anything but a tyranny or an ignorance twice as powerful " (p. 1).

This is the arsis. And now comes the thesis. Labour, either our own or of others, is the source of wealth and revenue. The wealth of a nation consists in its preserved labour, or rather in its preserved surplus labour, that is, labour beyond its usual and necessary consumption. Surplus labour, then, means all the labour of the individual beyond what is exclusively appropriated to the maintenance and enjoyment of himself and family. Such labour is capital (p. 3).

And as this surplus labour is not owned by those who produced it, but by those who allowed the labourer the necessaries while he was producing it, therefore, capital is surplus labour taken away from the producer.

Capital has the power of reproduction. All political economists have for their object to suggest means to increase capital. But it will be shown that the accumulation of capital is very limited if we look at the condition of the whole population, and not at the opulence of the few, or at the high rate of interest which the labourers have to pay to the capitalist for the loan of the means of production.

The author assumes that profit is merely another name for interest ; the usurer lends money, the capitalist lends fixed and circulating capital to the labourers, who only leave to themselves as much of the produce of their labour as to enable them to subsist and perpetuate the race, while the rest goes as surplus labour to the lender of capital, *i.e.*, the capitalist.

Notwithstanding these appropriations, capital accumulates but slowly, since a high rate of interest has to be paid by the producer for its use. And this slow accumulation of capital is the immediate cause of the distress of the nation.

In order to grasp the meaning of this cause and find out its source, let us suppose a simple society where the whole labour of the country is just sufficient to support the whole population. In this case there is no surplus labour, and consequently no accumulation of capital. Suppose now the whole labour of the country can raise as much in one year as would maintain it two years, then either one year's produce must perish or the population must cease work for one year. But, of course, nothing of the kind will take place. The appropriators of the surplus produce or capital will, for one year, employ the labour on commodities not directly consumable, *i.e.*, on buildings, machinery, roads, etc. But the third year will again be devoted to productive labour, and, with the aid of the machinery built last year, the population will produce much more than in the first year, and consequently the surplus labour will be greater. It would follow still more that either the surplus commodities should perish or the population cease labour until the commodities were consumed. However, the labouring population will never be asked how to get rid of the surplus produce, but the capitalists will accumulate it. Looking at the reproductive power of capital and at the readiness of the great mass of the people to apply their labour to it, capital ought to go on increasing until no man would have any difficulty in getting it. And the falling rate of interest shows the tendency in that direction, but so long as capital can command interest at all, society cannot have arrived at the maximum production of wealth. When that maximum is reached society will not go on to exert its productive power as before, but will reduce its hours of labour from twelve to six. This beginning of general ease would be the beginning of real prosperity.

Wealth of the nation does not mean the opulence of the few, but facilities of living for all. " Wealth is liberty—liberty to recreation—liberty to enjoy life—liberty to improve the mind. Wealth is disposable time, and nothing more " (p. 6).

Considering all the facilities for production and the great benefits which would accrue from it to the nation at large, the question is, why has society never arrived yet at this prosperous situation ?

The first dead weight that impedes the progress of production is the possessor of capital who, as soon as surplus labour is available, ceases to work and maintains himself on the interest, or the surplus labour of others. He becomes an idle consumer. The increase in the production of wealth is marked by an increase of idle persons, and their menial servants and parasites. Thus, the momentum of wealth production is slackened. Moreover, the idle classes, besides exacting surplus labour for lending real capital, inflate the capital of the country by issuing fictitious paper money and stock,—fictitious because not covered by gold and silver or increase of real capital ; and for this fictitious paper capital they exact interest from Labour. Finally, they destroy enormous amounts of real capital by wars, and they waste real capital by exporting it to foreign countries in exchange for luxuries. We may safely assume that if capital does not decrease in value as it increases in amount, the capitalist exacts from the labourer the produce of every hour's labour beyond what is possible for the worker to subsist on. The less useful the capitalist becomes, the stronger his lust for appropriating and accumulating the surplus labour of others ; the more he wastes, the greater the exactions from the producers.

What are the exactions from Labour ? These can only be roughly estimated. According to Patrick Colquhoun's *Resources of the British Empire*, a labouring family consisting of four persons receives £45 annually, or £11 per head. We may, therefore, assume that the mere labour of any member of society is not worth more than £11 per annum ; and all income beyond that sum represents interest on the capital outlay for education, apprenticeship, training, etc. If a clergyman or a lawyer receives two, three, or four hundred a year, it is because two, three, or four thousand pounds is presumed to have been expended on his education. Taking now from Colquhoun the number of the heads of families of other classes and allowing to each the worth of mere labour, £45 per annum, we are able to separate the worth of this labour, or the just wages, from the interest they derive from capital, as the following table shews :—

The total income of these classes amounts to about 276 millions sterling, the value of their labour is about 41 millions' sterling. Consequently, they exact as interest on capital no less a sum than 235 millions, or six times as much as their labour is worth (pp. 35–6).

Number of Heads of Families.	Rank, Degree, Occupation.	Income per Family. £	Just Wage per Family. £	Interest on Capital. £
68,937	Royalty, Nobility ...	67,753.590	3,102,165	64,651,425
621,000	Professions, Farmers ...	92,830,000	27,945,000	64,885,000
35,000	Bankers, Merchants ...	30,064,000	1,575,000	28,489,000
9,250	Shipowners, etc. ...	5,652,000	426,250	5,225,750
44,900	Manufacturers, etc. ...	36,099,600	2,020,500	34,079,100
183,750	Shopkeepers, Traders ..	35,875,000	4,268,750	31,606,250
35,874	Teaching profession ...	7,664,400	1,614,330	6,050,070
	Total	275,938,590	40,951,995	234,986,595

The effect on society is deplorable.

" The increase of trade and commerce opened a boundless field to luxuries ; the splendour of the luxurious enjoyments of the few excited a worthless, debasing, and selfish emulation in all. The attainment of wealth became the ultimate purpose of life. . . . Their appetite was corrupted in their infancy that it might leave its natural and wholesome nutriment, and feed on the garbage of Change Alley. . . And the consummation of their hopes was characterised by misery and ignorance, the dissolution of all social virtue and common sympathy among individuals, and by a disunited, feeble, despotic, and despised government " (p. 18–19).

We have reached a stage of social life when Colquhoun wants the working men to feed on potatoes instead of bread. To such a pass has the nation been brought through injustice and bad policy. None the less, the political economists do not cease to write about the wealth of the nation and to exalt capital. In reality, the progress of a nation is marked by reduction of the hours of labour and rise of wages. These are unmistakable signs of prosperity ; and growth of capital would bring this about if we could eliminate the factors that retard and check it. Moreover, the emancipation of labour depends on abundant capital. When capital is increased in such masses that the rate of interest sinks to zero, the hour of freedom for all mankind will have arrived.

As to the measures to bring this flood of wealth over the earth the author hardly suggests any. He denies that he is " for levelling all classes and distinctions, or reducing the pay of a judge to the wage of a labourer, or any other such foolish speculations." He merely demands abolition of the Corn Laws, reduction of the interest on the National Debt, " for the loans to the Government were made in depreciated currency, which has now been restored to its full value," reduction of rentals and a general rise of wages.[1]

This anonymous pamphlet may have had some influence on John Gray.

[1] *Cf.* Karl Marx, *Theorien über den Mehrwert*, III., pp. 281–305.

2.—PIERCY RAVENSTONE

One of the seminal minds of the period was the author of the remarkable book, *A few Doubts as to the Correctness of some Opinions Generally Entertained on the Subject of Political Economy* (1821), and of a pamphlet, entitled *Thoughts on the Funding System and its Effects* (1824). He signed himself " Piercy Ravenstone," but it is very doubtful whether this was his real name ; it is rather probable that it is a pseudonym. Of his life nothing has been ascertained. In the Goldsmiths' Economic Library (London University) there are two copies of the book, one bearing the autograph " Henry Brougham, Esq. From the Author." The other copy is from the library of Sir Robert Peel. However, no matter what the name and history of the life of the author were, his works exercised a great influence on that group of writers and working class agitators, who, though averse from socialism, were intensely anti-capitalist, and laid the foundation of the class-warfare theory.

Ravenstone was essentially a Tory Democrat, but without any ulterior motives, without any other end to serve than what he considered justice and national welfare. Of an ardent temperament, a religious and cultured mind, his whole being was in revolt against capitalist and Stock Exchange dominion. He must have been in an advanced age when he wrote his first book, for the experience which he brought to bear upon it was full of pessimism, caused evidently by the French Revolution, the Napoleonic Wars, and the terrible years 1816 to 1820. He was then firmly convinced that England had run her course, and, loaded with debt and torn with dissensions, was tottering to the brink of the grave-trap in which exhausted nations disappear from the scene of history.

His ideal was a nation consisting in the main of peasant proprietors, handicraftsmen, and other useful labourers, with a minimum of government and taxation under the control of those who serve the community by hand and head. Like Cobbett, he hated the " accumulating, centralising, and amalgamating band of Malthusians and political economists." He was indeed Cobbett *édition de luxe*—a Cobbett who could think systematically and consistently, whose knowledge of history was more comprehensive and accurate and less vitiated by prejudice, and whose style was as vigorous as that of the *Political Register*, but of a polish and refinement which only a superior classical education can produce. We can imagine him an independent squire with an Oxford or Cambridge education, who knew his Thucydides, Tacitus, Montesquieu, Gibbon, the histories of the Italian republics, and the deeds of the Dutch, and who was impelled by a burning zeal to warn his countrymen of the impending fall of England, and to analyse and define the economic and social causes of it.

The events of the last hundred years, he declares, the changes they have wrought in the mode of existence of every nation of Europe, and the complications they have introduced into all relations of society, have given to the science of political economy an importance to which it could have never before pretended. As the classes into which nations are divided have multiplied, as the space allotted to the movements of each individual has been more circumscribed, their different interests have brought men more frequently into collision, and it has required no small amount of skill to state and regulate the claims of each (*Funding System*, p. 1). Political economists, or the scientists of the essentials of society and government, have undertaken to interpret those changes and to teach us how to re-adjust society. What is the system they have built up ? " A cold and dreary system which represents our fellow-creatures as so many rivals and enemies, which makes us believe that their happiness is incompatible with our own, which builds our wealth upon their poverty, which would persuade us to look on the world in the light of a besieged town, where the death of our neighbours is hailed with secret satisfaction, since it augments the quantity of provision likely to fall to our own share " (*A Few Doubts*, p. 17). It is time to put an end to that cheerless system which represents society as a jungle of wild animals always ready to devour each other.

In searching for the fundamental principle of society we find that every man brings into the world the capacity for procuring his own sustenance. Man gives existence to food, clothing, and shelter. Subsistence grows with the growth of numbers, or with the amount of labour employed on its production ; where the population is most numerous wealth is abundant. The increase of population allows of division and subdivision of labour, which, in their turn, raise production, and give leisure to some, who employ it to extend the bounds of knowledge. Increase of population, division of labour, opportunity for research, and the necessity of easing the labour of production, lead to inventions which result in an infinite multiplication of the productive powers (*Ib.*, pp. 23, 119, 177). Without detracting from the merit of a Watt or an Arkwright, inventions are seldom due to the man who brings them forward ; they arise from the spirit, the experience, knowledge, and needs of the age. Had not the predecessors of Watt studied the power of steam and built contrivances to utilise it, had not the population grown faster than sheep, had there still been enough wool for clothing, the steam engine and the spinning-jenny would have never reached that stage of perfection which permitted them to revolutionise our manufactures. Invention always sleeps in thinly populated countries. Human ingenuity awakens and is impelled to activity by the growing needs of a growing population. Where population is making great advances, every day presents new combinations of machinery and calls into action powers that a few years before none would have dared to dream of. The elasticity of nature and mind, the constant tendency in every people to increase its numbers and to give more profitable employment to its industry, this exhaustless capacity of improvement is the true capital of nations ; thence flows, if properly understood and acted upon, their wealth (*Funding System*, p. 43). God, in bidding man increase and multiply, and eat bread by the sweat of his brow, pointed out to him the true source of the wealth of nations. Growth of population and industry is the real cause of riches and welfare (*Ib.*, p. 76).

If, then, the experience of particular nations appears to controvert this theory, if the means of subsistence have not increased as rapidly as the population, the defects and errors must be sought in their own institutions.   Not the principles of society are wrong, but the human regulations of society are at fault.   Such a state of things is decisive evidence that the constitution of that society is defective and therefore requires to be re-cast.

Which are the defects and errors that have led to the dispro-portion between the means of subsistence and the population ?

Rent, taxes, and capital (profit) are the great engines for bringing about this unfortunate change in the condition of society.   And rent, taxes, and profit have their origin in the right of property.

We do not condemn property as such, but there are two kinds of property, natural and artificial.   The natural right of property is identical with the reward of labour.   Ravenstone, following Locke, says that he who renders things useful and valuable by his labour and skill is, as it were, their creator and they are rightly his property.   This species of property is, however, very different from that " artificial right " which grows up in the progress of society, by which a man is enabled to appropriate to himself the ownership of lands which he does not occupy, and on which he has never exercised any industry ;   a right which enables him to live in plenty, without any labour of his own, and to exact from others a large portion of the fruits of their industry, for the permission to employ their labour in rendering productive lands in which all appear to have an equal right of property (*A Few Doubts*, p. 99).   This pretension of the landowner is the basis of the property of every description which is seen to multiply with the growth of civilisation.   On it are built the pretensions of the master manufacturer, tradesman, and capitalist.   No sooner has the landowner established his claim to share in all the earnings of those who exercise their industry in the cultivation of the soil, than the master manufacturer sets up a similar claim to a share in all the earnings of those whose industry is employed in wool, cotton, timber, iron, or any of the productions of human ingenuity.   From this moment labour ceases to be free.   The exercise of industry is effectually barred ;   everywhere the toll must be paid before industry is allowed to go to work. This toll is rent or profit, or the idle men's shares in the labouring men's earnings (*Ib.*, p. 225). These idle men live on the surplus produce of the workers (p. 311).

Ravenstone does not clearly show how and why these rent and profit gatherers succeeded in raising themselves to that position, but he appears to suggest that man is naturally weak and desires some sort of leadership. Leaders are appointed to regulate and promote the affairs of society, but finally end by tyrannizing society and promoting their own interests. Or, as he says : " In a well-regulated society, the landowner, the trades-man, and the manufacturer perform merely the functions of channels in a system of irrigation. They do not produce water, their business is only to distribute it equally through every part of the field. But if these channels be made so numerous that all the water is absorbed in its passage, they will rob the soil of its nourishment, they will destroy the fertility they were meant to assist, their existence must prove injurious " (p. 352). At first, rent and profit constitute a very small proportion of the income of a nation, but gradually the proportion comes nearly to constitute the whole. In the early stages of society, when men, bound to-gether by few ties, contribute little to each other's aid, it is as much as each can do with all his industry to keep himself from starving. In every subsequent stage of society, as increased numbers and better tools add to each man's power of production, the number of those who labour is gradually diminished. When one man's labour is barely sufficient for his own subsistence, there can be no property nor idle men. When one man's labour can maintain five, there will be four idle men for one employed in production. They appropriate his surplus produce. The usurpers come to be considered as proprietors of the whole. Finally, the industrious are supposed to live on the bounty of the idle, the producers to owe their existence to the loving-kindness of the appropriators. The productivity of labour results in the undoing of the labourers. They sink to the level of horses, the reward of whose efforts is a wage just sufficient to keep them in working order. On the other hand, the interests of the rich are identified with those of the nation ; they frame the laws, which of course sanction all these usurpations (p. 201). For it may be accepted as a rule that economics rule politics.

And yet labour is the reality, while capital is a metaphysical concept, and one of the cabalistic signs of political science. Its incorporeal nature for ever eludes our grasp. Where the political economists are at a loss to explain any of the problems of social progress they have recourse to the miracles supposed to be performed by capital. According to the political economists capital is at once the child and the parent of labour. It is preserved labour and yet labour can achieve nothing without capital. Capital builds our towns, cultivates our fields, it mans our ships, it marshals and feeds the army, it fills the world's markets with goods, it turns a desert into flourishing habitations of man. But whence came capital that creates all these prodigies ? Adam left none to his children. Capital is the creation of labour, it is the result of accumulation of preserved labour. How then can it be the cause of labour ? (*Funding System*, pp. 38–9. *A Few Doubts*, pp. 293–4.) Capital is merely an instrument of exchange ; it exchanges preserved labour for new labour. And exchanges can add no value to the produced goods. The only source of value is productive labour, particularly labour employed on necessaries. " How ridiculous, then, the alarm which has been attempted to be raised that if the employers are not sufficiently attended to they would leave the country, and carrying with them their capitals, would deprive it of the advantages afforded to industry ! " (p. 352). Much more real is the dread that if labour left the country the source of all wealth would be gone ; no amount of capital could save us from destruction. Notwithstanding all these considerations capital is extolled and labour downed. " It is, however, hopeless to expect that industry will be able to rescue herself from the oppression of capital when once the latter has firmly established its dominion. The contest is that of feebleness against power. It is the struggle of the horse against the rider. . . . Capital, when it has once got its legs round the neck of a nation, never loosens its hold till it has strangled its victim. It is only by a revolution in its state, by a new casting of its constitution that a people can ever escape from its thraldom " (p. 357). England is, indeed, on the eve either of a revolution or a total eclipse. The Napoleonic wars, with their legacy of a crushing national debt, funding system, paper commercialism, suppression of the old nobility in favour of a money aristocracy of low-bred upstarts and Jews, have infinitely aggravated her condition. " The struggle she is now making serves but to show her weakness. The weather-beaten hull of her commercial system still floats on the waves, . . . but every scheme to relieve her distress has failed. The straining of her beams, the exhaustion of the pilot, explain but too clearly even to the most inexperienced passengers that if the wind should at all freshen, she must either throw overboard her cargo or perish in the storm " (p. 366).

What's to be done ? The remedy cannot be looked for in communism. A communist society is an artificial and over-governed society. Such a community can never be upheld but either by angels or by the strictest regulations and the most vigilant police. It is, in fact, a tyranny exercised by fanatics (pp. 196–7). But some may reply that men are improving and ever tending towards perfection. This is quite true, but communism depends for its success on a perfection of human character, which, if attained to, would bring men to the final term of their existence. " When the procession arrives at the temple of the gods, the victim without spot is offered on their altars " (*Funding System*, p. 51).

The most ordinary and most rational principle on which society can be formed is that which, leaving every man master of his own requirements, only puts forth the united strength of the community to check the encroachments which each individual may be disposed to make on the acquisitions of his neighbours. In order to enable the present society to re-arrange its affairs in conformity with that principle, the following measures appear to be required—Reduction of the national debt by taxing the income of the stockholders, taxation of profit, reduction of rents, abolition of indirect taxation, representation of Labour in Parliament. The rights of Labour will be neglected so long as the

s

working classes have no share in electing the House of Commons. People who live on rent, interest, and profit will never legislate for Labour. There is no reason to fear the influence of the people on legislation. The great body of the nation can never have an interest distinct from and opposed to that of the nation. It is a contradiction in terms. They cannot adopt a foolish measure without themselves feeling the consequences. The cry against democracy has no foundation in historical experience. If historians represent popular governments as turbulent, it is only because they have misapplied the term ; they have considered government as democratic which had no claim to that character. The republics of Greece were essentially aristocratic, for even the most popular of their constitutions was based on slavery. Rome had no pretension to be regarded as a democracy ; for though all had the right of voting, the mode in which their suffrage was given secured all power to the possessors of property. The constitutions of the Italian republics of the Middle Ages were still more objectionable. In short, experience does not speak against democracy, and reason is in favour of it. A Parliament consisting of a majority of men acknowledging the right of property, and labour as its source, will guard the nation against excessive wealth and excessive poverty. In securing to each the fruits of his labour they will not impede the production of wealth, but will correct the maldistribution of it. They will not allow capital to fasten itself on industry.

Such legislation involves changes in the economic constitution of present society. But change is inseparable from our condition ; it is a law of nature, from whose operation we cannot escape. All the works of creation are continually assuming new forms ; so rapid are the shiftings that the eye is scarcely fixed on their contemplation when already they appear other than they were.

It should also be remembered that, in the end, the greatest innovators are those who oppose timely reforms.

3.—THOMAS HODGSKIN

(a) His Activity and Principles.

Circumstances and temperament turned the young naval officer Thomas Hodgskin (1783–1869) into a social critic, and the books of Piercy Ravenstone gave him, for a time, an anti-capitalist direction.[1] He was, however, too original a thinker to be a mere populariser of Ravenstone. He studied the political economists, particularly Ricardo, whom he, at first (about 1820) misunderstood and disparaged, but afterwards regarded as " an ingenious and profound writer " (*Labour Defended*, p. 24). Besides Ravenstone and Ricardo, John Locke's natural rights doctrines, laid down in the famous treatise on *Civil Government*, exercised a lasting influence on his social speculations.

Hodgskin's part in the history of British socialist thought is not inconsiderable. He supplanted Bentham by Locke. Instead of the formula of happiness as the test and end of human institutions he emphasized the rights of nature and grounded his reasonings on the antithesis of natural and artificial rights of property. Although a friend of Francis Place, the Benthamite, who endeavoured to attach him to the Utilitarian circle, Hodgskin withstood all temptations, and reasoned in all matters concerning government and property in the sense of Locke. He was, further, one of the principal founders of the London Mechanics Institution[2] (1823), whose first director was Dr. George Birkbeck. And in that Institution, which was attended by the most active minds of the metropolitan mechanics and artisans, Hodgskin lectured on political economy and spread his anti-capitalist and natural rights philosophy. Some of these students became later the leaders of the Chartist Movement ; for instance, Lovett and Hetherington, to name only the most prominent. What George Mudie did for Owenism, Hodgskin

[1] For a biography of Thomas Hodgskin, based on original research, see Élie Halévy, *Thomas Hodgskin*, Paris, 1903. Ravenstone is mentioned by Hodgskin in *Popular Political Economy*, p. 77.

[2] Francis Place, Add. MSS. 27823 ; *Mechanics' Magazine*, June 16, 1827 ; *Mechanics' Weekly Journal*, 1823–4, p. 112.

accomplished for Ravenstone, Locke, and the anti-capitalist deductions from Ricardo. He transmitted the teachings of these pioneers to the British working classes who were soon to enter on one of their revolutionary periods.

Hodgskin's most active years were from 1820 to 1830 ; in this decade he wrote the pamphlet *Labour Defended Against the Claims of Capital, or the Unproductiveness of Capital Proved,* published anonymously in 1825; two years later, *Popular Political Economy,* based on his lectures delivered at the London Mechanics' Institution ; and, in 1832, he published anonymously *Natural and Artificial Right of Property Contrasted,* which had appeared, in 1829, in the shape of newspaper letters addressed to Henry Brougham.   In February, 1833, he was still in touch with the Labour Movement and encouraged the editor of the *Poor Man's Guardian* in his journalistic exposition of the natural rights doctrines.   And this is the last trace of his career as a popular agitator.   He disappeared from the public scene at a moment when the working men, inspired by the doctrines of Owen and natural rights, organised themselves in huge federations and unfurled the banner of class warfare and social revolution.

(b) His Labour Economics.

Through the intercession of James Mill, the friend of the editor of the *Morning Chronicle,* Hodgskin was engaged, at the end of 1822, as reporter of that paper.   His start was similar to that of Mudie.   He soon came in contact with the metropolitan mechanics, took an interest in the struggle of Francis Place for the abrogation of the Combination Laws,[1] and attended the House of Commons in 1824–5, when the Bills concerning that subject were debated and passed.   The speeches which Hodgskin heard were on the whole not favourable to the claims and prospects of the working classes.   None the less, the repeal was carried through, and the forward movement of the working classes began.   The rising spirit of Liberalism in the council of the nation undoubtedly accounts a good deal for this legislative measure in favour of the

[1] Graham Wallas, *Life of Francis Place,* chap. 8.

wage workers. The policy of concession in preference to force becomes from that time one of the main characteristics of the history of the relations between Liberalism and Labour. The idea of political equality, flowing from a purely doctrinal and humanitarian source, expresses itself in Parliamentary measures and softens the clash of antagonistic interests, which originates in field, factory, and mine, and finds its expression in trade unionist action. Hence it comes that the economic action of Labour, in passing through the atmosphere of Liberal Parliamentary politics, loses its revolutionary edge and temper. The hard-bargaining and unsentimental capitalist-employer becomes in Parliament a Liberal, and the revolutionary Labour leader, when elected to Parliament, turns into a reformer. This is the cause and source of the frictions between Labour in the workshop and Labour in Parliament. And this is the cause of the hatred of the ultra-conservative and the revolutionary against Liberalism. On the one hand, Liberalism facilitates the rise and movement of Labour, and is, therefore, hated and branded as subversive by Conservatives ; on the other hand, Liberalism prevents the rising and moving working classes from falling into the extremes of purely economic and revolutionary action, and is, therefore, hated and branded as hypocritical, by Revolutionists.

Hodgskin was, of course, unable to foresee this development, which required a century to mature. He reasoned on the basis of economics and cared little for politics. To him, all the Parliamentary debating proved but too clearly the irreconcilable opposition between capital and labour, as he was taught by the deductions from Ricardo's theory of value and wages, fortified by the doctrines of Ravenstone. In this mood and sense he wrote *Labour Defended*, one of the most aggressive and closely reasoned pamphlets of the labour and socialist movement.

Throughout the country, he declares, there rages at present a contest between capital and labour. The workmen of almost every trade have combined to obtain higher wages, and their employers have appealed to Parliament for protection. The contest will be decided not only by physical endurance, but by argument and reason.   To suggest some arguments in favour of labour and against capital, is the main purpose of the pamphlet.

The workman does not receive as wages the produce of his labour ; he only receives and has ever received as much as will enable him to subsist. Although, by his increased skill and knowledge, he produces now probably ter times more than two centuries ago, he must be contented with the same reward as two centuries ago.   All the advantages of the improvement go to the capitalist and landlord. And when the workmen claim their share and combine in order to give weight to it, they are punished or regarded as a danger to the nation.   " Capital," says Mr. Huskisson, " will be terrified out of the country, and the misguided workmen, unless they are stopped in time, will bring ruin on themselves and on us."   And the Marquis of Lansdowne says, " Capital must be protected, else it will leave for some more favoured country." The political economists, like McCulloch, James Mill, and Malthus, hasten to confirm the surpassing importance of capital, and assert that without circulating and fixed capital no wealth could be produced.   Under the influence of such ideas Labour is forced back to its old position of a bare subsistence wage, and all the rest of the produce of labour goes to the capitalist under the name of profit and rent for the use of his capital (pp. 1–6). Capital thus appears to be a substance of some wonderful properties, considering the fact that it has so many advocates and that Labour pays so exorbitantly for it.

Let us see what it does, whether it does anything, or whether it has any independent existence at all.

Without circulating capital, or food and clothing, say the economists, the labourer could never engage in any undertaking which did not yield an almost immediate return.   The advantage, then, of circulating capital is that by it the labourer is enabled, he being assured of his present subsistence, to direct his power to the greatest advantage.   The fact, however, is that that assurance is not the effect of circulating capital, but of co-existing labour.   The capitalist does not possess any such stock of commodities necessary to feed and clothe the labourers.   He only possesses money or credit, by which he commands the labour of the poor, of whom one set of workers produces machinery and raw materials, and the other set produces food and clothing. This gives the employer as well as the employed the assurance that they will be fed and clothed. It is thus co-existing labour, and not circulating capital, which makes it possible for the labourer to bend his energies on the production of wealth (pp. 9–11). The labourer, having no stock of commodities, undertakes none the less to bring up his children and teach them some useful art, always relying on his own labour. And various classes of persons undertake tasks, the produce of which is not completed for a long period, relying likewise on the labour of other men to procure them in the mean time what they require for subsistence. All classes of men carry on their daily toils in the full confidence that while each is engaged in his particular occupation, some other will prepare whatever he requires, both for his immediate and future wants. Co-existing labour is a fundamental fact of social life, and is made use of by the capitalist to magnify his own importance. So much as to circulating capital.

Fixed capital consists of tools and instruments of labour, or means of production. But what produces these instruments, and in what degree do they aid production independent of the labourers, so that the owners of them are enabled to receive by far the greatest part of the whole produce of the country? Are they, or are they not produced by labour? Are they not so much inert, decaying matter, of no utility whatsoever, but as they are guided, directed, applied, and vitalized by skilful hands? It is admitted by the advocates of capital that fixed capital is the product of previous labour, and is entitled to profit on account of having been stored up or preserved or saved. But the manufacture of machinery, tools, and instruments is quite as uninterrupted and constant as that of food and clothing. They are not stored up, and are not intended to be so, but are brought into use, and the quicker they are brought into use the better for the capitalist, for only when used do they yield a profit. They are made solely for the use of the labourers, and directly they come into the hands of the labourers, they return or repay the sum they cost him, and over and above this the labourers must give him an additional sum corresponding to the prevailing rate of profit.   It is plainly not the previous creation which entitles them to profit, for most of them diminish in value by being kept in storage. Fixed capital does not derive its utility from previous, but present labour ; and does not bring its owner a profit because it has been stored up, but because it is a means of obtaining a command over labour (p. 15).   The capitalist lends it to the labourers and they pay him a compound interest (p. 22). To make the evil effect of capital more apparent let us take the following simple example :—

The real price of a coat, or a pair of shoes, or a loaf of bread— all that nature demands from man in order that he may have any of these necessary articles—is a certain quantity of labour. But, for the labourer to have either of these articles he must give over and above the quantity of labour which nature demands from him, a still larger quantity to the capitalist. He must pay interest to the owner of the sheep, the buyer of the wool, the owner of the spinning mill, the owner of the weaving shed, the cloth-merchant, the master of the tailoring shop. How much more labour the working man must give to have a coat, or a loaf of bread, than the coat or the loaf cost, is impossible to say, but it is probably six times more (p. 22). Here is the source of evil, and not in taxation or Corn Laws ; these exactions do not concern the labourer ; they but diminish the profit of the capitalist, for if food and clothing are made dearer by reason of those exactions, the wages must rise, and profit and wages vary directly. But no matter how great or small the taxes are, the labourer will have to pay the same quantity of labour for his loaf or coat.

Hodgskin, as we see, is of opinion that there is an iron law of wages, and all socialists or social critics who believe that law to be operative must needs reject all palliatives.   If the labourer receives no more than a mere subsistence wage it does not matter to him how high or low prices, taxes, and house rents are, for if they rise wages must also rise to the subsistence level ; and if they fall wages must also fall correspondingly   All reform agitation appears thus as an attempt to divert the working classes from their revolutionary aim of getting the whole produce of their labour, or abolishing the capitalists.

Hodgskin continues to say that the power of the capitalist is so great that he mobilizes the greatest part of the nation to hurl anathemas against the Corn Laws and imbue it with respect and awe for capital, the most injurious enemy of labour (pp. 22–3). The capitalist permits the labourers to have but the means of subsistence, because he cannot do without labour, contenting himself very generously with taking every particle of produce not absolutely necessary to that purpose. It is the overwhelming nature of the demands of capital, sanctioned by the laws of society, which keep, which have ever kept, and which will ever keep, as long as they are allowed and acquiesced in, the labourer in poverty and misery (p. 24).

And yet, capital, both circulating and fixed, has no independent existence. It is nothing but a cabalistic sign used by certain men to stultify the labouring masses in order the better to deprive them of their surplus produce.

For a nation to acquire wealth and to make good use of it, three things seem to be requisite. First, knowledge and ingenuity for inventing machines. Secondly, manual skill and dexterity for carrying these inventions into effect. Thirdly, skill and labour to use them after they had been made. All these requisites of genius, talent, and labour have been attributed with an extraordinary perversion of thought to fixed and circulating capital, in order to justify the existing order of society, which is founded on property or possessions, and oppression of the labourers who form unhappily part of these possessions. It is therefore evident that the interests of the capitalist, or master-manufacturer who performs no labour, are decidedly opposed to those of the labourers (pp. 17–19, 27).

How should this sort of distribution be righted? That the whole produce of labour ought to belong to the labourer is quite evident and true, but how to apply this principle in practice, is difficult to say. Each article is the result of combined labour, and no individual labourer can put his hand on any commodity and say that it was made by him only. It is hard to find a satisfactory principle or rule for dividing the produce of joint labour among the various individuals who concurred in its production, but the judgment of the individuals themselves ; that judgment, depending on the value men set on different species of labour, can never be known nor dictated. As well might we dictate to others what they shall like or hate. There is no other way of deciding but by leaving it to the unfettered judgment of the workmen themselves. If all kinds of labour were perfectly free, if no prejudice invested some parts with great honour, and branded other parts with disgrace, there would be no difficulty on this point, and the rewards of labour would be justly settled by competition or what Adam Smith calls the " higgling of the market " (p. 24-5). Our labourers possess already in a high degree the skill to execute, and they are acquiring also the skill to contrive ; they are forming Mechanics' Institutions, studying physical and moral science ; they will soon engage in the investigation of the problem, why they only, of all classes of the nation, have always been poor ; they will examine into the foundations of society and see whether they were laid in justice and are worth preservation. And it is certain that the contest between labour and capital will go on and ought to go on, that there will be neither peace on earth nor good will among men, until the triumph of labour is complete, until productive labour is rewarded with wealth and idleness with poverty, until he who sows shall reap, in short, until labour shall possess and enjoy the whole of its produce (pp. 29-33).

This is the substance of Hodgskin's pamphlet, which may be said to have been the Manifesto of British Labour in the memorable year 1825, the commencement of the organized and systematic struggle of the British working class, either in the form of large trades unions, or Chartism, or labour politics, co-operation and Socialism.

Hodgskin himself was no socialist. He preferred competition in the midst of institutions and opinions as free as man can form them. For this attitude he was taken to task by William Thompson, who regarded the difficulties which the author of *Labour*

Defended pointed out with regard to just distribution as a confession of failure. He, therefore, wrote *Labour Rewarded, or the Claims of Capital and Labour reconciled through Co-operation*. As a true Owenite he saw in competition one of the main sources of evil, and therefore, could not but scornfully reject the " higgling of the market " as a solution. He calls Hodgskin " my friend and fellow-labourer," with whose defence of the right of labour to the whole produce he fully concurs, saying that all the industrious " are indebted to him for the step he has made," but he tells him that, in adhering to individual competition, he is in bad company, since all the advocates of it are on the side of capital and against the claims of labour (*Labour Rewarded*, pp. 1, 5, 97).[1]

(c) *His Philosophy of History.*

The economic teachings contained in *Labour Defended* are further elaborated, and somewhat softened, in the *Popular Political Economy*, but the latter book includes also some speculations on the natural laws of human society or science of history, which are dealt with more comprehensively in *Natural and Artificial Right of Property contrasted.*

Society, according to these theories, is a natural phenomenon endowed by the Creator with laws which regulate it. The business of the political economist, or, as we should say to-day, the business of the sociologist, is to inquire into and ascertain these laws, and to warn against their being infringed. Were they acted upon by men, were their operation not impeded by human laws, the moral and material improvement of social conditions would have been much greater. For, the natural laws are beneficial, human laws a mere interference and injurious meddling.

The foundation of all national greatness is the increase of the people ; it renders division of labour possible, and promotes observation and knowledge, thus augmenting the productive forces in a compound ratio of the increase of labourers multiplied

---

[1] *Cf.* Karl Marx, *Theorien über Mehrwert*, 1910, III., pp. 313–80.

by the effects of division of labour and increase of knowledge. The increase of the people in this country within the last century, by creating a demand for agricultural produce, has led not merely to an extension of cultivation, to enclosures and breaking up of heaths, but also to improved agricultural processes. The growing wants of society act as a stimulus on the mind of the inventor— necessity is the mother of invention. The endeavour to trace the discoveries and inventions to natural laws does by no means detract from the merits of genius, it merely attempts to place him as a link in the endless chain of causation. For every individual has his character, sentiments, passions, thoughts, yea, even his intellect itself, fashioned by the time in which he lives and by the society of which he is a member. Every man is deeply indebted for whatever he possesses of knowledge, skill, inventive power to his present and past generations. Inventors and discoverers gather and accumulate within themselves the nascent truths, the products of numberless previous researches and improvements, and connect them by a comparatively small additional discovery or invention. Such minds arise naturally and necessarily from the general progress of knowledge and increase of human wants (*Pol. Econ.*, pp. 87–9).

Hodgskin, then, appears to regard increase of population, wants, knowledge, and inventions as the dynamic factors of human society.

The political organisation of society depends very largely on the mode in which property is distributed. Wherever the right of property is placed on a proper foundation, slavery, oppression, and legalised robbery cannot exist ; wherever this foundation is rotten, freedom cannot exist nor justice be administered. Economics precedes politics. Property makes laws, and not laws property. And this is the difference between Locke and Bentham. According to the former property was anterior to government ; it is a natural law that useful labour shall be rewarded with wealth. According to the Utilitarian, government or human laws make property. With Locke, the legislator's task is to prevent natural rights being transgressed, while the Utilitarians deny the existence of natural laws and look to government to determine the welfare of mankind (*Nat. and Art. Right*, pp. 35, 42, 152).

In accepting Locke's theory of property, Hodgskin separates himself expressly from the Owenites and declares that he regards individual property as natural and essential to the welfare and existence of society (*Ib.*, pp. 35, 41).

Neither socialism, nor capitalism, but the natural right of the labourer to his whole produce, is the remedy. This natural right has been violated by human legislation. Legislation has originally been founded in conquest, and it has ever continued in utter ignorance of its results. It is hostile to the course of nature. Who are the law-makers ? Men who do not labour ; the law is actually made by those who derive from nature no title whatever to any wealth (*Ib.*, pp. 63–7). Laws are always made by others than labourers, and are intended to preserve the power of those who make them, or to enable them to appropriate wealth to themselves. The law-makers are the landed aristocracy, the bishops, and the capitalists, or rent, tithes, and profits. To this violation of the natural right of property, to this creation of the artificial right of property we owe most of our social miseries, and as long as plunder and oppression last, there will be misery, fraud, mistrust, crime, and murder.

Who will make an end to the artificial right and restore the natural right of property ?

Hodgskin's reply is rather halting and contradictory. In *Labour Defended* he attributed that mission to the working-classes. In his *Natural and Artificial Right* he thinks it will be the middle-classes who will accomplish it. At any rate, it will not be done by law-makers. All real progress to freedom has been caused by the development of history and forced on the law-makers. Hodgskin may have meant that progress was effected by a sort of re-assertion of the outraged divine-natural laws. In attempting to explain his meaning he gives a short and very fragmentary outline of the stages of historical development. He begins by putting the question, " Who brought the capitalists to power ? " The law-makers ? No, for they upheld the landed interests against the monied interests. " It came about by itself." The changes form an interesting part of the history of civilisation. When feudalism weakened, the serf gradually outgrew his bondage, ceased to be the property of the warrior noble, and acquired a right of property in what he created. The capitalist then emerged into notice and, obtaining from the landlord interest and profit on his property, shared his power. Now we find that a large middle class, completely emancipated from bondage and destitution, has grown up in every part of Europe, uniting in their own persons the character both of labourers and capitalists. They are fast increasing in numbers, and we may hope that, as the beautiful inventions gradually supersede unskilled labour, they will gradually reduce the whole society to equal and free men, and extinguish all that still remains of slavery and oppression. Changes are going on which are overthrowing injustice. All these changes are sometimes attributed to the discovery of America, the rounding of the Cape of Good Hope, the sagacity or rulers and philosophers, or to any thing else rather than to the divine government of the moral world.

IX

SOCIAL CONSERVATIVE CRITICS

I.—COLERIDGEAN INFLUENCES

SEVEN years after Edmund Burke, in his *Reflections on the Revolution in France*, had defended the organic view against the mechanical conception of society, and two years after Erasmus Darwin, in his *Zoonomia*, had laid the foundation of the evolutionary view of nature, the German philosopher, F. W. J. Schelling, in his *Ideen zu einer Philosophie der Natur* (1797), began to spread in his country the concept of organism, the inner growth and connection of living matter as opposed to the mechanical atomism, and gradual evolution in opposition to sudden creation. The same thoughts, which, in England, had a historical and a scientific setting, assumed in Germany a mystical appearance and an idealistic meaning. It was no longer nations that developed organically their institutions, nor nature that evolved from stage to stage to higher forms, but the Absolute who in ceaseless productivity brought forth natural formations and historical periods. Nature was the Odyssey of the Absolute, and History His epic poem. Religion, tradition, intuition, and mysticism gradually gained predominance over sober science, critical reason, and logical prose.

The rapid transition from the liberal philosophy of Kant and the national socialism of Fichte to the romanticism of Schelling was the effect of reaction against and dire disappointment with the course of the French Revolution. The intellects of Germany, who had hailed the storming of the Bastille and the victory at Valmy as the dawn of human freedom, who had expected external actions and spectacular dramas to bring salvation to humanity, now immersed their minds in the inner depths of things and

271

looked inwardly to the eternal forces which, inscrutable to the reason of man, mould and govern this infinite Universe.

Coleridge, who had gone through similar mental experiences, visited Germany at the time when that transition took place. He at once felt its vibrations and remained all his life in harmony with them. And, like Schelling, who never succeeded in formulating a systematic philosophy of history, Coleridge never did go beyond enunciating religio-philosophical aphorisms, which since about 1820 began to attract the inquiring minds of the British youth ; since about 1820—the same date when Owen's co-operative schemes and the anti-capitalist economics began to find adherents. Thomas Carlyle has left us a short sketch of this period of Coleridge's life. He relates : " Coleridge sat on the brow of Highgate Hill, in those years, looking down on London and its smoke-tumult . . . attracting towards him the thoughts of innumerable brave souls still engaged there. His express contributions to poetry, philosophy, or any specific province of human literature or enlightenment had been small and sadly intermittent ; but he had, especially among young inquiring men, a higher than literary, a kind of prophetic or magician's character. . . . The practical intellects of the world did not much heed him, or carelessly reckoned him a metaphysical dreamer ; but to the rising spirits of the young generation he had this dusky sublime character ; and sat there as a kind of Magus, girt in mystery and enigma, . . . his Dodona oak-grove whispering strange things, uncertain whether oracles or jargon." [1]

But while Carlyle goes on entertaining his readers with Coleridge's " sum-m-jects " and " om-m-jects," a far superior thinker, John Stuart Mill, tells us the real reason of Coleridge's attraction. The awakening of the spirit of philosophy and of inquiry into the laws of human existence and the growth of society, was the work of the Germano-Coleridgean school. " This doctrine expresses the revolt of the human mind against the philosophy of the eighteenth century. . . . They were the first who inquired, with any comprehensiveness and depth, into the

[1] Thomas Carlyle, *Life of John Sterling*, I., chap. 8.

inductive laws of the existence and growth of human society.
. . . They thus produced not a piece of party advocacy, but a
philosophy of society, in the only form which is yet possible, that
of a philosophy of history. The brilliant light which had been
thrown upon history during the last half century, has proceeded
almost wholly from this school. The disrespect in which history
was held by the Encyclopædists is notorious ; one of the soberest
of them, D'Alembert, we believe, was the author of the wish that
all records whatsoever of past events could be blotted out."[1]

This Germano-Coleridgean school brought the political and
philosophic thought of England in touch with socialistic schools
and the aspirations of the masses, either by leading men's minds
back to the pre-individualistic times when society was organised
in corporate bodies with special responsibilities towards their
members, or by turning the attention of the possessing and ruling
classes to the social ethics of Christianity, or by showing history
to be a long and continuous process of the development of social
institutions, in which the concept of property and the relation of
the classes changed, and have been changing from period to period.
It taught men that such laws as those of supply and demand,
wages, capital, and other economic categories were by no means
eternal and immutable, nor was their absolute rule desirable.
Finally, it induced some of the noblest spirits of the nation to
look at Chartism as not a mere rebellion of drunken helots to be
ruthlessly suppressed by bullets and gallows.

Coleridge inspired Frederick Denison Maurice, later the
guide and philosopher of Christian Socialism, particularly of
Charles Kingsley. And Cardinal Newman, in his controversy
with Kingsley, relates that the " Oxford Movement," too,
owed much to Coleridge, who, " after all, instilled a higher
philosophy into inquiring minds than they had hitherto been
accustomed to accept. In this way he made trial of his age,
and succeeded in interesting its genius in the cause of Catholic
truth."[2] Hurrell Froude, one of the founders of that Move-

---

[1] J. S. Mill, *Dissertations*, I., article Coleridge ; *Autobiography*,
1873, pp. 160–2.
[2] J H. Newman. *Apologia*, 1864, p. 185-6.

T

ment, undoubtedly read Coleridge; his poem "Farewell to Toryism" is distinctly Coleridgean.[1] And there was much social reform and even democratic sentiment among its leaders.[2]

These were the influences of Coleridge. But he has left no book which would give an adequate summary of those teachings. The nearest approach to such a book is his *Constitution of Church and State* (1830), which, besides a trenchant criticism of utilitarian liberalism, contains some of his views of an ideal commonwealth. He desired to see an English realm, " where the integral parts, classes, or orders are so balanced, or inter-dependent, as to constitute, more or less, a moral unit, an organic whole." The landed interests, or the principle of permanence and law, should work harmoniously with the monied interests, or the principle of progression and freedom. The possessions of both orders, taken collectively, should form the Property (pp. 117–18), which must be connected with especial duties and should be regarded as a trust rather than as arbitrary and unconditional ownership (p. 45). The Church should comprise the whole scholarship and the educators of the nation, which means, that the arts and sciences should be headed by theology. In short, his ideal commonwealth was a nation ruled by the spirit and letter of Christianity. Only in such a State will the conquests made by reason redound to the moral benefit of the nation. To-day reason governs in opposition to Christianity. And what are the results? " My eye at this moment rests on a volume newly read by me, containing a well-written history of the inventions, discoveries, public improvements, docks, railways, canals. . . . We live, I exclaimed, under the dynasty of Understanding : and this is the golden age. It is the faculty of means to medial ends. With these the age, this favoured land, teems ; they spring up, the armed host, from the serpent's teeth sown by Cadmus. . . . Sea and land, rock, mountains, lake and moor, yea, nature and all her elements, sink before them, or yield themselves captive ! But the ultimate ends ? . . .

[1] R. Hurrell Froude, *Remains*, I., p. 429.
[2] *Ib.*, p. 312.

> O voice, once heard
> Delightfully, increase and multiply !
> Now death to hear ! For what can we increase
> Or multiply, but woe, crime, penury.

. . . We have game laws, corn laws, cotton factories, Spital-
fields, the tillers of the land paid by poor rates, and the remainder
of the population mechanised into engines for the manufactory of
new rich men ; yea, the machinery of the wealth of the nation
made up of the wretchedness, disease, and depravity of those who
should constitute the strength of the nation " (pp. 63–7). The
history of a century of wealth-making is a history of vulgarisation of thought and politics : " The mechanico-corpuscular
theory raised to the title of the mechanic philosophy. . . . A
state of nature, or the Ourang Outang theology of the origin of
the human race, substituted for the first ten chapters of the Book
of Genesis. . . . Our state-policy a Cyclops with one eye,
and that in the back of the head ; our measures become either
a series of anachronisms, or a truckling to events. . . . Meantime, the true historical feeling, the immortal life of the nation,
generation linked to generation by faith, freedom, heraldry, and
ancestral fame, languishing and giving place to the superstitions
of wealth and newspaper reputation. Talents without genius ;
a swarm of clever, well-informed men : an anarchy of minds, a
despotism of maxims. Hence despotism of finance in government
and legislation. . . . and hardness of heart in political
economy." And he saw " government by clubs of journeymen ;
by saint and sinner societies, committees, institutions ; by reviews, magazines, and above all by newspapers " (pp. 67–70).
The cure for this vulgarisation and anarchy is religion, moral
discipline—Christian ethics and faith.

2.—SOUTHEY'S PROSPECTS OF SOCIETY

While Coleridge was thundering against the mechanisation of
the country and creating an anti-liberal phraseology which made
the fortune of many an anti-capitalist writer after him, Southey
was communing with the spirit of Sir Thomas More on the evils
of the time. The trend of conservative and religious minds to-

wards mediaevalism became pronounced, as it always will in Christian countries in times of spiritual and social anarchy, or after a surfeit at the feasts of reason and materialist conceptions of nature and life. The great European minds have, since the Renascence, been oscillating between Olympus and Golgotha, moving to and fro in search either of happiness or redemption. According to Cardinal Newman also Southey contributed much to the stock of ideas and sentiments that led to the Oxford Movement.

Both Sir Thomas More and Robert Southey speculated in the joy and freedom of their younger years upon the possible improvement of society ; and both in like manner lived to dread the effects of that restless spirit which insults Heaven and disturbs the earth. In the eyes of Southey, the nineteenth century exhibited characteristics similar to those of the age of the Reformation, and he thought to hear the voice of the author of *Utopia*, saying, " By comparing the great operating causes in the age of the Reformation, and in this age of revolutions, going back to the former age, looking at things as I then beheld them, perceiving wherein I judged rightly and wherein I erred, and tracing the progress of those causes which are now developing their whole tremendous power, you will derive instruction " (*Sir Thomas More, or Colloquies*, I., p. 19).

To him, as the representative of Catholicism who could not believe in the salvation of any Protestant nation, is assigned the part of the social critic, while Southey himself represents the optimistic social reformer who believes in the moral and material progress of man. Sir Thomas warns him against short cuts to the Millennium, for this has always " been the ruling fancy of the most dangerous of all madmen " (p. 34). And there is hardly anything in the present age to warrant such a belief. " The prevailing opinions of this age go to the destruction of everything that has hitherto been held sacred. They tend to arm the poor against the rich ; the many against the few ; worse than this, for it will also be a war of hope and enterprise against timidity, of youth against age. . . . You surely do not expect that the Millennium is to be brought about by the triumph of what are called liberal opinions ; nor by enabling the whole of the lower classes to read the incentives to vice, impiety and rebellion, which are prepared for them by an unlicensed press " (p. 35). But, even granted that there is now more knowledge and more wealth in England than there was in former times, surely there is also less wisdom and less happiness. Finally, Southey accepts the assumption that the condition of the labour- ing classes was, perhaps, better in the age of More " than it ever has been either before or after. The feudal system had well-nigh lost all its inhuman parts, and the worse inhumanity of the commercial system had not yet shown itself." To which More rejoins that " it was, indeed, a most important age in English history, and till the Reformation so fearfully disturbed it, in many respects a happy and an enviable one. But the process was then beginning, which is not yet completed."

This remark gives Southey the occasion to present the Catholic view of the social development of English history from the Reformation to the first quarter of the nineteenth century, in which the Factory system took its rise. On this point both More and Southey are at one in condemning it, but they differ as to its origin. Southey is of opinion that " it has been the growth of circumstances, not a system fore-planned, foreseen and deliberately chosen. Such as it is we have inherited it, or rather have fallen into it, and must get out of it as well as we can. We must do our best to remove its evils, and to mitigate them while they last, and to modify and reduce it till only so much remains as is indispensable for the general good." More, however, replies : " The fact will not warrant you in saying that it has come upon the country unsought and unforeseen. You have prided yourselves upon this system, you have used every means for extending it ; you have made it the measure of your national prosperity. It is a wen, a fun- gous excrescence from the body politic ; the growth might have been checked if the consequences had been apprehended in time ; but now it has acquired so great a bulk . . . that to remove it by absorption is impossible, and excision would be fatal " (pp. 171–2). Fraud and gamble have taken the place of work and wealth. Paper notes, stock, and the funding system, or the so-called securities, have rendered the whole system insecure. It is but certain that the poverty of one part of the people seems to increase in the same ratio as the riches of another part. This is the effect of competition. Every man oppresses his neighbour ; the landlord racks his tenant ; the farmer grinds the labourer ; great capitalists ruin the small traders,—like pikes in a pond which devour the weaker fish. There is no stability anywhere. A nation on the move—from village to town, from town to oversea countries. The great majority of these poor people are willing to work, to go anywhere where they may be able to provide for themselves. Whatever means may be devised for their benefit, they are ready to co-operate, and perform their part. They can dig and sow, weave and spin, forge and mould iron and steel, make bricks and build houses. But how they should be set to work, how the beginning should be made, is what we must not expect to learn from any professor of political economy. And Sir Thomas More adds : " The wisdom of the heart is wanting there. Statesmen . . . have not yet had faith enough in goodness to believe in the moral miracles which benevolence and zeal are able to perform ! If at any time they have entertained a serious wish for bettering the condition of their fellow-creatures, the difficulties which they see before them have appeared like mountains in the way ; and yet, had they faith but as a grain of mustard seed, these mountains might be removed. There is abundant room in this country and its colonies for any possible increase of population till the end of time ! Only let the poor be placed where they may ' labour for that which satisfieth,' and ' the earth will give seed to the sower and bread to the eater—they shall build houses and inhabit them ; and the solitary place shall be glad, and the desert shall rejoice ' " (II., pp. 263-5).

Meanwhile the evil is growing and the revolution is spreading. Society has its critical periods, its climacterics. The present age is a critical one. " A new principle, a *novum organum* has been introduced, the most powerful that has ever yet been wielded by man. If it was first *Mitrum* that governed the world, and then

Nitrum, both have had their say—gunpowder as well as the triple crown. Steam will govern the world next, and shake it too before its empire is established " (I., p. 199).

And the shake came in the form of Chartism, the first social-democratic and revolutionary movement of the British working classes as the pioneers of European and American Labour. Southey heard their tramp and the voices of their commanders. Austin, then a famous jurist, lecturing in 1829 on the condition of England, complained that the working classes were not favourable to the system of private property. And two years later the London artisans were taught that " Property is the cause of all evils. Create it not ; make it but sufficient for yourselves— and that not to possess it, but to enjoy it. . . . No personal liberty or happiness for the people can exist until at least there is no individual property in the soil."[1]

[1] *Poor Man's Guardian*, June 4, August 20, 1831. *Cf.* Graham Wallas, *Life of Francis Place*, p. 274, for similar views expressed by London artisans in 1831.

X

THE BIRTH OF CHARTISM

I.—ESSENCE, AIM, AND NAME

THE two currents of social economic thought generated and developed by the school of Owen and the anti-capitalist criticism reached, in the years from 1825 onwards, the thinking portion of the British working class and created Chartism, which constituted a series of social revolutionary attempts to re-organise the United Kingdom on a socialist and labour basis. This movement assumed gradually national proportions, and was in full activity in the second quarter of the nineteenth century, but it was only in the year 1838 that it received the name " Chartism," which merely signifies democratic parliamentary reform. The name, like that of many of the great movements and parties of the United Kingdom, does not cover, either chronologically or intrinsically, the history and essence of this movement. The years 1825 to 1830 were the period of its incubation ; from 1831 to the end of 1834 it developed its theories and exhibited great intellectual vigour ; from 1837 to 1842 it received, as far as the Corresponding Act permitted, its practical and organised form ; and from 1849 onwards its vitality was rapidly ebbing away and it died in 1855, leaving only here and there scattered stragglers who obstinately refused to believe that Chartism was extinct. Its theories, traditions, and legacies were either taken up by continental socialists, like Karl Marx and Frederick Engels, who, ten years later, formed the International Working Men's Association, or by the co-operators and trade unionists of Great Britain, who transformed them according to their education and experience.

Chartism, in its essence and aim, resembled the international socialist and labour movement of the present day. But, having had no precedent to be guided by, and, indeed, forming a kind of socialist seminary and an experimental laboratory of working-class revolution, it was deficient in coherence of thought and systematic policy. It presents itself as an elemental class-war, rising and falling in curves between enthusiastic upheavals and apathetic inertia, between riotously profuse creations of ingenious ideas and pitiful relapses into barren and obsolete theories ; only its immediate aim—the conquest of political power—appears to have been grasped with unmistakable distinctness and energy, but owing to lack of a national organisation and popular education it was impossible for it to become a permanent and victorious movement. To the eye of the historian it takes the form of a pioneer movement of socialists and masses of work-men—a valiant and desperate contest for the material, moral, and intellectual uplifting of Labour. From its experimental and, on the whole, practical character it follows also that there could be no uniformity of opinion as to the ultimate shape of the social revolution and social reconstruction. During its theoretical period (1831–34) illuminating ideas flashed out with meteoric suddenness and disappeared just as abruptly, leaving scarce a trace behind ; and even to the present day doubts, erroneous assumptions, and misunderstandings are still prevalent with regard to the originators and the import of their ideas. And during the practical period (1837–49) theoretical discussions were not favoured, lest they should be a hindrance in the struggle for the immediate aim—to seize the reins of government as quickly as possible : " Peaceably if we may—forcibly if we must."

As already indicated, the ultimate socialist aim was not estab-lished with unanimity. A judgment on this point can only be formed by a study of Chartist newspapers and pamphlets, and of their intellectual sources and ramifications. There were three lines of policy in the question of the ultimate aim : one was communistic and parliamentary, at any rate up to the year 1845, until the disastrous break-up of Queenwood, the last Owenite colony ; it strove for political power in order to trans-form Great Britain into a certain number of communist colonies ; and with its adherents the question of the common ownership of the land took precedence of every other consideration. This line of policy dominated among the working classes of the North of England. The second was, indeed, Owenite in its critical attitude to social problems, but it aspired after political power in order to utilise it for paving the way for social reform, for trades unionism and the political organisation, education and enlightenment of the working classes, so as to fit them for reforming the country in a socialistic sense. These were the ideas which centred in the intellectual working men of London and Scotland, who probably did not form more than ten per cent. of the British working classes. The third line of policy was in the direction of trades unions, and adhered to the theory of natural rights, viz. that the workman should receive the full produce of his labour, and in actual practice made the demand : " A fair wage for a fair day's work." A sharp separation of these lines of policy was never attained. Excepting for the years 1833 and 1834, in which economic action in the syndicalist sense was most strongly marked, the organised workers and the Chartists were of opinion that the fundamental condition for emancipation from wage slavery lay in the conquest of political power, and that therefore all their energies ought to be concentrated on this purpose. The parliamentary and democratic idea dominated the movement so completely as to give it its name. The movement received the name Chartism from its democratic programme : the People's Charter, which was originated in the year 1837 to 1838 by the London Working Men's Association, and was drawn up by the joiner, William Lovett. The People's Charter was nothing more than a plain and clearly written Bill, containing the following six points in the form of sections and paragraphs : (1) Universal Suffrage, (2) Equal Electoral Districts, (3) Abolition of Property Qualifications for parliamentary candidates, (4) Annual Parliaments, (5) Ballot, (6) Payment of Members of Parliament.

2. STAGES OF DEVELOPMENT

Chartism, as a collective term for the revolutionary struggle of the British working class, passed through several stages, as already stated in the preceding section. The years 1825 to 1830 formed its period of incubation. They were years in which Great Britain cast off its agricultural character, and passed over to industrialism on a large scale. To the revolution in production was added that in commerce and transport. Through the repeal of the Bubble Act (1719) in the year 1825, capital could henceforth form joint-stock companies and inaugurate the era of extensive and collective enterprise which revolutionised commence and transports. The middle classes became intoxicated with the prospect of infinite possibilities ; and it flashed upon the working men that, as a class, they played a more indispensable part even than capital in the process of production. At the same time the operatives gained the depressing conviction that there was no possibility of their ever becoming capitalists themselves ; they saw the vast scale of industrial production, with which no independent craftsman could compete. The middle classes hastened towards their political victory, the working classes began their class war. This great transition period was depicted by a Conservative writer in 1826 in a naïve yet broad and fascinating manner :

" The age which now discloses itself to our view promises to be the age of industry, to which no monarch shall affix his name —it shall be called the age of comfort to the poor,—if the phrase had not been so ill applied of late, we should say—the age of the People. By industry alliances shall be dictated and national friendships shall be formed. . . . The prospects which are now opening to England almost exceed the boundaries of thought ; and can be measured by no standard found in history. . . . The manufacturing industry of England may be fairly computed as four times greater than that of all the other continents taken collectively, and sixteen such continents as Europe could not manufacture so much cotton as England does. . . ."[1]

At the same time the working classes appeared upon the stage of history, self-conscious economically, but with hesitation from a political point of view. The following declarations are charac-

[1] *Quarterly Review*, June to August, 1826, pp. 92–99. *Cf.* also Ure, *Philosophy of Manufacture*, Introduction.

teristic of this appearance. A meeting of the unemployed in Leeds, passed the following resolution on November 23, 1829[1] :—

" We, the Operatives, by no means wish to assume a situation that does not belong to us, yet we are well aware that labour is the only source of wealth, and that we are the support of the middle and higher classes of society."

The first political weekly newspaper of the working classes of Lancashire announced in its programme :

" Labour is the source of wealth ; the working men are the support of the middle and upper classes ; they are the nerves and soul of the process of production, and therefore of the nation."[2]

The same paper, however, declared at the same time for joint political action with the Liberals.

On the other hand they were taught that " the natural tendency of wealth " was " for the rich to become richer, and for the poor to become poorer. Trade carried out on a large scale has driven out trade on a small scale. The result is that a large proportion of the community has to depend on their labour only, whilst machinery is superseding labour. . . . The effect of wealth is to divide society into classes, between whom the distance is so great that they have lost touch with each other, and are in danger of becoming enemies to each other." [3]

The first result of this knowledge was that from a trade unionist point of view the workmen strove for comprehensive class-organisations, but politically for an alliance with the middle classes. In the years 1830 to 1832, when the struggle for the Reform Bill was raging, the workers for the greater part marched as allies of the middle classes.

The alliance between the working and the middle classes was the first stage of Chartism. But already during this period of alliance there was a small minority of workers who defended the standpoint of class-war with extreme acrimony, and were opposed

[1] *Leeds Patriot*, November 29, 1829.

[2] *Voice of the People*, Manchester, January 1, 1831.

[3] *Sheffield Courier*, quoted by the *Midland Representative*, September 17, 1831. The latter paper was edited by Bronterre O'Brien.

to every alliance with the middle classes. Regardless of consequences, they transferred the economic antagonism of the middle and working classes into the political arena and pointed with inexorable logic to the fact that labour and capital must always remain irreconcilable opponents. This minority existed in London ; its organisation was the " National Union of the Working Classes," and its paper was the *Poor Man's Guardian*. This remarkable organ was one of the first unstamped newspapers ; it appeared first of all as *Penny Papers for the People*, from October 1, 1830, to the end of December, 1830 ; then it received the sub-title, *By the Poor Man's Guardian;* from July 9, 1831, until it ceased on December 25, 1835, it appeared as the *Poor Man's Guardian*. It refused to pay the newspaper stamp. "Unstamped" at that time meant the same thing as illegal. By reason of the " Six Acts " of the year 1819 every periodical which published news had to pay a stamp-tax of fourpence a copy, and since paper was also burdened with a high tax and the publisher had to give security, the publication of a newspaper involved heavy expenses. The stamped papers could not be sold at less than sevenpence a copy,—a price which only few working men could pay. Henry Hetherington, the publisher of the *Poor Man's Guardian*, defied the law and published the paper at the price of one penny. Below the heading of every number was the announcement : " Established contrary to Law to try the power of Might against Right." The editor of the *Poor Man's Guardian* was after the middle of 1831 or the beginning of 1832, Bronterre O'Brien. Most of the social-revolutionary thinkers of those years contributed either anonymously or under a pseudonym to the paper, and made it an arsenal of revolutionary ideas. Among the anonymous contributors there was one who championed the idea of class-war with a determination which few followers of Marx could have surpassed. For a long time the articles of the anonymous correspondent were ascribed to the editor, but it will be pointed out later on that they proceeded from the pen of a self-educated weaver, most probably a hand-loom weaver, who had been ruined by machinery. He hurled polemics against the alliance between the working and middle classes. The best of his articles were reprinted later on as standard documents. They initiated the schism between the workers and the middle class ; they made a profound impression upon the thinkers of the working class of Great Britain.

At the same time the idea of a general strike came into being ; a London shoemaker, publisher and coffee-house proprietor, called William Benbow, gave expression to it in a pamphlet that appeared in January, 1832. Benbow likewise belonged to the minority which rallied round the *Poor Man's Guardian* and the National Union.

Finally, Owen in 1831 took up an attitude to parliamentary action which not only signified disdain, but even contempt and abhorrence.

The combined effect of these influences became all the stronger from the fact that the Reform Bill, which had become law after a year of violent conflict, agitating the whole country, left the workers as unenfranchised as before. The working class which had to a great extent furnished the physical energy for the movement of reform came away with empty hands.

Disappointed and embittered by the negative result of the agitation for reform ; their self-consciousness strengthened by the help they had given to the middle classes ; influenced by the class-war idea of the anonymous weaver, by the general strike advocated by Benbow and by Owen's anti-parliamentary attitude, the organised working class turned syndicalistic. The tempestuous course of the class-war idea and of direct economic action not only swept away all notions of the solidarity of the classes or of alliances between them, but, at least for two years, it destroyed all ideas of parliamentary action or of democratic parliamentary reform. The organised workers became revolutionary and anti-parliamentary, and hoped for everything from the direct economic action of the masses. This period embraced the year 1832 to 1834 ; it formed the second stage in the history of the growth of Chartism ; its characteristic was *Syndicalism.* At this stage of development strenuous intellectual efforts were made to emerge from the socialism of natural rights, to make an end to Utopian experiments and to form a conception of history based on class-war and evolution, in short, to accomplish what Karl Marx took in hand ten years later. In 1833 discussions took place in English working men's clubs about the descent of man from the animal kingdom, or as it was called at that time : the Simian theory.[1] And a year later the *Pioneer and Official Gazette* (September 20, 1834),[2] the organ of the revolutionary trades unions, published an essay which pointed out that class-war is the necessary consequence of the natural evolution of Society from capitalism to socialism, and that it heralds in the growth of a new form of society. The intellectual history of this period has remained unknown to the present time. It is essentially the history of the separation of the workers from orthodox Owenism. Its documents lie scattered in the weeklies, the *Crisis, Pioneer*, and *Pioneer and Official Gazette*. But at that time no thinker arose to strike the intellectual balance of those remarkable years. In the summer of 1834 British syndicalism broke down, and at the same time its mental activity sank into complete oblivion. However, mental struggles are never wholly fruitless. Even if their results are only appreciated by posterity, yet they also furnish their contemporaries with suggestions and ideas which are turned to good use for future progress. This, indeed, was the case in Great Britain in the years subsequent to 1834, when social reform, trades unionism, and parliamentary action became re-united. Only the orthodox Owenites remained as sectarian independents, and they were known at that time as socialists, and were few in number. The gist of the contests and discussions of the years 1825 to 1835 consisted of the following declarations :

The workers form a class whose interests are opposed to those of all the other classes ; their ultimate emancipation can only be obtained by a revolution in the socialist sense ; the means for this purpose is to seize political power. The embodiment of these

---

[1] *Crisis*, September 28, 1833.

[2] Only one number of this weekly journal has been preserved. All that we know about it otherwise occurs only in extracts printed by the *Poor Man's Guardian* in August, 1834.

ideas constitutes Chartism from 1837 onwards.[1]   The struggles, disappointments, Owenite experiments and syndicalist efforts which preceded it were the cause of the last stage of Chartism assuming in the main the character of *independent parliamentary action*   In addition to these principal causes the following secondary causes were contributory, viz. the dissatisfaction with the Poor Law of 1834 in the North of England, and the demand for factory legislation for the protection of women and children.

3.—ORGANISATION AND DOCTRINE

From 1837 onwards Chartism became a movement of the masses, a revolutionary struggle implying many a sacrifice, for the purpose of seizing political power. It suffered, however, up to the very last from the following weak points : the impossibility of conferring upon the masses a firm and unified organisation, since the Corresponding Act (1817) did not permit of founding a national organisation with branch societies. The Chartists were only allowed to form local societies, but not to enter into union with each other. This led sometimes to the formation of secret leagues, which only caused the government spies to promote existing insurrectionary tendencies, and to bring the Chartists to trial for high treason, and resulted in heavy sacrifices. As a rule the leaders and the speakers were the connecting links between the local organisations. On this account such a preponderating part in the movement fell to the share of the leaders that it would hardly be possible to write a history of Chartism without a thorough study of the life-histories of the leaders and of the trend of their thoughts. The leaders and speakers were, however, only human, and afflicted with human weaknesses. Disunion in their ranks implied the splitting and breaking up of the Chartist societies, the formation of cliques and hero-worship, which raised serious difficulties in the way of any well-organised progress of the Chartists on a large scale.

The other source of weakness lay in a relapse into the historical

---

[1] These ideas were later secured for Socialism by Engels and Marx. Both expected great things from this movement, if not from its leaders. *Cf. infra* XIII. 2 ; also the *Northern Star*, December 4, 1847.

conception of natural law. The following are a few characteristic extracts and references on the subject, occurring in the authoritative organs and documents of Chartism :

" We base our demands upon natural equity : All men are equal and can demand equal rights and liberties.[1]

" A receipt for making eye-water for the benefit of Englishmen, Irishmen and Scotchmen : Take of the Law of Nature, 6 drams ; of the Rights of Man, 4 drams ; of Reason, 3 drams ; of Agrarian Justice, 5 drams ; of Commonsense, $\frac{1}{2}$ grain. Mix them up in the Cup of Liberty."[2]

" The abstract political rights of man are founded on natural and moral justice. All presumed rights not founded on the above are usurpations. . . . Every community has a right to be governed by the concentrated wisdom and intelligence of its members."[3]

Even a Tory and Social Reformer, like Richard Oastler, exclaimed :

" Every man born in England has a natural right to live well in England. It is a law of nature and a law of God that the husbandman that laboureth must be the first partaker of the fruit."[4]

The central organ of the Chartists treated the law of nature almost from the commencement as the foundation-stone of the movement.[5] All the great manifestoes of Chartism, e.g., the Declaration of Rights of 1831 and 1839, the three petitions of the Chartists of 1839, 1842, and 1848, refer to the law of nature as the irrefutable proof of the justice of their democratic demands. The leading spirits of Chartism : O'Brien, O'Connor, Lovett, M'Douall, always had recourse to the law of nature as the source of their knowledge and action. And most of the Chartist speeches for the defence on the trials for high treason in 1839 and 1840 bore the impress of the law of nature.

---

[1] *Poor Man's Guardian* (Penny Paper), May 26, 1831.

[2] *Ibid.*, January 12, 1833. The names of the specified ingredients are the titles of Thomas Paine's works.

[3] *Carpenter's Monthly Political Magazine*, February, 1832, p. 229.

[4] *Poor Man's Guardian*, August 15, 1835.

[5] *Northern Star*, May 14, 1842.

U

The whole trend of Chartist thought was dominated by the idea that the weal and woe of society depends in the last resort upon the character of the laws of the State.   The law can build up and destroy, can both heal and wound.   With the exception of the germinating idea of evolution in history in the year 1834 Chartism lacked the faintest trace of any insight into the growth and decay of right and law, or the dependence of legislators upon social forces and changes.   And this insight is of necessity absent in adherents of the law of nature.   According to this conception of history it was originally men who, after having made a social contract, promulgated laws, because they enjoyed sovereign power.   Simply by human decrees corporate society and private property were brought into being.   Subsequently a single individual or a small minority of men made the laws after having usurped the sovereign power.   But what is the essential nature of sovereignty ?   What enables it to produce revolutions wholesale ?   What is it that enables it quite arbitrarily either to further the common weal or to degrade the masses ?   To these questions the law of nature gives the answer, Force.   Whoever possesses force exercises sovereign power and can make laws at will.   Force, sovereignty, and legislation form, according to natural law, the Trinity of the State, all-powerful and absolute : it can change public property into private property, or private property into public property, or can mould society into any form it likes.[1]   Accordingly, the main object of revolutionaries and reformers must be to obtain power.   If they possess the forces of the State the main problem is solved.   They considered sovereign power to be creative.

The law of nature holds also another answer to our question.   Since the time of the Physiocrats and Adam Smith, the old Stoic opinion of the law of nature held the ground, viz. that definite laws are inherent in the universe, and that if these laws of nature were not hindered by human laws, they would ensure the happiness of all.   The originators of human laws were the despots and the oligarchs.   If they could be swept away then

[1] This idea is very clearly expressed in Pascal's *Pensées*, ed. 1850, Pt. I. Ch. XII. § 7.

the inherent laws of nature would resume their functions.
Accordingly the work of the revolutionaries and reformers was
purely negative. Their real work lay in the removal of usurpers
and their laws. As soon as this takes place the social problem is
solved. In any case—so the Chartists reasoned—the main task of
the movement lay in seizing the power of the State, so as to destroy
the oligarchy and then at least to approximate to the law of nature.

4. LINES OF POLICY

The Chartist movement revealed two different lines of policy,
the advocates of which were known as the Physical Force Party,
and the Moral Force Party. They were opposed to each other,
and between the two there existed elements which oscillated
backwards and forwards. The policy of Physical Force was
insurrectionary and militant, with proclivities to conspiracies,
secret societies, and violent talk. The policy of Moral Force
directed its aim towards slow and thorough organisation within
the law, towards peaceful trades unions, political and educational
societies. The militant party were more revolutionary in their
phraseology, more determined in their attitude, and much more
hostile to the middle classes than the adherents of moral force.
The mass of the proletariat supported the militants, whilst the
smaller number of intellectual workers associated themselves
with moral tactics. The representative of the militant tactics
was the Irish landowner, Feargus O'Connor, who indeed always
condemned on moral grounds the abortive attempts at insurrection, yet continually fostered them anew by his insurrectionary
language. The representative of moral tactics was the London
carpenter, William Lovett. The contest between the two lines
of policy lasted for several years, and was decided in favour of
militant tactics : Lovett had to give way to O'Connor.

The insurrectionary policy seems to have originated from the
historical conception of the law of nature. The following considerations may throw some light upon the question of Jacobinism
and Blanquism.

The whole democratic and socialist movement, which is based
on considerations of the law of nature, considers the evil of the

existing order of things to be the result of bad laws based on usurpation. Certain cunning despots are supposed to have got hold of society in order to oppress and to exploit it for the benefit of a small minority. This whole system of government is therefore a misuse and violation of the social contract and of natural equity. This conception appeared with classic clearness in the conspiracy that is connected with Babeuf's name. The people are justified and in duty bound by all great principles to do everything in their power to sweep away the unnatural, unjust, and pernicious state of things. The fight against this condition is a holy war for the restoration of the law of nature, the social contract, the ancient constitution, innate rights and liberties,—a holy war against usurpers, who destroyed and subverted the old conditions. What need is there of further arguments ? What is the use of philosophising, of educating and enlightening the masses when everything is all as clear as daylight ? The aim of society is the happiness of all and the protection of all. This aim would have been realised if despotism and oligarchy had not destroyed the ancient rights and pledges. The existing order is full of manifest evils ; each of the evils is an indictment against the usurpers and an argument against the minority who gained their power by robbery and destruction. Nature created men in a state of freedom, the rulers threw them into chains.

Such conceptions are just as much calculated to incite violent insurrections of the mass of the people as the feelings of the robbed against the robber. The passions become much more easily roused to action if claims are made upon ancient rights which have once been possessed than if new rights are demanded. In the first case no further evidence or further arguments are required ; force alone is necessary to overthrow the robbers *i.e.*, the Physical Force argument. On the other hand, if rights are demanded which have not hitherto been enjoyed, or if indeed reliance is placed upon new rights in order to contest obsolescent and moribund rights, then the demand for these rights must be based on theory. In this case the feelings play a much smaller part than reason, research, and education.

O'Connor's victory was inevitable ; his tactics corresponded more exactly than Lovett's to the fundamental ideas of Chartism.

The history of Chartism as outlined in the preceding four sections will be treated in detail in the following chapters.

XI

THE ALLIANCE BETWEEN THE WORKING CLASS AND THE MIDDLE CLASS

I.—THE REFORM BILL AND THE POLITICAL UNIONS (1830 to 1832)

From the last third of the eighteenth century until 1830 Great Britain was in the throes of a transformation, which altered the face of the country, brought new classes into being and created men with new interests. Scattered hamlets became vast industrial districts ; trading villages became populous centres, feverish with activity. The increase in the population of the towns is illustrated by the following figures :

	1801	1821	1841
London	959,000	1,379,000	1,950,000
Liverpool	82,000	138,000	286,000
Manchester	77,000	129,000	243,000
Birmingham	71,000	102,000	183,000
Leeds	53,000	84,000	152,000
Sheffield	46,000	85,000	125,000
Nottingham	29,000	40,000	52,000
Bradford	13,000	26,000	67,000
Newcastle	33,000	—	70,000

Yet in spite of this increase the parliamentary representation of the nation in 1830 remained the same in character as it was in 1760. The entire economic revolution appeared incapable of affecting the composition of parliament in the slightest degree. Even in November, 1830, at the opening of William the Fourth's first parliament, the Duke of Wellington, the head of the Tory government, explicitly declared that the existing franchise could not be altered. The time was, however, ripe for a political change. In a debate on a subject of minor importance the ministry was defeated and had to resign. A Whig ministry took its place with Lord Grey and Lord John Russell for its chief members.

A premonition of a coming political crisis swept over the country. No one exactly gauged the significance of the coming events ; there was only a general feeling that English history had reached a crisis. A Radical press came into being to give expression to these feelings ; enthusiasm was rife, and when news reached London of the July revolution in Paris, the people burst into a frenzy of delight that knew no bounds.

On February 18, 1830, the Marquis of Blandford introduced a Reform Bill in the House of Commons, to confer the franchise on householders. The Bill was thrown out. It was a whole year later that Lord John Russell introduced the great Reform Bill. It passed the second reading by a majority of one, and was thrown out in Committee. It was followed by a dissolution of parliament, and the fresh elections gave the government a majority of over 130 votes. A second Reform Bill was introduced ; it passed the House of Commons and was thrown out by the Lords on October 8, 1831, but the government answered them by re-introducing the Bill. The attitude of the Lords roused the whole country to a pitch of indignation that increased from day to day, and led to rioting and the Bristol conflagration.

In the meantime political unions had been formed in most of the towns and by speeches and writings hastened on the agitation for reform. The first political union was founded by Thomas Attwood and his adherents in Birmingham, and it comprised members from both the middle and the working classes. The paper-money reformers in Birmingham had endeavoured for over a decade to press their views upon government, but without any result, and they now saw no other way out of the difficulty than to agitate for a reform of parliament itself and to call in the workers to their help. On January 25, 1830, a meeting took place in Birmingham of 20,000 people, to whom Attwood, the principal speaker, expounded his views. The working men attended the meeting in great numbers, since they were in agreement in demanding that parliament should be reformed. Their idea, however, was less to reform the currency than secure legislation for the protection of labour. Moreover, the fact that they possessed no franchise was unendurable, and they were seeking for the means of obtaining it.

Attwood, in the course of his speech, outlined the scheme of a political alliance between the middle and the working classes. He had already observed the growing independence of the workers and the development of antagonism between capital and labour. He therefore utilised the general demand by the masses for reform to restore harmony between the two classes. The following was the programme he drew up for the political union :—

" 1. To obtain by every just and legal means such a Reform in the Commons House of Parliament as may ensure a real and effectual representation of the lower and middle classes of the people in that House.

" 2. To enquire, consult, consider, and determine respecting the rights and liberties of the industrious classes, and respecting the legal means of securing those which remain and recovering those which are lost.

" 3. To prepare petitions, addresses, remonstrances to the Crown and legislative bodies, respecting the preservation and restoration of public rights, and respecting the repeal of bad laws, and the enactment of good laws.

" 4. To prevent and redress, as far as possible, all local public wrongs and oppressions, and all local encroachments upon the rights, interests, and privileges of the community.

" 5. To obtain the repeal of the beer and malt taxes ; and in general to obtain an alteration in the system of taxation, so as to cause it to press less severely upon the industrious classes of the community and more equally upon the wealthy classes.

" 6. To obtain the reduction of each separate tax and expense of the government in the same degree as the legislative increase in the value of money has increased their respective values, and has reduced and is reducing the general prices of labour throughout the country.

" 7. To promote peace, union and concord among all classes of His Majesty's subjects and to guide and direct the public mind into uniform, peaceful and legitimate operations, instead of leaving it to waste its energies in loose, desultory, and unconnected exertions, or to cater to its own objects, unguided, unassisted, uncontrolled.

" 8. To collect and organise the peaceful expression of the Public Opinion, so as to bring it to act upon the legislative functions in a just, legal, and effectual way

" 9. To influence by every legal means the election of Members of Parliament so as to promote the return of upright and capable representatives of the people.

" 10. To adopt such measures as may be legal and necessary for the purpose of obtaining an effectual Parliamentary investigation into the situation of the country, and into the cause of its embarrassments and difficulties, with the view of relieving the National Distress, of rendering justice to the injured as far as practicable, and of bringing to trial any member of either House of Parliament who may be found to have acted from criminal or corrupt motives."

Nearly the whole of the English press published long reports of this meeting, and all over the country political associations of the middle and working classes came into being, adopting the Birmingham programme. By electoral reform the workers understood universal suffrage, or at least a very wide extension of the franchise which would include a great part of the workers. The organised operatives of the North of England held the same opinion as their comrades in Birmingham. When the committee of the Birmingham political union supported the Marquis of Blandford's proposals to enfranchise house owners and tenants, the operatives of Birmingham protested against this unfriendly attitude of the middle class to the working class. A working man called Bibb, who spoke on behalf of his comrades against the action of the committee, declared :

" . . . . If the suffrage be confined to householders the poor would almost entirely be shut out from the exercise of the rights of the people to annual parliaments or universal suffrage.

People say we should have no right to vote because we don't pay direct taxes. But who are the classes of the people who pay taxes ? The working men. The source of taxation is the produce of labour. What the master pays in taxes is taken off the produce of labour. Profit on capital, profits on trade come from labour. Even those small shopkeepers who pay rates recoup themselves on the consumers for taxation. Finally it is the workmen who pays. In this manner taxes are dragged out of the vitals of the workmen. (Loud cheers) . . . I ask therefore what can the poor expect from the middle classes should they obtain the desired rights, if when there ought to be a similarity and union of feeling from common wrongs, they shrink from their support ? "

During the discussion Attwood and other speakers defended the action of the committee, whereupon Bibb withdrew his protest and at the same time declared :—

" I took this step reluctantly, for I am convinced the declaration you are going to sanction would ultimately destroy the chief, the most important means by which the lower classes might expect to obtain equal rights with their superiors." [1]

Among the Birmingham workers we find the same consciousness of their economic *rôle* and of their political dependence as in the case of the operatives in Leeds and Manchester. From January 1, 1831, the operatives of Lancashire ran their own paper, the *Voice of the People*, which was also the organ of the trades unions as well as of radicalism and Owenism. The Lancashire workers, who aspired after comprehensive economic class-organisation and coquetted with co-operative experiments, came under the political influence of the Benthamites. Only the hardest thinkers of the Lancashire workers, in particular John Doherty, the leader of the textile operatives, dreamed of creating a political Labour Party with the trades unions for its units. According to this plan the local and district unions were to be affiliated for the sole purpose of dealing with matters affecting trades unions, but all the unions should together

[1] *Birmingham Journal*, January 31, 1830.

form a National Association to undertake the emancipation of the working class by means of parliamentary and socialistic action.[1] This plan only became realised in the year 1899–1900 by the formation of the Labour Party. It is obvious that the founders of the Labour Party had no conception that seventy years earlier the idea of a similar organisation had originated. At that time it remained a mere dream, for during the agitation for the Reform Bill the workers formed a part of the political union of the middle and working classes.

It was only in the summer of 1832 that organised Labour dissolved its alliance with the middle classes, and this was partly owing to the stormy character and negative result of the agitation for the Reform Bill, and partly to the propaganda of the intellectual section of the workers of London, who banded together in opposition to the political unions founded on the Birmingham plan and in hostility to the reforms suggested by the Whigs.

2. THE LONDON NATIONAL UNION OF THE WORKING CLASSES

This union, founded in the year 1831, was the birthplace of Chartism. Here the first contests took place between class-war and the solidarity of classes, and here after a long struggle the ideas were formulated of independent action on the part of the operatives, of decisive democratic reform, of revolutionary agitation by the masses and of the general strike.

This union stood in the most intimate connection with the *Poor Man's Guardian*. The development of the movement can be closely followed in its discussions, and their sounding-board was formed by the whole of the thinking portion of the working men of Great Britain. Its immediate history extends as far back as the year 1829, when the British Union for the Diffusion of Co-operative Knowledge was founded. In a manuscript document that is still extant one of its founders makes the following remarks on the subject :—

" During Owen's absence in America, the leaders of the working men who were in favour of Owenism and also of political

[1] *Voice of the People*, June 11, 1831.

Radicalism, met together and opened co-operative shops ; finally they founded the British Union, for enquiries reached London from all sides for information concerning co-operative matters. A special office for supplying information became necessary therefore ; for the correspondence connected with the co-operative establishments had increased to such vast proportion that it could no longer be grappled with after business hours. Our work was both practical and theoretical and we extracted from Owenism as much as we had in common and discarded all points of difference. All the leading men were workmen. When Owen returned from America and saw our co-operative undertakings, he disapproved of them and contemptuously called them Trading Associations, frankly declaring that buying and selling had nothing in common with his co-operative commonwealth. But when he discovered that numerous members of these unions were inclined to support many of his views, he entered into relations with them and took a keen interest in their deliberations." [1]

The meetings of the workers took place at that time either in the large hall of the Mechanics' Institute or in Carlile's Rotunda (Blackfriars). One of these meetings—the fourth quarterly meeting of the British Union for the Diffusion of Co-operative Knowledge—was held at the Mechanics' Institute in October, 1830 ; the report yields a good insight into the mental progress which the workers had made in socialistic thought.

The fundamental ideas were Owenite, but the tone of the speeches was full of a fighting spirit and revolutionary verve. The wage system was condemned root and branch, capitalism was denounced as obnoxious and execrable, whilst labour and co-operation were regarded as the pillars of civilisation. " We by our labour produce all and we ought to enjoy it." The committee's report laid stress upon the rapid rise of the co-operative idea ; the main point was to eradicate the belief from the workers' heads that they were dependent on money or on the possession of capital. Labour was to supplant capital, co-operation was to take the place of individual competition.

[1] Lovett's *Memorandum* in Place MSS. 27791, III.

When the report had been read and discussed, a debate was opened on the subject : " Machinery under competition and under co-operation." Among the speakers were Hetherington, Lovett, Cleave, and Watson, all of them subsequently leaders of Chartism, and their speeches resounded with the theme that machinery is a curse under the system of capital, since all the advantages of mechanical progress fall to the share of the capitalists ; machinery on the other hand will become a blessing under the system of co-operation, since in this way the acquirements of the human mind will benefit the whole of society. Side by side with ideas of co-operation and attacks on capitalism most of the speeches contained hostile aspersions on the Church. If the word socialism were substituted for co-operation, it would be easy to imagine that this report referred to any large social-democratic meeting of workers at the present day.[1]

These were also the doctrines which the leaders of the British Union disseminated in 1829 and 1830 all over the country in the furtherance of co-operation.

In February or March, 1831, the leaders of this association were requested by some joiners to assist them in founding a general union of London operatives.   The joiners were acquainted with the doctrine of co-operation and to all appearances were bent on founding a political trades-unionist organisation based on the ideas of the leaders of the Lancashire working classes. Hetherington and his friends immediately met them half way, and in March, 1831, the " Metropolitan Trades Union " sprang into life.   Hetherington wrote out a prospectus for it, laying down two aims for the organisation, viz. to obtain universal suffrage and to carry out trades-unionist and co-operative measures.[2]

The prospectus was despatched to 150 working men's clubs in London, many of which joined the Union.   In a few weeks its meetings were so largely attended that the Union moved to larger premises, and met in the Rotunda, which could accommodate 1000 people.   The meetings in the Rotunda were always

[1] *Magazine of Useful Knowledge and Co-op. Misc.*, October 30, 1830.

[2] *Penny Papers (Poor Man's Guardian)*, March Numbers, 1831.

overcrowded, so that hundreds could not obtain admission. The subjects which were discussed immediately after the foundation of the Union hinged upon universal suffrage and questions of organisation. In a few weeks the name " Metropolitan Trades Union " disappeared to give place to the name " National Union of the Working Classes and Others." It is obvious from this addition that non-workers were also received within the Union. But the words " and others " were only used at the very beginning. Afterwards we read only of the " National Union of the Working Classes." The non-workers found themselves in a dwindling minority ; among them were Julian Hibbert, a member of a rich Liberal philanthropic family ; T. J. Webb, a practical surgeon ; William Benbow, at that time a coffee-house proprietor ; Benjamin Warden, formerly a saddler's apprentice, but now an independent master.

The National Union rapidly increased in members and prestige, so as to justify Hetherington's exclamation that the Union was on the right road to become national. On May 25, 1831, it received its constitution, which had been drawn up by Lovett and Hetherington, and to all appearances with O'Brien's assistance. The main declaration was a nearly verbal copy of the first part of the French " Rights of Man," 1789. It merely contained the following alteration—emphasised here by spacing : " The members of the National Union of the Working Classes are convinced that forgetfulness of and contempt for the Rights of Man in a municipal state of society[1] are the only causes of the crimes and misfortunes of the world."

This was followed by the aims and objects of the Constitution :—

" 1. To avail itself of every opportunity in the progress of society, for the securing for every working man the full value of his labour and the free disposal of the produce of his labour.

---

[1] " Municipal state of society " means the same as " civilised or artificial state of society," in contrast to the original or natural state. This expression, so far as social criticism is concerned, is only used by Ogilvie and O'Brien (*Carpenter's Political Letters*, January 18, 1831).

2. To protect working men against the tyranny of masters and manufacturers by all just means as circumstances may determine.

3. To obtain for the nation an effectual reform in the Commons House of the British parliament : annual parliaments, extension of the suffrage to every adult male, vote by ballot, and especially no property qualification for members of parliament.

4. To prepare petitions, addresses and remonstrances to the Crown and both Houses of Parliament.

5. To concentrate into one focus a knowledge of moral and political economy, that all classes of society may be enlightened by its radiation, the National Union feeling assured that the submission of the people to misrule and oppression arises from the absence of sound moral and political knowledge amongst the mass of the community."

Finally the constitution of the National Union took over most of the provisions from the statutes of the "Birmingham Political Union." The addition of the statutes of the Birmingham Political Union shows that the London National Union at the time of its foundation held no decided opinion in favour of class-war. The very first discussion, however, evoked a declaration on the subject. In electing the committee some of the workers proposed the following motion :

"Since the Union aims at rescuing the workers from their degradation and in raising them to a higher level, it is necessary that the workers should set themselves the task of attaining this object. Therefore no member of the Union shall be elected on the Committee who is not a producer, or who does not earn his living by labour."

Warden and Hetherington opposed this resolution. They expressed the opinion that holding office did not depend on a man's trade but on ability, talent and allegiance to principles, and that the National Union had not been founded in order to lay stress on differences of class. The meeting agreed with these views, and the resolution was rejected. The leading men in the Union were Owenites, and consequently opposed to class-war. This position, which Hetherington and Warden had taken up drew upon them a sharp attack by the anonymous champion of class-war (to whom reference has already been made) in a communication addressed to the *Poor Man's Guardian*. His first letters allow the critical reader to form an estimate of the personality of their author. In the first place solecisms escape from his pen which could not possibly proceed from a practised writer like Bronterre O'Brien, who had received a college education, but might very well be written by a self-taught working man. For instance, the anonymous writer interchanges the verbs " teach " and " learn ; " in the second place he mentions " his loom " on one occasion ; thirdly he opposed co-operative enterprises, whilst O'Brien even in 1830 was one of Owen's admirers ; fourthly, he regards trade unionism as one of the foremost weapons of the fighting working class, while O'Brien, in 1831, held the opinion that trade unionism was " a folly and waste of money and time, leading but to discord and riots ; "[1] finally, the anonymous writer was hostile to any joint action between the operatives and the lower middle classes, whilst O'Brien was in favour of an alliance between them. This correspondence could, therefore, not have proceeded, either in its wording or its tenour, from O'Brien, but must have come from a hand-loom weaver, ruined by modern machinery, who had had the advantage of a little schooling in his youth. The most determined fighters of Chartism came from the handicraftsmen who were ruined by the growing Factory System.

Now for the " communication."

The anonymous correspondent inveighed in long diatribes against the Reform Bill, which he considered to be even more reactionary and pernicious than the old franchise. Then he addressed himself to Hetherington (the publisher of the *Poor Man's Guardian*) and Warden :—

" People who live by plunder will always tell you to be submissive to thieves. To talk of *representation*, in any shape, being of any use to the people is sheer nonsense ; unless the people have a House of working men, and represent themselves. Those

[1] *Midland Representative*, May 28, 1831, p. 8. (Review of *Knight's Working Men's Companion*.)

who make the laws now and who are intended, by the new reform bill, to make them in future, all live by profits of some sort or other. They will, therefore, no matter who elect them, nor how often they are elected, always make the laws to raise profits and keep down the price of labour. Representation, therefore, by a different body of people to those who are represented, or whose interests are opposed to theirs, is a mockery, and those who persuade the people to the contrary are either idiots or cheats. . . . The people should drop all contention, therefore, about electing a legislature in its present shape, and contend night and day, every moment of their lives for a legislature of their own, or one made up of themselves. This is the *primum mobile*, the grand *desideratum*, and in the absence of this there is not a shadow of a chance of getting a shadow of justice, but that of keeping the plunderers in continual dread, thereby raising a sufficient portion of fear to counteract their vicious desires. They will then respect the people for the sake of themselves. . . . Co-operation is of no use, unless the people would get the raw materials without going to the land-stealer, then dispense with the use of money, and live by bartering their manufactures with each other. No one could then get either rent, tax or profit out of them, but as they cannot do this, co-operation has little or no other effect than that of feeding the rich, and starving those who can scarcely live. . . . As soon as it becomes generally understood that the co-operators can live a shilling a week cheaper than before, their employers will reduce their wages to that amount ; and thus will their employers reap all the advantages of their co-operation. . . .

" *The Trades Union.*—This was a most important union, but unfortunately strangled in its birth. The first resolution of the Union that was proposed was to this effect—' That as this Union is intended to raise the working classes from their present degraded condition, it is necessary that it *be done by* themselves. No person, therefore, shall be eligible to act on the committee unless he be a wealth-producer, that is, one who gets his living by labour.' This resolution spoke a volume, by showing the people's desire to take the lead in favour of themselves. This

w

resolution you and Mr. Warden destroyed. . . . You and
Mr. Warden then will do well in withdrawing yourselves from
their committee, and every one else who is not absolutely a man
who works for a master, or working man. Attend their meetings,
hear what they have to say, report their proceedings, and encourage them to go on ; but at the same time give them the lead,
learn them to go alone, and encourage them to be no longer slaves,
but men."[1]

The anonymous correspondent addressed to the *Poor Man's
Guardian* other letters full of the logic of the working man.
From the very beginning this organ advocated universal franchise, but it considered the alliance between the middle and
working classes to be necessary. A few days after the introduction of the Reform Bill this newspaper wrote :

" . . . In conclusion, we hope and trust this reform measure
will not be carried ; at the same time we feel convinced, that
even those who are now so more than satisfied, will soon find out
its complete inefficiency even for their own purposes ; but it
will retard the progress of real reform considerably ; for a time,
the middle classes will be removed from the side of the people at
large, and, it must be admitted that they are a great loss, inasmuch, as when united in one common cause, they can afford to
give publicity to their wants, which the people cannot."[2]

This attitude appeared to the anonymous writer to be dangerous. He protested in a blazing letter to the editor against any
compromise between workers and capitalists. The economic
contrasts between the two classes were so deep-seated that the
workers could not possibly expect any political help from the
middle class. And he addressed himself to the working people
as follows :—

" What justice or what mercy can you expect at the hands of
the employers when they shall have acquired their elective
privileges of forming the legislature, whose very preliminary step
consists in divesting you of your dearest and most *sacred right ?*
We have a hundred rotten boroughs at the present day, but

[1] *Penny Papers* (*Poor Man's Guardian*), April 29, 1831.
[2] *Poor Man's Guardian*, March 12, 1831 (leading article).

pass this Bill with this obnoxious clause and the whole kingdom will be rotten to the very core. . . . The landowner, the merchant, and the tradesman will hereafter possess the sole right (or rather privilege) of making the laws. The interest of all these people is directly opposed to yours. Mark then what I say : If this Bill pass in its present shape, that is, with this obnoxious clause, *house rent will rise*, wages will be still further reduced, and the prices of everything else will be advanced. You are now to be forsaken, rejected, and to become entire outcasts in the world. . . ."[1]

" As a proof of what kind of materials the House of Commons is to be composed, two candidates have already been named by the profit-men or middlemen, for our town. One of them everybody knows, and therefore I shall say nothing about him ; the other, I am informed, is a Cockney, of the name of Young, a shipbuilder, who possesses as much information as *my loom.* . . . It is but common justice that the people who make the goods should have the sole privilege of making the laws." [2]

During the discussions and the enormous mass demonstrations of the people in favour of the Reform Bill, the Whigs succeeded in intimidating the Lords, and in exacting from the King a promise to create a batch of peers if necessary. In March, 1832, a decisive victory for the Reform Bill was at last in sight. The anonymous writer took all his knowledge and ability in both hands and wrote the following article for the *Poor Man's Guardian* :—

" TO THE WORKING PEOPLE OF ENGLAND "

" FELLOW COUNTRYMEN,

" I have given you my opinion in several letters, at various times, on the present measure of Reform. I have in these letters uniformly told you that that measure, if carried into effect, will do you an incalculable deal of harm. I have told you that the evils under which you labour are not produced by taxation. I have shown you that the whole expense of the government, from

[1] *Penny Papers (Poor Man's Guardian)*, April 9, 1831.
[2] *Poor Man's Guardian*, November 19 and 26, 1831.

the King to the common soldier, does not amount to more than one halfpenny a day upon each individual in the two kingdoms ; and that the abolition of the whole government would relieve you to the amount of only that one halfpenny a day. I have told you that the remote cause of your poverty is your not having seats, personally, in that which ought to be your house ; and that you are thereby prevented from assisting, like the land-stealers, the merchants, the manufacturers, and the tradesmen, in your own persons, to make the laws by which you are governed ; and I told you that the *immediate* cause of your poverty is the exorbitant rents, tithes, interest on money, profits on labour, and profits on trade, which are imposed on you by laws made by the land-stealers, merchants, manufacturers, and tradesmen in that house from which you are excluded, and by which exclusion you are prevented from making laws to regulate your wages. I have told you that the government taxes are only a natural consequence arising out of the rents, interest, and other profits which are imposed on you—that those taxes are, in short, only a sum of money given to the government to beat and torture you into a submission to those rents, tithes, interest, and profits, by which you are robbed to more than twenty times the amount of those taxes. I have told you these things before, and I tell you the same now, and in so doing I tell you the truth.

" I have told you that the influence of those men who impose those rents and profits, is to be increased in making the laws, and that your influence is to be diminished by this Bill. I told you, and I shewed you that every increase of these rents, tithes, and profits is equal to a reduction of your wages to the same amount ; and that by this Bill these rents and other profits will be still farther increased, and your wages, in consequence, still farther reduced. I told you these facts before, and I repeat it again now, that this Bill will augment your poverty to an incalculable degree.

" I told you, and I shewed you existing facts to prove that the taxes, in every country in the world, are always increased in exact proportion as the influence of the land-stealers, merchants, manufacturers, and tradesmen is increased in making the laws ;

and as I am determined to assert nothing without proof, I will now shew you the reason why those taxes are so increased. For instance, as soon as the land-stealers, merchants, manufacturers, and tradesmen acquire the privilege of law-making, they begin to legislate for their own individual interest ; that is, to increase their rents and profits, by which they deprive you of the produce of your industry ; and in proportion as their influence in law-making is increased, so are those rents and profits increased, and so likewise is your burden increased accordingly. In proportion as your poverty is increased, so do you become more and more tumultuous for the want of food. In proportion as you become tumultuous, so do these land-stealers and others strengthen the government to keep you down ; and in proportion as they strengthen the government to keep you down, so do they increase the taxes to support the government. So here then you *see*, in a few words, the real cause of that increase of taxes in all countries, which I only *told* you of before—that these taxes are nothing more than the natural consequence or offspring of exorbitant rents, tithes, interest, and other profits ; and that these rents, and so on, are the real cause of your poverty ; yet the influence of these men who live by these impositions, is to be increased in making the laws, by this Bill, more than ten-fold ! ! Will you believe now that you have any interest in the passing of this Bill, or that your interest does not consist in its being kicked out, as it was before ? I am told that you cannot be worse off than you are now. I say yes. The Irish people are three times worse off than you are, bad as you are, and that you are capable of being as bad off as they. I therefore conjure you to prepare your coffins if you have the means. You will be starved to death by thousands, if this Bill pass, and thrown on to the dung hill, or on to the ground, naked, like dogs. I now proceed to other matters connected with this measure.

" Of all the Bills, or plots (for it is nothing else), that ever was proposed on earth, this is the most deceptive and the most mischievous. This Bill proposes to extend the number of electors to about five times the present amount. This, on the face of the measure, appears, at first sight, a most liberal alteration What !

extend the number of voters from 150,000 to 600,000 or 700,000 ?
Most liberal indeed ! ! ! But now, when we come to see that the
liberality is all on one side, and none on the other—when we
come to see that those whose influence is already tenfold too
great, are to have that influence tenfold increased, while you
whose influence is already tenfold too little, are to have that
influence (through the great increase of the other) incalculably
diminished, it is the most *illiberal*, the most *tyrannical*, the most
abominable, the most infamous, the most hellish measure that
ever could or can be proposed. Your number is four-fifths of the
whole population. Your influence, therefore, at elections (in
addition to your right of being elected yourselves) ought to be
four times as great as all the rest of the community. Yet your
influence will not be more than *one-twentieth part* of that which
will be exercised by those who live on the fruits of your labour.
You will in reality, therefore, from fear and fewness of number,
have no influence at all.

" This Bill proposes to disfranchise a number of rotten boroughs,
and to transfer the elective franchise to large populous towns.
This is another of the supposed liberal features of the Bill.
Do you not see that the interest of a few wealthy individuals at
Gatton, and Old Sarum, who live on the fruits of your labour, is
the same as the interest of as many millions, in any other part of
the kingdom, who live by the same means, and that the interest
of one working man is the same as that of all others—that is,
to get rid of his burdens ? But then it will be said : those
wealthy individuals at Gatton and Old Sarum live by high rents,
while the same description of people in the large towns live
by profits on manufactures, and on trade. Oh ! then these
individuals in these large towns want to get as large profits on
their manufactures as the others do on corn, and thereby im-
poverish you three times as much as you are. Their profits,
already, are three times as great, aye, ten times as great, in those
towns, as they ought to be. These profits are the main cause
of your poverty in those towns now. So much for the liberality
of disfranchising small towns to enfranchise large ones ! The
increase of poverty by this *liberality* will be in exact proportion

to the increased number of working men who will be affected by those profits. What liberality !

"When I hear master manufacturers and tradesmen say—We must get large profits to enable us to pay you high wages, my blood curdles within me, and I wish at once that I were a dog, or anything else, rather than a man. Those large profits are the sole cause why wages are low. They are got by keeping wages down. Shall I say anything more on this subject ? Is it necessary, seeing that we are rational beings and ' lords of the creation ! ' . . . The profit is that which is retained and never paid back. The manufacturer's profits, therefore, like the land-stealers' rent, and tithe-stealers' tithes, and all other profits, was obtained solely by keeping wages down. . . . There is no common interest between working men and profit-makers. This fact, like the sun, for ever stares us in the face—that in exact proportion as these large capitals are obtained, so is the poverty of the working people most *capitally* increased. . . .

"It is supposed that the members for the manufacturing towns will be enabled successfully to attack and abolish the corn-laws. Nothing can be more delusive. They must be holders of stolen land themselves before they can become members. Besides, if they were not, a sufficiency of land-stealing members has been secured by the division of counties to make head against the large towns, and for the loss of the rotten boroughs, so that, in short, the corn laws will be equally as secure as ever, while the manu-facturing members will increase their profits like the profits of the land-stealers, and therefore I am justified in saying that the Bill will retrograde from, instead of approaching towards Reform.

"Do you not see then that all that you want is high wages and low profits ? You must get your own wages up, and then these rents, tithes, interest, and other profits must fall. The Reform Bill has nothing to do with this policy of the working man. I therefore warn you, if the Bill be kicked out, be you as peaceable and as still as mice. I know you will never get anything without exertion ; but then the example of France, Belgium, and all other countries, will convince you that no sudden convulsion will relieve you. Your exertion must be constant, uniform, and as silent and as perpetual as the conduct of your enemies, till they pay you as much wages as will purchase you your fair proportion of everything you produce. If you want to know who is your greatest enemy—it is he who has the greatest income, no matter what he may say to deceive you, nor to what sect or party he may belong, nor from what source his income may be derived. With this warning I take my leave with the assurance that if the Bill pass, I will tell you something of greater importance than anything else I have told you before.

" ONE OF THE OPPRESSED."[1]

Manchester, March 19, 1832.

The power of the style and the argument of this anonymous social thinker are so striking that little comment is necessary. The article reveals all the strong and weak points of a keen but one-sided brain : ruthless logic, transparent clearness, inclination to prophecy, the omission of all factors not bearing on the economic side of the question, however important they might be in themselves, which, however, subsequently prove strong enough to overturn all the economic prophecies. The essay shows distinct traces of Hodgskin's way of thinking. Its author was obviously influenced by the latter.

It is highly probable that the same anonymous writer is responsible for the following verses which were printed in the *Poor Man's Guardian* (January 7, 1832) :—

> " Wages should form the price of goods ;
>   Yes, wages should be all,
> Then we who work to make the goods
>   Should *justly have them all ;*
> But if their price be made of rent,
>   Tithes, taxes, profits all,
> Then we who work to make the goods
>   Shall have—*just none at all.*"

The verses contain the entire theory and deduction of natural rights, viz. that the price of work is by right the product of the work ; but under civilised conditions the worker only receives

[1] *Poor Man's Guardian*, April 14, 1832.

for his wages the minimum of the means for existence, since capitalism, landlordism, State and Church appropriate the greater part of the proceeds of labour.

The *Poor Man's Guardian* also published opinions drawn from labour and socialist circles in support of the Reform Bill. A labouring man wrote :—

" You are certainly correct in your opinion of the ' Reform,' which literally does *nothing* for us, the labouring classes ; but are you not wrong in advising us to have all we demand or nothing ? Should we not get as much as we can ? I do not say, accept this reform, which gives us worse than nothing, but let us get any advantage, however trifling it be, by the aid of which we might benefit ourselves more and more, step by step. This strikes me to be better advice than what you offer."

Allen Davenport, an old Spencean, wrote to the paper as follows :—

" I feel inclined to support the present Reform Bill in spite of all that can be said against it. I consider the Reform Bill, if carried into law, will be the commencement of a legal revolution, whose movement will not be so easily arrested as some persons imagine. I calculate more on external than internal energy, when every thing has changed around us it will be impossible for us to remain stationary." [1]

The National Union fostered international solidarity with particular ardour. It celebrated the anniversaries of the French Revolution and of the Polish insurrection, and opposed Palmerston's foreign policy, which it severely stigmatized as dictated by the Tsar. From the summer of 1831 onwards the influence of the National Union upon the *élite* of the British working class was

[1] *Penny Papers* (*Poor Man's Guardian*), March 18 and May 27, 1831. Allen Davenport was born in 1775, as the son of an agricultural labourer. He grew up without having been to any school, served in the army, became converted to Spenceanism in 1817, subsequently to Owenism, wrote poems, pamphlets, and a short biographical sketch of Thomas Spence (1836). He died in London in 1846, poor but universally esteemed (*Reasoner*, 1847, pp. 16, *sqq.*).

very considerable.[1]   Delegates from the Midlands and North of
England appeared at their meetings.   The whole mental activity
of British socialism was disseminated thence by the leaders of the
British working men.   In October, 1831, their members were
already regarded as communists holding the opinion that " private
property had no right to exist at all, since it could only be harmful
to the worker." [2]   They were not Owenite communists but
socialists, waging class-warfare ; they were unable to dissociate
themselves from militant tactics, and at the end of October, 1831,
the *Poor Man's Guardian* published instructions on making
barricades and on street-fighting against soldiers.   That was the
time also in which the Reform Bill agitation reached its greatest
height and in which the social-revolutionary idea of the general
strike and of convoking a national convention began to take
root and was soon formulated by William Benbow.

3.—WILLIAM BENBOW AND THE GENERAL STRIKE

The later months of 1831 saw the birth of the idea of a social-
revolutionary general strike.   Its originator was William Benbow,
shoemaker, publisher, bookseller and coffee-house proprietor,
a man of great eloquence and mental energy, but with a violent
temperament and exaggerated self-consciousness.   The patho-
logical trait of his nature was in all probability the result of a
nervous affection, partly due to his ceaseless self-tuition under
unfavourable material conditions, mostly to persecution on
account of his violent agitation and speeches.   Hitherto, little
has been known of his life history.   The movements in which
he was engaged used him up without caring for his personality.
William Benbow represents the same mental type as Richard
Carlile and Thomas J. Wooler.   This type was a product of a
mental tendency, characterized by democratic radicalism, free
thought and the law of nature, which prevailed in the last decades
of the eighteenth century and the first decades of the nineteenth
century.   At that period the cleverest artisans and operatives

---

[1] Place MSS., 27,791, pp. 333, *sqq.*, 343, 412.
[2] *Ibid.*, 27,790, p. 23.

acquired considerable literary and political knowledge by dint of iron will-power and unquenchable enthusiasm, and they utilised this knowledge to enlighten the masses. Benbow appears to have been born in Manchester in 1784. In April, 1840, when he had to defend himself before a jury in Chester for having made seditious Chartist speeches, he stated at the end of a ten-hour speech in his defence that he was already an old man and at the very best had only ten years more to live.[1] He was apprenticed to a shoemaker,[2] showed capacity for public speaking, and preached in Nonconformist chapels. He took part, after 1815, in the Radical movement and was arrested. He is also known to have been a printer and publisher from 1817 to 1825. His publishing house had Lord Byron's head for a sign and was called " Byron's Head " in consequence. Here he printed for Richard Carlile the drama *Wat Tyler*, by Robert Southey, which drew upon him the latter's eternal enmity.[3] Benbow printed cheap editions of the English poets, especially of Byron. In 1823 he brought out a work in parts which was a chronicle of clerical scandals. It bore the title, *Crimes of Clergy*, and belongs to the class of scurrilous literature. Two years later he published a polemic against Southey and in defence of Byron. This pamphlet, *A Scourge for the Laureate*, is well written and shows that Benbow was a man with a trenchant style and with no inconsiderable literary knowledge. At that time he had already served a term of imprisonment. In 1831 and 1832 we find him to be a member of the National Union and one of the most violent speakers in the Rotunda. At that time he owned a coffee-house at No. 205, Fleet Street, where he penned his pamphlet on the social-revolutionary general strike. It bears the title : *Grand National Holiday and Congress of the Productive Classes*. It appeared towards the close of 1831 or in January, 1832, and was dedicated to the workers in the following brief sentences :—

[1] *Northern Star*, April 25, 1840; *Chester Gazette*, April 11, 1840.

[2] *Gaols and Prisons :* Accounts and Papers, Vol. 38, 1840, No. 600, pp. 691, *sqq.*

[3] This statement is based on Benbow's evidence only. I could find no *editio princeps* of Southey's *Wat Tyler*, and therefore I am unable to confirm it.

"Plundered Fellow-sufferers! I lay before you a plan of freedom; adopt it and you rid the world of inequality, misery and crime. A martyr in your cause, I am become the prophet of your salvation. A plan of happiness is pointed out and dedicated to you. With it I devote to you my life and body, my soul and blood.

"WILLIAM BENBOW."

"Commercial Coffee House,
205, Fleet Street."

His speeches in the National Union were often printed in the *Poor Man's Guardian*. From 1834 to 1838 we hear nothing of him. It is only in 1838 that he appears again in Lancashire, where he travelled about with horse and cart, holding open-air meetings and pushing the sale of his pamphlet on the general strike. He must have left London about the year 1837, in order to betake himself to the centre of the Chartist agitation. For at that time the leading radical and socialist agitators, such as O'Connor and Owen, left London for Yorkshire and Lancashire, whither the political centre of gravity had followed the industrial centre. In the beginning of August, 1839, Benbow was arrested in Manchester and spent eight months in prison awaiting his trial since he could not give security; it is curious that he could not induce any one to bail him out. He was popular enough among the workers, without, however, receiving any degree of confidence at their hands. Positions of trust were not conferred upon him. In all the many conferences, conventions and other functions of the Chartists he never appeared as a delegate. All this neglect greatly contributed to embitter him still further. He believed himself to be persecuted alike by friend and foe. Yet his pamphlet on the general strike exercised a powerful influence between 1838 and 1842. There were probably few Chartists who had not read it; its phrases were on every lip; Chartist speakers made use of it; and all the debates on a general strike and all attempts at its realisation in that decade are to be traced to Benbow's pamphlet.

Benbow's main ideas are as follows :—

The labour of the mass of the people is the source of wealth, but it is only a privileged few that obtain it. The people is the source of all power, but the oppressors of the people make use of it ; the mass of the people fight both by land and sea, but the usurpers carry off the laurels and the booty. How has this become possible ?

By the ignorance and disunion of the people.

The worst result of ignorance is the assumption that others will do for us what we ought to do ourselves. It is sheer lunacy for working men to ask their masters to undertake the task of emancipation.

The working men must emancipate themselves. And if the working-men understand this they will win. From Wat Tyler to Thistlewood the martyrs of truth have always been found among the people.

But how can the people obtain this knowledge and unity of action ? By proclaiming a national holiday ; by stopping work. We suffer from overproduction, so we are told. Good. Let us stop producing. The masters will soon find out that an over-abundance of goods is no misfortune. We suffer from over-population, so we are told. Good. Let us count ourselves ; let us find out the large numbers of the working men and the small numbers of the privileged class. The very act of the masses stopping work will give the latter the consciousness of their strength, the magnitude of their united action. The month's holiday must be a month's congress of the working men ; a people's month for taking stock of the social conditions ; a national congress to put tyranny to flight.

Before the national holiday is proclaimed, preparation for it must be made. Every locality will elect a committee to direct the agitation and to enlighten the masses concerning the objects and significance of the national holiday and of the national congress.

Every family of workers must provide food for a week. A longer period is not necessary. If the working class of the whole country is united and resolute for only a single week, success is certain.

All money and property which were originally destined for the support of the people and have been appropriated by various corporations and churches must be restored to their original destination. Land and live stock originally belonged to all. The committees appointed by the people will have to see that the present owners restore part of the fruits of the earth and the live stock to the masses resting from their toil. And behind the committees there must stand a people strong in morals and resolute in action. Above all the masses must not be squeamish. Both right and might are on the side of the people.

The object of the national congress is to reform society root and branch by a better division of wealth, by a uniform circulation of goods so as to set the whole body of society in a state of harmonious activity.

Benbow's plan can therefore be reduced to the following ideas : The general strike is the best means of bringing the workers to a sense of their power ; the object of the agitators is to make use of a propitious moment to induce the workers to act together *en masse*. Consolidated action on the part of the workers would transform their power into violence which would lead the people on to victory and happiness by producing economic equality.

Benbow himself never used the term " general strike," but spoke always of the national holiday ; the Chartists generally used the term " sacred week " or " sacred month " ; it was the trades unions who discarded all those terms and spoke of the general strike. We find this term for the first time in the *Herald of Rights of Industry* (April 5, 1834, p. 66. col. 2). This paper was edited by John Doherty.

4.—THE REFORMED PARLIAMENT AND DISILLUSIONMENT

In June, 1832, the Reform Bill was made law and in the middle of August parliament was dissolved. The posting of the lists of electors and the preparations for the elections had a sobering effect. The exhilaration of the Reform agitation had evaporated, the wildest hopes gave way to the deepest disappointment. In November and December the elections took place, but they only resulted in a great victory for the Whigs. In February, 1833, the first Reformed parliament was opened by a King's speech, which, as Thomas Attwood, the member for Birmingham, remarked, might just as well have been read by the Emperor of China, since it had so little connection with the problems of the day or the wishes of the people.

The first year of the Reformed parliament was, however, not quite so barren as its critics maintained ; negro-slavery was abolished in the West Indies and a factory act was passed for the textile industry of Great Britain, which marks the actual commencement of legislation in protection of the working man. It was absolutely forbidden to employ children under nine years of age, the working hours for children from nine to thirteen years were restricted to eight hours, a maximum of sixty-nine working hours a week was established for young people, night-work was forbidden for both categories and an inspection of factories was introduced. The law, however, only affected the North of England and had hardly any application except for textile-workers. Not a single labour paper of the day printed a leading article on the factory law. On the other hand, ample use was made of the material of the Committees of Inquiry, which had preceded this law and had revealed the frightful exploitation of child-labour. The feeling of disillusionment was intensified by the Act of 1834 amending the Poor Law, which swept away the old Poor Law administration, erected bastilles for the poor, and stigmatised poverty as a crime. The old Poor Law had a social reform character ; the support of the unemployed out of the parish-rates was regarded as a duty, the claim to support was considered as the right of the citizen who had fallen on evil times. The new law completely reversed this conception and asserted the individualistic idea by which it was the duty of every one to look to himself and to make no claim whatever to the help of his fellow-men. The majority of the Reformed parliament swore by Malthus and the political economists, who knew no other remedy for poverty than celibacy and regarded unemployment as the result of laziness or as an unavoidable evil with which no social remedy could contend.

The new franchise, which conferred parliamentary representation upon the middle classes, but left the working classes unenfranchised, disclosed at one blow the apparently unbridgeable chasm that existed between capital and labour. The operatives had realised the economic antagonism for decades, but owing to the middle classes being just as much without representation up to 1832 as the working classes, the opposition between the classes was to some extent obscured and, accordingly, both classes fought side by side for reform as allies. After 1832 this alliance was no longer possible. The division was obvious in every direction. To cap it all, the severity of the new Poor Law changed the estrangement into open enmity.

The anonymous champion of class-war in the *Poor Man's Guardian* had, so it seemed, predicted all this in advance ! And a working class poet expressed the feelings of Labour in the following lines :—[1]

'Tis twelve months past, just yesterday, since earth, and sky, and sea,
And rock, and glen, and horse, and man rang loud the jubilee;
The beacons blazed, the cannons fired, and war'd each plain and hill
With the Bill—the glorious Bill, and nothing but the Bill !

Our taxes, by the glorious Bill, were all to sink and fade,
Our shipping was to prosper, and think, oh ! what a trade !
Our agriculture and our looms, our pockets were to fill,
By, ah ! you rogues, the Bill, the Bill, and nought but the Bill !

But now each holds up his hands in horror and disgust
At this same document, once termed the people's trust,
That at last was to bring grist to all the nation's mill.
Ah ! curse the Bill, ye rogues, the Bill, and nothing but the Bill!

The working men in their desperation condemned not only the Reform Bill but the whole institution of parliament. The workers now asked the question : " What have the political unions done for us ? "

Nothing at all ! Worse than nothing ! And they shattered their gods of reform and even turned away from the prophets who had warned them against the false gods. The London National Union lost its members and prestige so rapidly and the *Poor Man's Guardian* its readers, that both of them only carried on a precarious existence and died out in 1835.

[1] *Glasgow Liberator and Trades Union Gazette*, September 14, 1833.

The people again looked for their salvation to Owen, who had become entirely anti-parliamentary, and to trades unions, which gradually assumed a revolutionary or syndicalist character. The operatives looked to them not only for an amelioration of the conditions of labour but for emancipation from wage slavery.

Yet an alliance between Owenism and syndicalism presented difficulties both in theory and practice. Owenism depended on the co-operation of classes ; it only distinguished between erring and enlightened human beings. Trades unionism, with its social-revolutionary character, depended on class-war and only recognised exploiting and exploited classes. Owen made the attempt to displace private industry and competition by means of peaceful co-operative establishments and wherever possible by a union between the workers and the capitalists. The object of syndicalism was to expropriate the capitalists by continued hostilities and to get the factories, workshops and agricultural industries into the hands of the trades unionists. The intrinsic opposition between the two aspects of society was not immediately recognised. The fusion of Owenism and syndicalism led to conflict and confusion ; and this period did not last long enough to furnish investigators with the opportunity of producing a clear separation of the two points of view.

XII

SEPARATION OF THE MIDDLE AND WORKING CLASSES

1.—LABOUR EXCHANGES AND CO-OPERATIVE SOCIETIES

At the time when the Reform Bill agitation reached its high-water mark and Great Britain was brought to the verge of civil war, Owen again took up his plan for guiding the country into the path of a peaceful economic revolution. He interpreted the whole political agitation as the blind yearning of the nation for redemption, and as the tempestuous approach of a momentous crisis in history.

Without delay he grappled with his task. First of all labour exchanges were to be instituted, in order to enable producers suffering from a stagnant market to exchange their goods for others which they might require. Then the individual producers were to be induced to band themselves together in co-partnership, so as to emancipate the operatives from their dependence on capital. As a first step in this work of emancipation Owen in November, 1831, conceived the idea of founding an association for the intelligent working men of London in order to initiate them in the doctrine of co-operation, and to train up leaders for carrying out his great work. A committee for this purpose was formed as early as December 3, and a certain Bromley placed at Owen's disposal, without any compensation, his business-premises in Gray's Inn Road, known as the " Royal Bazaar." On December 12 and 19, 1831, a crowded public meeting was held in these premises, and led to the foundation of the " Association of the Intelligent and Well-disposed of the Industrious

---

[1] The plan of labour exchanges is mentioned, for the first time, in the *Co-operative Magazine*, 1827, p. 511.

Classes for removing Ignorance and Poverty."[1] The objects of the association were announced to be the education of the children of working-men, and the purchase of land for agricultural schools, as well as " to receive provisions, clothing and other property, and services of every description to be exchanged on the equitable principle of labour for equal value of labour, through the medium of labour notes ; also to establish a bank in which to exchange the labour notes for the currency of the country." [1]

The ideas on value and money which Owen had expounded in the Lanark *Report*, published in 1820, were now to be put into practice. The committee accepted Bromley's offer without securing it by a contract. The Institute was opened. Its organ was a weekly, the *Crisis*, of which the first number appeared on April 14, 1832. Its first editor was R. Dale Owen. From the very beginning, not only in the association but also in the *Crisis*, active propaganda was set on foot in favour of the labour exchanges which Owen regarded as only introductory to the work of emancipation. The following ideas were at the root of the scheme of the labour exchanges :

The producers suffer from the drawback of not knowing the markets for their produce ; they are not acquainted with the people who would be ready and willing to exchange their goods for others. Therefore, they betake themselves to contractors, middlemen, and retailers, who pay them money for their goods after deductions for profits and rents. With the money thus obtained they have recourse again to middlemen to procure the goods they require, and in their purchase they have again to pay profits and rents to the non-producers. Before the producer, therefore, can obtain what he wants he has to hand over to non-producers the major part of the produce of his labour. In order to guard against these evils labour exchanges were to be set up where the producers can deposit their goods and can estimate the average amount of time taken in their production. When this is done, the producers receive vouchers stating the amount

[1] *Times*, December 20, 1831 ; Carpenter, *Co-operative Congress*, 1832, p. 128.

of labour time on deposit. By means of these vouchers they can obtain, at the same place, at any time, goods to the same average amount of labour time that has been expended in their production. In this manner supply and demand are brought into close relation with each other, and an exchange takes place without any loss.

Owen's labour exchange was not the first of these institutions. Even at the close of 1831 a bank of exchange was founded at the Gothic Hall in Marylebone ; the second was situated in the north-west of England. Owen's was the third, but was the most notable of its kind, owing to its founder's reputation. The Institute in Gray's Inn Road became the Mecca of all interested in co-operation and peaceful social reform. During the last week of April, 1832, the third Co-operative Congress was held in its rooms. The first congress sat in Manchester in May, 1831, the second in Birmingham in October, 1831. In the third Congress, in London, 65 co-operative societies were represented, and 29 of these were manufacturing societies. Here Owen expounded his plan of a labour exchange and proved at the same time that he himself was the originator of the idea and not John Gray. Gray's ideas were indeed anticipated in the Lanark report. William Thompson, too, was present as a delegate, and confirmed Owen's opinion of his priority over Gray.[1] In this congress a clash of views occurred for the first time between the parliamentary, democratic socialists and the non-political, co-operative socialists, and in general Owen's Institute and the *Crisis* on the one hand were often in conflict with the Rotunda and the *Poor Man's Guardian* on the other hand. It was in this Congress also that Owen demanded State-assistance to the tune of five million pounds for co-operative undertakings.[2]

On September 3, 1832, the labour exchange was opened at the Institute. During the first four months its success was not inconsiderable. Every week goods to the average value of £600 were deposited and exchanged, and the Institute received 8.5 per cent. of this sum for covering the expenses of administration.

[1] Carpenter, *Co-operative Congress*, 1832, p. 43.
[2] *Ibid.*, p. 42.

At the same time a branch institute was started in Blackfriars Road near the Rotunda. Several trades unionist organisations of London also proceeded to engage their unemployed members in co-operative undertakings and to exchange in the Institute the goods which they made. These undertakings could, however, only benefit the operatives who were in fairly good circumstances. The really poor workers could neither attend the meetings and socials at these institutes, since they had to pay for admission, nor could they enjoy the advantages of the labour exchanges, since they were unable to produce any article at their own cost. These institutes offered a great advantage to Owen, for they brought him into close relations with the intelligent members of the working classes.

Owing to misunderstandings between Owen and Bromley, the Institute had to vacate the premises in Gray's Inn Road about the middle of January, 1833. The enterprise moved for the time being to the branch institute near the Rotunda. The disturbance of moving, adverse rumours in the London newspapers, and the resultant losses caused a moral disorganisation from which the association never quite recovered. Finally it moved to 14, Charlotte Street, Tottenham Court Road, and was opened on May 1, 1833, by Owen in an apocalyptic speech. This district has ever since served as a resort for all political refugees who, on account of their political or communist convictions, have been forced to seek asylum in London.

In June, 1833, the operatives and the Owenites opened a labour exchange in Birmingham, which also enjoyed only a moderate degree of success.

For the whole year Owen lived in a state of ecstasy. The rapid rise of the trades unions, the diffusion of the idea of co-operation, the thorough contempt for parliamentary action, and the growing solidarity of the working classes were all considered to be harbingers of the imminent emancipation of the world from error and injustice. He handed over the labour exchanges to the workers, and went on a tour of propaganda to Lancashire, Yorkshire, and Staffordshire, where he came in touch with the workers' leaders. His propagandist tour revealed to him the possibility of uniting all the trades unions and co-operative societies of the United Kingdom—the productive classes, as he called them—into a single organisation, and of transforming them in a communistic sense so as to place the whole country upon a co-operative basis.

A colossal plan! A few years were to see the completion of the work. Its entire creation lay all ready made in his constructive brain. But ideas and facts soon began to come into conflict with each other.

2.—THE SYNDICALIST PHASE

Up to the year 1832 the trades union movement passed through the following stages of development : organisation for the purpose of mutual support, organisation of a single trade for purposes of strikes and mutual support, finally organisation of allied trades (trades unions). These economic unions were non-political ; their members were either Tory or Whig, or adhered to Radicalism and vied with the members of the other classes in struggling for a definite political programme. In any case, the economic unions of the workers only pursued aims which did not go beyond daily interests, and which did not seriously affect the stability of the prevailing system of society.

From 1832 onwards the position was changed. The organised workers became anti-parliamentary for a time. They cut themselves off from parliamentary politics, not for the purpose of observing neutrality, but in order to fight against parliamentary action, and to attain by means of trades unions what had hitherto been only considered possible of attainment by legislation. At the same time Robert Owen came on the scene with his anti-parliamentary views and placed before the trades unions the aim of converting society from capitalism to socialism by means of productive co-operation.

Owing to its alliance with Owenism, however, trades unionism assumed a Utopian character antagonistic to its essential nature. The economically organised working class possessed no preconceived system of society. It regarded class-warfare as a means of raising wages and lowering profits.

For the time being it was not concerned with what would happen
if the profits sank to zero. As soon as the struggle had strengthened the workers' organisation sufficiently for them to check-
mate capital, they would take over the business of production
and would conduct it for the benefit of the workers. They are,
to use Henri Bergson's or Belfort Bax's phraseology, *alogical*.

Owen did not understand this point of view. His system was
the product of rationalist logic. It rested, moreover, on the
idea of the solidarity and co-operation of Capital and Labour.
His remedy and his aim were in point of fact the reconstruction
of society.

Convinced of the absolute truth of his views, and buoyed up
by the conviction that absolute truth is irresistible, when
uttered at the right time distinctly and resolutely, Owen communicated his plan to the leaders of the workers. He found
the relatively highest degree of understanding to exist among the
operative builders, who at that time formed one of the most
powerful organisations. This was no mere chance. The builders
suffered greatly at the hands of middlemen, contractors, and sub-
contractors, who intervened between the employers and the
workers, and derived their profit entirely at the expense of the
working man. " Down with the middlemen and the contractors " was the watchword of the operative builders. Why
should profit-hunters push their way in between the producer
and the consumer so as to diminish the just wages of the
workers ? We, the workers, said the operative builders, could just
as well make the contract so as to receive the full amount of pay
for our work.

These ideas and precepts were closely allied to Owenism.
Owen's economic doctrine for the major part laid stress upon the
parasitic nature of the middle man, upon the necessity of close
relations between producer and consumer, and finally he considered that the actual solution of the social problem consisted
in the producers taking over the management of production.[1]

As soon as Owen received information of this state of things

[1] *Pioneer*, September 7, 1833. *Cf. Character of Trades Unions*,
1834, p. 45.

from his adherents he entered into communication with the builders' organisations. The leaders called a conference, which met in Manchester in the last week of September, 1831. No less than 500 delegates were present, and after long discussions Owen's plans for labour exchanges and co-operative societies were adopted.[1] Owen, however, remained in ignorance of the fact that the workers still adhered to their policy of class-war.

Three weeks after the conference of the operative builders they started a weekly, *The Pioneer*; its motto, " The day of our redemption draweth nigh." Its editor was James Morrison, a young, self-taught operative builder, who began with Owenism and ended with syndicalism. Beyond all doubt Morrison must be regarded as the originator of the syndicalist conception of class-antagonism on the part of the working-classes. Little is known of his life. He came from Birmingham, but was of Scottish descent. In 1832 he was active in the workers' movement and after two years of intense intellectual work he died, owing to overwork and poverty, at the end of September, 1835, in Manchester. His wife continued to work for a long time afterwards as a socialist agitator in Salford.[2] His friend and intellectual companion, James E. Smith (1801–1857),[3] was more fortunate. Smith came of a family of weavers ; he was a mystic, a theologian with broad views, and a metaphysician, and came to London from Glasgow in September, 1832. He became converted to Owenism, gave lectures in the Owenite Institute, and became editor of the *Crisis*. Smith was an original thinker. His main line of thought was mysticism and opposition to dogma. His mind was extremely active but somewhat lacking in stability, and was susceptible to all heterodox theories. The tenets of socialism soon captivated him, at least for some time, so long as they presented him with fresh problems and roused his incessant search after truth. He exercised a great influence as a speaker in the Owenite community in 1833 and 1834 on account of his philosophical culture, his remarkable power of

[1] *Crisis*, October 12, 1833.
[2] Holyoake, *History of Co-operation*, 1875, I. 211.
[3] W. A. Smith, *Life of J. E. Smith*, London, 1892.

oratory and his artistic style. He soon exhausted Owenism and pursued his search in other directions. He met Morrison, who, in his capacity of editor of the *Pioneer*, frequented the same printing-office. Smith became fascinated with the syndicalist ideas of the young operative builder, and gave them definite shape in his lectures and leading articles. Morrison and Smith, therefore, gradually withdrew from orthodox Owenism, and in 1834 became actively opposed to Owen. Smith then became a follower of Saint-Simon, subsequently of Fourier, and finished as an ordinary journalist; but to the very end he retained an attitude hostile to parliament, and friendly towards trades unionism. Indeed, his belief in the efficacy of trades unions was one of the few positive ideas which this restless spirit was able to assimilate. His philosophical and historical writings show clearly traces of Schelling's influence. Smith evidently believed in a theory of evolution, tinged with mysticism. Up to the present time little was known of this man's activity in the co-operative and syndicalist period. His biographer accumulated a mass of material which concealed rather than revealed this activity.

The first duty of the editor of the *Pioneer* was to comment upon the great conference at Manchester :

" Our Union Bark is once more safely out at sea. She has proudly triumphed over the troubled waters. . . . The new arrangements are likely to insure the permanent prosperity of the Union. We are not permitted to go into detail, but from what we have seen of the regulations, we believe they will produce an immediate effect on the district lodges. The builders' parliament have had a long session, but we hope the result of their labours will give satisfaction to the whole of their constituents. There has never been a period when the working classes were so intent on bettering their condition, and the silent progress they are making in legislation will secure them from ever being gulled with the party politics of the old school. . . . We are in earnest in saying that the builders have initiated the task of the emancipation of the world."

The chief result of the conference seems to have been the

unanimous resolution that the operative builders should form a co-operative body in order to "render the employer super-fluous."[1]

In the second week of October, 1833, a Congress was held in London of delegates of co-operative societies and trades unions in order to discuss the question of amalgamation. On the evening before the congress a mass meeting took place at Charlotte Street, where Owen was the principal speaker and discussed the relations between socialism and trades unionism. According to the information he had obtained during his tour of propaganda the workers would be won over within six months' time to the great truths of co-operation. He added : " I will only briefly sketch the outlines of the great revolution in preparation, which will come upon society like a thief in the night."[2]

Everything was to be consummated without strife or violence : the unions would be transformed into co-operative societies, and would combine into associations to exchange goods reciprocally by means of labour exchanges. A general congress, to sit in London, was to take the place of parliament and to regulate the production of the whole country.

A great part of the time of the congress was taken up with reports. The main task, viz. the amalgamation of the co-operative societies and trades unions, was deliberated with closed doors. The congress must have made a very favourable impression upon all who visited or participated in it. Even the

[1] *Pioneer*, October 5, 1833.

[2] It may not be without some interest to compare this theory of sudden development in sociology with the analogous theory in biology. Just eight days before this speech of Owen's the *Crisis* printed a report by the Owenite and geologist, W. D. Saull, on the progressive development of man from the animal world. Saull had spoken on this subject in meetings of working men. The *Crisis* called it the " Simian hypothesis," with which it could not agree. The editor declared : " Man, it is allowed, is of recent origin ; and as is also evident that he has come suddenly into existence ; and this suddenness of appearance is rather a formidable argument against the supposition that Nature gradually converts one species of animals into another " (*Crisis*, September 28, 1833).

Poor Man's Guardian (October 19, 1832), was full of praise and admiration for the proceedings :

"A spirit of combination has grown up among the working classes, of which there has been no example in former times. A grand national organisation, which promises to embody the physical power of the country, is silently, but rapidly progressing ; and the object of it is the sublimest that can be conceived, namely—to establish for the productive classes a complete dominion over the fruits of their own industry. Heretofore, these classes have wasted their strength in fruitless squabbles with their employers, or with one another. They have never sought any grand object, nor have they been united for those they sought. To obtain some paltry rise, or prevent some paltry reduction in wages, has been the general aim of their turn-outs ; and the best result of their best combinations, even when successful, was merely to secure their members against actual want in the day of sickness, or of superannuation. These and the like objects were only worthy of slaves ; they did not strike at the root of the evil ; they did not aim at any radical change ; their tendency was not to alter the system, but rather to perpetuate it, by rendering it more tolerable ; nay, they in some respects only aggravate the evils of the workman's condition, as for instance, in benefit societies, of which the tendency is to pinch the bellies and backs of the contributors to the fund, in order to save the poor-rates, that is to say, the pockets of the affluent classes, from the just claims of broken-down industry. . . . But far different from the paltry objects of all former combinations is that now aimed at by the congress of delegates. Their reports show that an entire change in society—a change amounting to a complete subversion of the existing ' order of the world '—is contemplated by the working classes. They aspire to be at the top instead of at the bottom of society—or rather that there should be no bottom or top at all ! "

Morrison exclaimed : " Well, brothers, we have now macadamized the road to success, or rather, we have laid a railroad to prosperity. . . . The crisis of our condition is at hand—close upon us. The contest affects all alike ; and woe unto the man who deserts his post. The question to be decided is, Shall Labour or Capital be uppermost ? "[1]

The delegates and agitators returned to their districts or started on missionary tours : the committees of the trades unions sent out circulars and the secretaries and organisers set about the task of realising the plan which had been drawn up in London. At the present day it is difficult to realise exactly what took place at this juncture. The trades unions experienced a growth that was more rapid and comprehensive than any before or since. Battalions of trades unionists seemed to rise out of the ground ; the spirit of redemption swept through the working classes and intoxicated them with boundless hopes. In November, 1833, as many as 800,000 workers are said to have been organised,[2] and the continual additions to the organisations showed no signs of decrease. The boundless hopes at one pole of society were counterbalanced by excessive apprehension at the other pole, viz. among employers and all who were interested in capital. The centres of industry, trade, and commerce became transformed into hostile camps. Class-war raged from south to north, and from east to west. Strikes, lock-outs, coercion of the men to join the trades unions or to leave them, were all in the order of the day. The part played by the agitation for the Reform Bill in 1831 and 1832 was now transferred to the struggle for and against the trades unions. The excitement was even greater than before, since it concerned no longer a political, but a social revolution.

The vigour with which such large numbers of operatives threw themselves into the cause of class-war filled their friends partly with enthusiasm, partly with dread, but it only inspired their enemies with fear and hatred. The whole press of the kingdom busied itself with the question and took up various attitudes to the trades unions according to their interests in class or party. The Whig newspapers poured the vials of their wrath upon the class they had hitherto despised ; the papers of the radical middle class were fairly friendly but expressed the wish that the operatives should not disdain politics ; the Tory press called

[1] *Pioneer*, October 12, 1833.   [2] *Crisis*, October 12, 1833.

for the police and the public prosecutor or else they tempted the operatives to join their cause so as to lead them against the Whig government.[1]

In this atmosphere charged with enthusiasm the operatives adopted Benbow's plan of a general strike. On October 5, 1833, a resolution to this effect was passed in a large meeting of Glasgow operatives. The idea of a general strike was the subject of much discussion :—

"There will not be insurrection ; it will simply be passive resistance. The men may remain at leisure ; there is, and can be, no law to compel them to work against their will. They may walk the streets or fields with their arms folded, they will wear no swords, carry no muskets ; they will present no multitude for the Riot Act to disperse. They merely abstain, when their funds are sufficient, from going to work for one week or one month ; and what happens in consquence ? Bills are dishonoured, the *Gazette* teems with bankruptcies, capital is destroyed, the revenue fails, the system of government falls into confusion, and every link in the chain which binds society together is broken in a moment by this inert conspiracy of the poor against the rich." [2]

A journeyman shoemaker writes at this time to the *Poor Man's Guardian* :—

"If organisation goes on like that there will soon be no more than two classes : non-producers and producers—the first will no longer be permitted to revel in wealth, for by law of nature and common justice wealth and power belong only to those who produce it." [3]

The idea of class-war finds its clearest expression in an anonymous letter to the *Poor Man's Guardian* of August 30, 1834 :—

"The battle of labour against capital is not to be fought with guns and swords ; the capitalists themselves do not go into the fight ; they send ignorant labourers against enlightened labourers.

---

[1] *Tait's Edinburgh Magazine*, January, 1834, p. 389 ; *Cobbett's Political Register*, December 7, 1833 ; *Newcastle Press*, December 21, 1833 ; *Times*, November 4, 1833.

[2] *Glasgow Liberator* (*Trades Union Gazette*), February 1, 1834.

[3] *Poor Man's Guardian*, November 2, 1833.

The people's press must be the chief weapon of our warfare. When the labourer knows his wrongs, the death-knell of the capitalist has been sounded. In order to work out the salvation of the working classes I would recommend that strikes should be repeated as often as possible, especially against employers who stand forth most prominently as the enemies of labour. The men cannot lose by a strike, for the work wanted must be done at some future time ; and the men ought to exercise their power of annoyance against their enemies by choosing their own time for doing the work. The great advantage of a strike is that it increases the enmity between labourers and capitalists, and compels workmen to reflect and investigate the causes of their sufferings. There are thousands of labourers in England who go on from year to year in perfect contentment with masters who allow them a bare subsistence in exchange for their incessant toil. A strike of a week's duration among such labourers would make them ask the question by what laws they were compelled to toil and to starve in order that their masters may idle and roll in wealth. The fruit of such reflections would be a violent hostility against the capitalist class ; and the new converts would be prepared to second the efforts of emancipation made by labourers in other quarters of England. Such a movement would inspire the capitalists with fear and would make them yield."

All this has a remarkably modern sound. In general, ever since 1833, the whole phraseology is modern. The terms social democrat, trades unionism, strike, general strike, bourgeoisie and proletariat, politics and anti-politics, class-warfare and solidarity of classes, etc., have been in general use ever since that period. Occasionally, and especially in reading the *Poor Man's Guardian* and the *Pioneer*, it is possible to imagine one's self transferred to the present day.

As soon as organised workers entered into the socialist agitation it ceased to be an Owenite sect and became a great movement of the working classes. Owing to special circumstances, it shunned parliamentary action for the time being and staked everything upon the direct action of trades unions.

Owen was horrified to see the masses abandoning his aims

and his policy. The spirits which he had helped to call up from the deep began to refuse obedience. He therefore redoubled his exertions to prove that the redemption of the country could only be obtained by the united action of the operatives and the propertied classes. He urged that capital was also a producer and that it deserved to receive friendly overtures from the operatives instead of meeting with hostility.[1] Alarmed at the rapid revolutionary growth of the trades unions, Owen, on the suggestion of John Fielden, founded the " National Regeneration Society " at a meeting in Manchester on November 25, 1833. Its object was to introduce an eight-hour day on March 1, 1834, by the joint action of the employers and the operatives. But the trades unions believed that the general strike would commence on March 1 in order to wrest the eight-hour day from the manufacturers. Owen soon began to throw the whole blame upon Morrison and Smith, and considered that the whole state of confusion was to be ascribed to their machinations and class-war policy. The incompatibility between peaceful socialism and fighting syndicalism, hitherto hidden and unrecognised, began to make itself noticeable from about the end of 1833.

Morrison and Smith had now to fight on two fronts, against Owen and his adherents on the one hand, and against the parliamentary socialists on the other hand. Smith considered Owen's influence on the trades unions to be pernicious,[2] and Morrison lost all respect for Owen.[3]

Owen's authority was, however, still considerable among the masses and many of their leaders. Syndicalist ideas were still of so recent growth and were known to so few of the working classes that Morrison and Smith were unable to achieve any success in opposition to Owen, for when the conflict came to a head Owen secured the dismissal of both (June, 1834). They, meanwhile, found greater opportunities and a more favourable scene of action in their polemics against the parliamentary socialists, who were headed by O'Brien, the editor of the *Poor Man's Guardian*.

[1] *Crisis*, December 7, 1833, January 11, 1834.
[2] W. A. Smith, *Life of J. E. Smith*, p. 104.
[3] *Pioneer*, January 25, 1834.

3.—CONTROVERSIES BETWEEN SOCIAL DEMOCRATS AND SYNDICALISTS

J. E. Smith, prior to his conflict with Owen, declared in his lecture of August 25, 1833, that parliamentary politics could not suffice for the people either from an intellectual or practical point of view, since they furnished no opportunity for action. The political unions merely developed a power of eloquence in their members and the drafting of useless resolutions. The main point is economic action :

" Politics must gradually change as the working men rise into importance ; and the operatives will then soon discover that, by looking exclusively to their own affairs, they will control the movements of the government, as a rudder controls the movements of the vessel to which it belongs."

Smith had in his mind's eye both co-operative societies and trades unions. After the congresses of the working classes in September (Manchester) and October (London), anti-parliamentarism assumed a purely syndicalist character both for Smith and for Morrison who in the meantime had become the editor of the *Pioneer*. The *Crisis* and the *Pioneer* became the organs of the intelligent section of the proletariat, whilst the *Poor Man's Guardian* lost its old prestige. O'Brien protested as follows :—

" In viewing the struggle which is now in progress between labour and capital there is one circumstance which fills us with astonishment and regret—we mean the disposition of the chief leaders of the workmen to disconnect their cause altogether from politics. This is the most futile and ill-judged proceeding that can be conceived. They see that if the workmen combine against the employers, the soldiers are called in. By whom are the troops paid ? By the people ! Who commands the troops ? The Government ! And in the composition of the Cabinet, just as in the making of the whole machinery of the State, the people have no share. Universal suffrage would place the magistracy and Parliament and consequently the disposal of the military

¹ *Crisis*, August 31, 1833.

and police forces in the hands of the entire body of the people, the workmen as well as employers. The Parliament being thus the representative of the whole, and the magistracy its principal executive, no particular part would receive more than its due share of protection. The present objects of the Trades Unions can never be attained under the existing Government. . . . Universal suffrage does not signify meddling with politics, but the rule of the people in the State and municipality, a Government therefore in favour of the working men. What seek the Trades Unions ? *Increase of wages* and a *diminution of the hours of labour;* that is to say, *to work less*, and to *get more for it*—in other words, *to produce less wealth*, and to *enjoy a larger portion of it.* Who does not see that this is to attack ' property ? ' But do *we* find fault with this ? Far from it ! To attack ' property ' is to attack robbery. But the question is, how are we to attack the capitalist in the safest and most expeditious manner ? We cannot attack him by *law*, for he holds the ' law ' in his own hands. How are we to attack him then ? We say, *in the way of the Trades Unions*, provided only that they add Universal Suffrage to their present avowed objects." [1]

These polemical statements were regarded by trades unionists as an attack upon trades unionism. The *Poor Man's Guardian* was treated by the workers as obnoxious and O'Brien was stigmatised as their opponent. An ordinary working man answered him (*Poor Man's Guardian*, December 28, 1833).

" Your remarks on the trades unions show lack of knowledge of trades unionism. The working people have found that political unions have not as yet been able to produce anything but the Humbug Bill, nor do they think they will ever be able to do anything. There are men mixed up with these unions whose interest it is to hinder the working man from enjoying the fruits of his labour. They are of opnion that in unions where all sorts of people are mixed up there never will be one united opinion or determination to do any real good. A remark has fallen from you last week that the workman in asking for higher wages and shorter labour time was attacking property. Now the trades

[1] *Poor Man's Guardian*, December 7 and 21, 1833.

unions do not seek to produce less wealth, but to equalise it by giving employment to the unemployed and full employment to the partially employed. Now I ask you, will this produce less wealth? With regard to the attack on property, I would ask whose property is it but the producers? And consequently why should he have no right to take his own? Also the whole talk about capitalists giving higher wages is nonsense. They never did and never will. What the working men mean by getting better wages is to enjoy the produce of their labour."

This was the opinion of ordinary working men in 1833. It was not difficult for O'Brien to show that he too was in essential agreement with these objections, but that " the natural claim of the working man to the product of his work must be recognised by the artificial law of the State," and this could only be effected by the help of universal suffrage. But at that time the working men of the trades unions were so permeated with distrust of the State and so full of the consciousness of their power and of faith in their own organisations that they treated every reference to the necessity of seizing political power as a depreciation of trades unionism. Both sections of thought ceased to understand each other, as if they had suddenly begun to speak two different languages. Such expressions as government, universal suffrage, self-government received different meanings. The parliamentary party referred these terms to political institutions, the syndicalists applied them to trades-unionist organisations. The former desired a democratic House of Commons ; the latter strove for a general Labour Chamber to direct the interests of the productive classes and of the whole nation. The former regarded the electoral districts as political units, the latter found them in the separate trades unions. Parliamentary politics and trades-unionist economics diverged completely from each other. The *Crisis* wrote :—

" A struggle is awaiting us, but it is a struggle in which we are sure to conquer. At present we are within the laws, and still we are making our rulers tremble. By and by they will make new laws and then reproach us for breaking them. Shall we consider it our duty tamely to submit to any new laws which

p. 126–7   X —·— X   (Some)

p. 130 –133
134 –   X — X (Some)

· p 164–5   X ~ X   (Some)

Vol Ⅰ p. 300 –1   X — X ✓ "
p. 309 –10   X — X ✓ "
p. 331 –   X — X ✓ "

✓ p 333   X — X ✓

p. 333 –4   X — X ✓

p 336 –7   X — X ✓

339 –40   X — X ✓

341 –3   X — X ✓

Beer II

✓ p. 13 — last para (same)

p. 14 ✓ 1st para (same)

p. 20 ✓ X —— X (same)

p. 28 X —— X (same

p. 30 X — X ,,

✓ p. 42-3 X —— X (same
(separately)

p. 45 X —— X

p. 46-7 X — X (same)

✓ p. 47 X — X (same)

p. 60 X — X (same

p. 51 X —— X ,,

p. 64-5 X —— X ,,

p. 87-8 X —— X ,,

may be made to check our progress to prosperity and social happiness ? Let them make laws for themselves if they are so fond of legislating. If they are so fond of imposing taxes let them tax one another ; but let them first ask our consent before they prescribe pills for our disease which we ourselves know much better how to cure. No ! The immediate consequences of any attempt to crush the efforts of the popular mind, at this present juncture, will be a most resolute determination on the part of the people to legislate for themselves. This will be the result. We shall have a real House of Commons. We have never yet had a House of Commons. The only House of Commons is a House of Trades, and that is only just beginning to be formed. We shall have a new set of boroughs when the unions are organised : every trade shall be a borough, and every trade shall have a council of representatives to conduct its affairs. Our present commoners know nothing of the interests of the people, and care not for them. They are all landholders. How can an employer represent a workman ? There are 133,000 shoemakers in the country, yet not one representative have they in the House of Commons. According to the proportion they bear to the population they ought to have twenty-five representatives. The same is with carpenters and other trades in proportion. Such a House of Commons, however, is growing. The elements are gathering. The character of the Reformed Parliament is now blasted, and like the character of a woman when lost, is not easily recovered. It will be substituted by a House of Trades."[1]

The democratic press misunderstood the opinions of the *Crisis* and the *Pioneer*, and this attitude evoked the following reply from Morrison :—

" . . . The political economists are so short-sighted that they look only to partial release,—the diminution of taxation, separation of Church and State, revision of pension list and such other milk-and-water favours ; and when they have received their boon, pray where are they ? Is the power of private capital and monopoly in any wise impaired ? Is the commercial system paralysed ? And finally, have the working classes ob-

[1] *Crisis*, April 12, 1834.

tained any practical knowledge by scrutinising the measures of government,?....No, nothing valuable is gained. There is only one way of gaining them, and that is by a general association of the people for the purpose of initiating themselves into the practice of conducting those affairs in which they have some experience. The Unions are of all the other means the only mode by which universal suffrage can safely be obtained, because it is obtained by practice, by serving an apprenticeship. Here they start to manage their own affairs on a small scale before they get management of larger affairs. The growing power and growing intelligence of a trades unions, when properly managed, will draw into its vortex all the commercial interests of the country, and, in so doing, it will become, by its own self-acquired importance, a most influential, we might almost say dictatorial part of the body politic. When this happens we have gained all that we want ; we have gained universal suffrage, for if every member of the Union be a constituent, and the Union itself becoming a vital member of the State, it instantly erects itself into a House of Trades which must supply the place of the present House of Commons, and direct the industrial affairs of the country, according to the will of the trades which compose the associations of industry. This is the ascendant scale by which we arrive at to universal suffrage. . With us, universal suffrage will begin in our lodges, extend to the general union, embrace the management of trade, and finally swallow up the political power.''[1]

Two weeks later Smith, who contributed to the *Pioneer* under the pseudonym " Senex," gave expression to this idea in the following classic words (*Pioneer*, June 14, 1834) :—

" Social liberty must precede political liberty. While we are in a state of social slavery our rights would be exercised to the benefit of our tyrants, and we should be made subservient to the parties who work us for their purposes. No, before the horse is turned out to enjoy freedom in the green meadow, he must be unharnessed from the shafts of the wagon ; the galling rein that holds back his neck in the collar must be loosened, the bit must be taken from his mouth, and the collar itself from his shoulders ;

[1] *Pioneer*, May 31, 1834.

nor will he go forth in the valley rejoicing in his strength, while the limber of the gear hangs over his loins and encumbers his feet. To say, indeed, we shall never be free until we have universal suffrage is saying nothing more than we never shall be free until we are free. . . . Our position, brethren, is not political, and it cannot become political with any benefit to ourselves until we have found means to obtain a greater independent weight in society. This can only be the result of Unions."

At the time that Morrison and Smith wrote these articles, the " Grand National Consolidated Trades Union," with which we shall deal presently, had come into existence. They endeavoured to complete the edifice of this great organisation in a syndicalist sense, whilst Owen exerted himself to endue it with a co-operative character and a spirit of national solidarity so that it should form the basis for a peaceful revolution of society.

4. GREATER UNIONISM.

In the third week of February, 1834, the delegates of the trades unions met in London for the purpose of founding the " Grand National Consolidated Trades Union." The proceedings took place in secret. So far as can be gathered from the statements in the *Pioneer* a number of delegates were opposed to centralisation ; in the same way the assumption is warranted that the Consolidated Union only comprised about one half of the organised operatives of Great Britain. The committee appointed by the conference resolved to waive the question of a consolidation of the funds of the different trades unions, but to secure a unity of action and management, especially in the spending of sums of money in support of members or individual unions who might fall victims to the relentless persecution of capitalists. Moreover, the committee drew up the following propositions, forming a kind of programme of future action :—

" 1. That as many different Trades Unions as possible do mutually agree under a perfect understanding with each other, to maintain a unity of action in all their proceedings with respect to their general laws and government, and also with regard to

Pioneer March 8. 1834

the levying and disposing of all funds raised for objects of presumed permanent utility.

" 2. As land is the source of the first necessaries of life, and as, without the possession of it, the producing classes will ever remain in a greater or less degree subservient to the money capitalists, and subject to the deterioration of the money value of their labour consequent upon the fluctuations of trade and commerce, this committee advise that a great effort should now be made by the Unions to secure such portions of it on lease as their funds will permit, in order that in all turn-outs the men may be employed in rearing the greater part, if not the whole, of their subsistence under the direction of practical agricultural superintendents, which arrangements would not have the effect of lowering the price of labour in any trade, but on the contrary would rather tend to increase it by drawing off the at present superfluous supply in manufactures. . . .

" 3. The committee would, nevertheless, earnestly recommend in all cases of strikes and turn-outs, where it is practicable, that the men be employed in the making or producing of all such commodities as would be in demand among their brother unionists ; and that to effect this, each lodge should be provided with a workroom or shop in which those commodities may be manufactured on account of such lodge which shall make proper arrangements for the supply of the necessary materials.

" 4. That great advantages would accrue by the formation, in each district lodge, of a fund for the support of the sick and aged.

" 5. That in all cases where it be practicable, each district or branch lodge should establish one or more depots for provisions and articles in general domestic use ; by which means the working man may be supplied with the best commodities at little above wholesale prices.

" 6. That each lodge do make arrangements for furnishing the means of mental improvement to their members, and for the cultivation of good habits among them, by affording them every facility for meeting together for friendly conversation, mutual instruction and rational amusement or recreation ; which arrangements might be rendered in a short period infinitely more enticing and agreeable than the delusive, pernicious, and dearly-bought gratifications sought after in the tap-room or the gin-shop.

" 7. ~~That~~ we should offer ~~the females~~ among the industrious classes every encouragement and assistance to form themselves into lodges for the protection of their industry."

The programme was therefore a compromise between the Owenite and trades-unionist aims, and kept closely in view the object of " freeing the working men completely from the tyranny of the capitalists."

Morrison's *Pioneer* was officially adopted as the central organ to start with.

Whilst the accoucheurs and nurses of the Grand Consolidated Union shouted for joy, the new-born babe hovered between life and death. The employers, the Press, and the State made every effort to deprive it of light and air. Lock-outs and strikes exhausted the funds of the Union, the Press demanded a strict inquiry into the union's by-laws, the law passed draconic sentences upon trades unionists. The conviction of the six Dorchester labourers for swearing and administering oaths on the admission of members was a deterrent example.[1]

The main policy of the employers was not to wait until the Labour forces were concentrated, but to attack at once and beat the separate columns of the Labour army before they had reached the converging point where the grand assault on property was to take place.

The unprotected condition of the funds of the Union was another obstacle. Defaulting officials could embezzle money with impunity, and this actually happened in the case of the " Grand Consolidated Trades Union," shattering the confidence of working men. As early as April the position of the organisation was critical. This was followed by the differences between Owen, Morrison, and Smith, who were no longer able to work together. Owen viewed everything from the standpoint of co-operation and solidarity of the classes and regarded all class strife as pernicious, whilst Morrison and Smith, on the other

---

[1] Webb, *History of Trade Unionism*, pp. 113. *seq.*, 1896.

hand, rejected all Utopian ideas and wished to utilise the instrument which the working class had forged in the Consolidated Trades Union by wielding it as a sword to overthrow the old state of society and to set up labour in the place of capital. In June, 1834, the antagonism between the thinkers of the working class could no longer be bridged over. Owen stopped the publication of the *Crisis* in order to turn Smith out of the labour movement, and he induced the committee of the Consolidated Trades Union to disown the *Pioneer*, to discharge Morrison, and to found a new paper as the central organ.

Owing to the secrecy of the committee's proceedings nothing further can be stated concerning this national confederation of labour. When the *Pioneer* ceased publication the committee founded its own paper, i.e. *The Pioneer and Official Gazette*. In September the committee broke off all relations with Owen [1] and refused his request for an interview. The organisation fell to pieces, but even in its dissolution it has handed down an important document of the intense activity of thought of this period. It occurs in the *Pioneer and Official Gazette* of September 20, 1834, the only copy extant of this newspaper. The leading article is obviously a kind of final survey of the struggles of 1832 to 1834, and they could not have received more suitable treatment. The article runs as follows :—

" *Thoughts on the growing spirit of union among the labour holders or operative classes.*—The spirit of union among the operatives of the industrious classes in the most advanced nations of Europe is the manifestation of a strong natural feeling, the remote causes of which are of greater magnitude and of more serious influence on the happiness of mankind than most people are disposed to acknowledge. From time immemorial this creation moves on, and works on, with us and within us. Man individual is at different times more or less actuated by the temporary arrangement of localities, or by the artificial circumstances that surround him ; but nature acting incessantly upon man species by the constant laws of assimilation which develop all organised substances, they consequently vary from

[1] Frank Podmore, *Robert Owen*, 1906, II., 453.

themselves imperceptibly at each instant of time, and no substance can rationally be said to BE, since all are passing from one modification to another modification. The condition of society at any given moment must always be considered as modifying itself, because the human species being composed of organised substances, generating new ideas by the successive modification of their nature, whilst the artificial rules of life (laws and regulations) do not undergo a corresponding gradual modification of their nature, man individual soon begins to feel new wants ; he finds, after a period, that he can no longer move in comfort and liberty in the same localities, under laws and regulations framed long since for substances and circumstances which no longer exist : hence it is that radical reforms in all things artificial become indispensable after a certain period of time. The most important duty expected by reason from all rational government is undoubtedly that of watching the effect of the natural changes thus operated upon whole populations, in order that after having ascertained the nature of the new ideas which have actually created new imperative wants, the laws and regulations may be so modified *in time* as to maintain political equilibrium. The performance of that important duty requires that rulers should possess three qualities most essential to sound legislation : 1, a knowledge of the age they live in ; 2, sagacity to discriminate right from wrong ; 3, impartiality to act with justice from a *national* point of view *only*. . . .

" The increasing competition between great and small masters has compelled some to become the unwilling petty tyrants over the operatives ; and the unionists appear to be equally unjust in compelling others not to work under a minimum of wages, fixed by no acknowledged authority. But in truth no one is actually to blame—it is nature all through. It is the Creator's law of progress working on for the greater happiness of mankind through the mind and the difficulties of individuals. . . . A new system of labour is coming into the world. The new system and the struggles between the classes are positive signs of new social arrangements. Boards of labour or committees of industry must assume the place now occupied by the great masters. Such arrangements will gradually pave the way to community of property. . . .

" Meanwhile the struggle goes on and the operatives are suffering. But we must have patience. The spirit of the age is an irresistible power—unions will continue ; more strikes and more blunders will succeed each other. However productive they may be of temporary mischief and misery, better associations shall be formed, and from the difficulties of the time the nation will learn. A new world will gradually unfold itself ; the financial delusions and blunders which clog and shackle society will become evident to every one ; a new kind of knowledge and of liberty will arise and spread itself, from that single reason that no remedy can be found in the old, worn-out basis of thought and action far too narrow for the mental fecundity and for the mechanical powers of the age now begun ! "

This was the last syndicalist manifesto. The movement collapsed, dragging down with it in the dust labour exchanges, co-operative societies, the movement for the Eight Hour Day, syndicalism, and even a great part of the Owenite Utopias and tenets of salvation. Among the ruins of the shattered syndicalist laboratory the labouring class lay in a state of exhaustion. John Francis Bray, the author of *Labour's Wrongs* (1839), has left us a vivid picture of the doubt and disappointment of that time :—

" The great body of the working classes believed that their late trades unions would be omnipotent in effecting their deliverance from the dominion of the capitalist ; for a more powerful engine was never made use of by the producers. From there being many trades united together, and supporting each other, when one struck a blow at tyranny, that blow fell with the accumulated monetary force of the whole mass. But, whether victorious or defeated, the workman was alike involved in losses and in difficulties—all his efforts for the permanent bettering of his condition were uneffectual—and this vast confederation was at length broken up and dissolved into its primitive trade societies. These have continued at times a desultory and unequal contest with capital—sometimes with partial success, but oftener with defeat and ruin. The capitalist and the employer have always ultimately been too strong for them ; and trades unions have become, amongst the enemies of the working class, a byword of caution or contempt—a record of the weakness of Labour when opposed to Capital—an indestructible memento of the evil working of the present system in regard to the two great classes which now compose society."[1]

Two years of recuperation and reflection enabled the working classes to rise up again into activity. They were awakened and roused from their apathy by the intelligent section of the London operatives, who were parliamentary Owenites and were convinced more than ever of the necessity for independent parliamentary action. In their meetings which were held either in favour of the liberation of the Dorchester labourers or in favour of the people's press, Lovett, Hetherington, Watson, Cleave, Hartwell, etc., spoke on the position resulting from the events of 1830 to 1838, and drew inferences for future guidance. Their main doctrines were : an independent labour policy, socialist aims, peaceful and educational methods.[2] The threads of social democracy which had been snapped by the events of 1833 and 1834 were now to be taken up again. Circumstances came to their help ; the Municipal Reform Act (1835) which adapted the parliamentary franchise to the municipalities and was intended to put an end to the old system of cliques, was opposed by the Lords and led to a conflict between the two Houses. This aroused once more the public interest in constitutional questions. The introduction by stages of the new Poor Law Bill incited the working class to political activity. The impending reduction of the newspaper stamp from fourpence to one penny put fresh life into the people's press. At the end of 1835 the approach of Chartism proper was perceptible.

[1] J. F. Bray, *Labour's Wrongs*, p. 100.
[2] Place, MSS. 27819, pp. 24, 229, *seq.*

INDEX

AA